A BOOK OF BIRDS

THE MACMILLAN COMPANY
NEW YORK · BOSTON · CHICAGO · DALLAS
ATLANTA · SAN FRANCISCO

A BOOK OF BIRDS

By

MARY PRIESTLEY

With 82 Wood Engravings by

C. F. TUNNICLIFFE

NEW YORK

THE MACMILLAN COMPANY

1938

To J. B. P.

"*And then, besides my work and my family,
I've my little hobbies—my birds, Stella.*"

PREFACE

Like many anthologies, the *Book of Birds* began as a private scrapbook. The happy present of a pair of Zeiss glasses, given to me at a time when I was spending some weeks of enforced rest on a balcony overlooking a garden full of birds, turned me into a bird-watcher. For the garden contained a yew-tree, and the flock of little birds I had thought of as sparrows suddenly turned with the magic of the glasses into a flock of brilliantly coloured goldfinches, chaffinches, and redstarts, and in the dark shade of the tree I found a spotted missel-thrush, whose bright eye I could vividly see. I found myself reading more and more about birds, and noting down short descriptions of any that seemed to me particularly vivid or amusing.

At first these passages were mostly modern, such as Ford Madox Hueffer on the Starling, and Ruth Pitter on the Stormcock, and Julian Huxley, and Robert Lynd looking at his first Humming-bird.

Inevitably, all manner of half-remembered passages— bits from poets and prose writers—began to haunt me, and I had to hunt them up and add them to my collection. These range from Chaucer to Meredith and Martin Armstrong. After that, finding a genuine anthology of bird literature taking shape in my scrapbook, I cast about a wider net. The eighteenth century gave me Gilbert White, with his pictures as lovely as any Girtin or de Windt; and also gave me the most entrancing mistakes, for instance a delightful one on the Eagle by Cuvier, or the first guess as to what happens to the Swallows in winter.

I added sections on migration, on the courtship of birds. Travellers, such as Wallace, and Ross in the Antarctic (1839–43) and Cuvier, and Beebe in the Tropics, and others gave me a full section. Then there is Doctor G. Murray Levick, who was in the Antarctic before the War, describing Adélie Penguins.

Naturalists to-day give some enchanting descriptions of new discoveries. Mr. Witherby describes a Long-tailed Tit building its nest; Edgar Chance describes the Cuckoo laying its egg in a Pipit's nest; and Miss Turner a fantastic experience with the Snipe.

Exact details are what the modern naturalist wants. Perhaps he knows that he can fill in the enchantment and magic for himself from his long days on marsh or shore, in woods or along the hedgerows. The general reader will prefer the literary extracts, feeling, quite rightly, that for him such lines as those of Tennyson on the Eagle are worth pages of scientific facts.

In short, I have tried to make this a companionable book, a book meant for anybody who has ever taken a moment's joy in watching a bird.

ILLUSTRATIONS

ILLUSTRATIONS

ILLUSTRATIONS

ILLUSTRATIONS

There sat I down among the fairë flow'rs,
And saw the birdës trip out of their bow'rs.

CHAUCER

A BOOK OF BIRDS

As I lay among the heather and gorse on the top of a hill on Sunday a green woodpecker flew over my head, with a yellow flash of tail, and dropped with a scream to the stem of a hawthorn-tree a few yards away. He clung to it, as if listening, and the sun gleamed on his green cloak and on the ruby in his crown. But he no sooner saw me than he screamed again and fled behind a thicket, beautiful in his ungainliness. The hill was also full of redstarts in their Joseph's coats, flying from covert to covert, and showing little of their beauty but the tail, that seemed to be on fire as they disappeared. They were, for the most part, but a melancholy voice crying "Coo-ee!" behind the leaves. Occasionally, however, cock and hen would settle on the tips of the branches and carry on their dialogue of alarm, he blue, black and red, exquisite as a Japanese painting, she more domestic in her brown dress. But at the slightest movement of one's head they became aware of the presence of man, the enemy, and were once more crying fugitives with tails of fire. Here, too, there is no way to see the world but by sitting still. On these terms alone will the procession of bright things go by. If you want an excuse for doing nothing, here is one ready to your hand.

ROBERT LYND from Solomon in All His Glory

Bb

The golden plover was then one of the abundant species. After its arrival in September, the plains in the neighbourhood of my home were peopled with immense flocks of this bird. Sometimes in hot summers the streams and marshes would mostly dry up, and the aquatic bird population, the plover included, would shift their quarters to other districts. During one of these droughty seasons, when my age was nine, there was a marshy ground two miles from my home where a few small pools of water still remained, and to this spot the golden plover would resort every day at noon. They would appear in flocks from all quarters, flying to it like starlings in England coming in to some great roosting centre on a winter evening. I would then mount my pony and gallop off joyfully to witness the spectacle. Long before coming in sight of them the noise of their voices would be audible, growing louder as I drew near. Coming to the ground, I would pull up my horse and sit gazing with astonishment and delight at the spectacle of that immense multitude of birds, covering an area of two or three acres, looking less like a vast flock than a *floor* of birds, in colour a rich deep brown, in strong contrast to the pale grey of the dried-up ground all round them. A living, moving floor and a sounding one as well, and the sound too was amazing. It was like the sea, but unlike it in character since it was not deep; it was more like the wind blowing, let us say, on thousands of tight-drawn wires of varying thicknesses, vibrating them to shrill sound, a mass and tangle of ten thousand sounds. But it is indescribable and unimaginable.

Then I would put the birds up to enjoy the different sound of their rushing wings mingled with that of their

cries, also the sight of them like a great cloud in the sky
above me, casting a deep shadow on the earth.

W. H. HUDSON from *A Hind in Richmond Park*

American Golden Plover

What, then, did I want?—what did I ask to have? If the question had been put to me then, and if I had been capable of expressing what was in me, I should have replied: I want only to keep what I have; to rise each morning and look out on the sky and the grassy dew-wet earth from day to day, from year to year. To watch every June and July for spring, to feel the same old sweet surprise and delight at the appearance of each familiar flower, every new-born insect, every bird returned once more from the north. To listen in a trance of delight to the wild notes of the golden plover coming once more to the great plain, flying, flying south, flock succeeding flock the whole day long. Oh, those wild beautiful cries of the golden plover! I could exclaim with Hafix, with but one word changed: "If after a thousand years that sound should float o'er my tomb, my bones uprising in their gladness would dance in the sepulchre!"

To climb trees and put my hand down in the deep hot nest of the Bien-te-veo and feel the hot eggs—the five long pointed cream-coloured eggs with chocolate spots and splashes at the larger end. To lie on a grassy bank with the blue water between me and beds of tall bulrushes, listening to the mysterious sounds of the wind and of hidden rails and coots and courlans conversing together in strange humanlike tones . . . to visit some haunt of large birds at that still, hot hour and see storks, ibises, grey herons, egrets of a dazzling whiteness, and rose-coloured spoonbills and flamingoes, standing in the shallow water in which their motionless forms are reflected.

w. h. hudson from *Far Away and Long Ago*

The Mother Bird

Through the green twilight of a hedge
I peered, with cheek on the cool leaves pressed,
And spied a bird upon a nest:
Two eyes she had beseeching me
Meekly and brave, and her brown breast
Throbbed hot and quick above her heart;
And then she opened her dagger bill:—
'Twas not a chirp, as sparrows pipe
At break of day: 'twas not a trill,
As falters through the quiet even;
But one sharp solitary note,
One desperate, fierce, and vivid cry
Of valiant tears, and hopeless joy,
One passionate note of victory.
Off, like a fool afraid, I sneaked,
Smiling the smile the fool smiles best,
At the mother bird in the secret hedge
Patient upon her lonely nest.

WALTER DE LA MARE

Annus Mirabilis (1902)

Daylight was down, and up the cool
Bare heaven the moon, o'er roof and elm,
Daughter of dusk most wonderful,
Went mounting to her realm:
And night was only half begun
Round Edwardes Square in Kensington.

A Sabbath-calm possessed her face,
An even glow her bosom filled;
High in her solitary place
The huntress-heart was stilled:
With bow and arrows all laid down
She stood and looked on London town.

Nay, how can sight of us give rest
To that far-travelled heart, or draw
The musings of that tranquil breast?
I thought—and gazing, saw
Far up above me, high, oh, high,
From south to north a heron fly!

Heron

CHICKADEES

Oh, swiftly answered! yonder flew
The wings of freedom and of hope!
Little of London town he knew,
The far horizon was his scope.
High up he sails, and sees beneath
The glimmering ponds of Hampstead Heath,

Hendon, and farther out afield
Low water-meads are in his ken,
And lonely pools by Harrow Weald,
And solitudes unloved of men,
Where he his fisher's spear dips down:
Little he knows of London town.

So small, with all its miles of sin,
Is London to the grey-winged bird,
A cuckoo called at Lincoln's Inn
Last April; in Soho was heard
The missel-thrush with throat of glee,
And nightingales at Battersea!

LAURENCE HOUSMAN

Meanwhile also came the chickadees in flocks, which,
picking up the crumbs the squirrels had dropped, flew
to the nearest twig, and, placing them under their claws,
hammered away at them with their little bills, as if it
were an insect in the bark, till they were sufficiently
reduced for their slender throats. A little flock of these
tit-mice came daily to pick a dinner out of my wood-pile,
or the crumbs at my door, with faint, flitting, lisping
notes, like the tinkling of icicles in the grass, or else with

sprightly *day, day, day,* or more rarely, in spring-like days, a wiry summery *phe-be* from the wood-side. They were so familiar that at length one alighted on an armful of wood which I was carrying in and pecked at the sticks without fear. I once had a sparrow alight upon my shoulder for a moment while I was hoeing in a village garden, and I felt that I was more distinguished by that circumstance than I should have been by any epaulet I could have worn.

THOREAU from *Walden*

In order to see birds it is necessary to become a part of the silence. One has to sit still like a mystic and wait. One soon learns that fussing, instead of achieving things, merely prevents things from happening. To be passive is in some circumstances the most efficient form of activity. You cannot command events: you can only put yourself in the place where events will happen to you. No impatient man has ever seen Nature. It is no use bustling after a kingfisher. I knew this and, though I have no great taste for patience, I sat down on the bank of the stream, idly watching flycatcher and wagtail, and the fresh green of the iris leaves. I did not hope for too much. I was content to lie at the edge of a stream that a kingfisher inhabited. The unseen kingfisher made the mud of the stream as pretty as though it were sitting there on a bough as in an illustration. So at least I thought, and I knew that I was going to return again and again to the shores of that stagnant streamlet until I had set my eyes on Solomon in all his glory or whatever a kingfisher most resembled. Then, suddenly, out of a turn of the stream under a

thicket of bushes, the blue flame appeared and fled past
me along the water, perching for a moment on the lower
branch of a willow and taking to flight again as soon as
it saw the cat-like eyes of a human being watching it
from a few yards' distance. Was I disappointed in the
spectacle? No. I am disappointed only because I am
unable to describe it. Can you imagine a blue that is

Kingfisher

more beautiful than any green, and a green that is more
beautiful than any blue, and both of them blended as
though into a magical light? Perhaps there are waters
of as wonderful a blue lying about the shores of some
undiscovered island. Perhaps there are waters of as
wonderful a green visiting the white caves on the shore
of that island.

There is surely no other bird that provides us in the
same degree with an Arabian afternoon's entertainment.

ROBERT LYND from *Solomon in All His Glory*

It is not often that one has so close a view of a shag as this. My head was but a foot or so off, and on a level with her own; my eyes looked into her glass-green ones. One thing about her struck me with wonder, and that was the intense brilliancy of the whole inside of her mouth, which, in a blaze of gamboge, seemed to imitate, in miniature, the cavern in which she sat.

EDMUND SELOUS from *The Bird Watcher in the Shetlands*

Artis has a cuckoo in his collection of stuffed birds, but I have not the sufficient scientific curiosity about me to go and take the exact description of its head, rump, and wings, the length of its tail, and the breadth from the tips of the extended wings. These old bookish descriptions you may find in any Natural History, if they are of any gratification. For my part I love to look on nature with a poetic feeling, which magnifies the pleasure. I love to see the nightingale in its hazel retreat, and the cuckoo hiding in its solitudes of oaken foliage, and not to examine their carcases in glass cases. Yet naturalists and botanists seem to have no taste for this poetic feeling; they merely make collections of dried specimens, classing them after Linnaeus into tribes and families, and there they delight to show them as a sort of ambitious fame. With them " a bird in the hand is worth two in the bush."

JOHN CLARE from his *Diary*

All that in after life he could recall was that from the first his father had taught him to look at birds, and that before he knew that the tops of the trees did not brush the skies, birds were for him "a frenzy." Years later he wrote of himself as a child, "None but aerial companions suited my fancy."

They suit the fancy of us all. What they feel they can voice, as we try to. They court and nest, they battle with the elements, they are torn by two opposing impulses, a love of home and a passion for far places. Only with birds do we share so much emotion. Man feels himself an infinity above those creatures who stand, zoologically, only one step below him, but every human being looks up to the birds. They seem to us like emissaries of another world which exists about us and above us, but into which, earth-bound, we cannot penetrate. It is not the strength of the lion that we give to angels, but wings.

And I think there is not any man to whom some bird call will not reach, to remind him of things he thought he had forgotten. The call of a crow makes me smell sunburnt grass, the chuckle of a wren has in it all the invitation of April, the running of Blue Ridge brooks, the honeyed odour of azalea, the light feet and heart of holiday. Any day that I hear the kingfisher's rattle it will be moonlight for me when I was lost once and lay blanketless upon the ground to sleep, and heard that war cry above the rushing of a nameless stream.

And there are joys and hours of trouble that, remembered long after, bring back the birds which flitted so unconsciously across them—there were two petrels, once, between the slippery hollows and the hissing hills of the sea, a thousand miles from land; if they could ride out their storms, I thought, then so might we.

DONALD CULROSS PEATTIE from *Singing in the Wilderness*

I always connect certain birds with various places according to the time of year, and in spring, in the river valleys and water meadows, I know exactly what I shall expect to see there. The lapwings are tumbling and swooping, incessantly uttering that plaintive wailing cry which could not be more agitated were I robbing their nest. But the nest is not here; it is on higher ground though the lapwing dearly loves the low meadows.

Lapwings

A pair of redshank is ever on the alert, imagining all kinds of danger and giving unnecessary warning to other birds with their petulant call.

On the ground, flitting about in their quiet busy way, are yellow wagtails, and the air is filled with the music of warblers and other birds, including the monotonous call of the cuckoo.

But there is one outstanding sound which is fine music above all other, the drumming of the snipe. It is impossible not to be impressed with this weird noise and to look for its origin. Perhaps the bird will be quite near, a mere speck in the sky overhead, or it may be almost half a mile away, yet the reverberating sound will reach our ears.

E. C. KEITH from *Woodcock and Snipe*

I had been fond of birds since a child; but it was when I was about fourteen that I became a real bird-watcher. The incident which precipitated the change was this. One morning of late winter, crossing the laundry-yard of my aunt's country house, I saw a green woodpecker on the grass only a few yards from me: I had just time to take in the sight of it before the bird was off to the wood beyond the hedge. The green woodpecker is a common bird enough; but I had never seen one close. Here I saw every striking detail: the rich green of the wings, the flash of bright yellow on the back when he flew, the pale glittering eye, the scarlet nape, the strange moustache of black and red; and the effect was as if I had seen a bird of paradise, even a phoenix. I was thrilled with the sudden realization that here, under my nose, in the familiar woods and fields, lived strange and beautiful creatures of whose strangeness and beauty I had been lamentably unaware.

JULIAN HUXLEY from *Bird-Watching and Bird Behaviour*

June 16. A fine distant view, yet wonderfully distinct through the glasses, of five spoonbills feeding. It is always the same, the down-stooped neck and head, with the beak—though a long one, sometimes almost hidden beneath the water—swept powerfully from side to side, giving an appearance of sturdy strength as though considerable resistance had to be overcome. They feed with the greatest alacrity, so that their eager and quick movements are somewhat at variance with the general majesty of their appearance. Anon they stand resting in a more or less straight line, at a little distance from one another. A nearer view, after a successful stalk, shows all five of them in a group standing and preening their beautiful white plumage. They often stand on one of the long black legs, with the other drooped half-way down, and an accustomed action with them, in the intervals, or, as one may almost say, as a formal accompaniment of preening, is to move their heads from side to side, by which the beak, moving in the same way throughout its length, but with a more leisurely motion—or so it seems—irresistibly reminds one of an elephant swinging its trunk—only with such majestic and ponderous creatures, if with any, is the superb spoonbill to be compared. Sometimes the foot of the drooped leg just touches the ground, the two together forming, then, a triangle of which the one side is perpendicular. How glorious is this for the true life-loving naturalist's eye to dwell upon! How massive looks the great depending foot!

EDMUND SELOUS from *Realities of Bird Life*

Nothing can look prettier than these little miniature terns as the glasses, wandering over the sandy waste, pick them up sitting here and there. They look very snug as they

sit, each in its little shallow depression, the head, with
its black velvet cap and yellow bill, the whole top of the
back, tail and tips of the wings showing quite plainly—
as does also the little white mark on the top of the black
velvet cap—but all the rest hidden in the trough of the
sand; for they look like prettily painted little ships at
sea,—or boats, for there are no masts—and belonging
to the classical period. They look so snug and cosy as
they sit in a little fleet, and so no doubt they are.

EDMUND SELOUS from *Realities of Bird Life*

O let your strong imagination turn
The great wheel backward, until Troy unburn,
And then unbuild, and seven Troys below
Rise out of death, and dwindle, and outflow,
Till all have passed, and none has yet been there:
Back, ever back. Our birds still crossed the air;
Beyond our myriad changing generations
Still built, unchanged, their known inhabitations.
A million years before Atlantis was
Our lark sprang from some hollow in the grass,
Some old soft hoof-print in a tussock's shade,
And the wood-pigeon's smooth snow-white eggs were laid,
High, amid green pines' sunset-coloured shafts,
And rooks their villages of twiggy rafts
Set on the tops of elms, where elms grew then,
And still the thumbling tit and perky wren
Popped through the tiny doors of cosy balls
And the blackbird lined with moss his high-built walls;
A round mud cottage held the thrush's young,
And straws from the untidy sparrow's hung.

And, skimming forktailed in the evening air,
When man first was were not the martins there?
Did not those birds some human shelter crave,
And stow beneath the cornice of his cave

Jay

Their dry tight cups of clay? And from each door
Peeped on a morning wiseheads three or four.

Yes, daw and owl, curlew and crested hern,
Kingfisher, mallard, water-rail and tern,
Chaffinch and greenfinch, warbler, stonechat, ruff,
Pied wagtail, robin, fly-catcher and chough,

Missel-thrush, magpie, sparrow-hawk, and jay,
Built, those far ages gone, in this year's way.
And the first man who walked the cliffs of Rame,
As I this year, looked down and saw the same
Blotches of rusty red on ledge and cleft
With grey-green spots on them, while right and left
A dizzying tangle of gulls were floating and flying,
Wheeling and crossing and darting, crying and crying,
Circling and crying, over and over and over,
Crying with swoop and hover and fall and recover.
And below on a rock against the grey sea fretted,
Pipe-necked and stationary and silhouetted,
Cormorants stood in a wise, black, equal row
Above the nests and long blue eggs we know.
O delicate chain over all the ages stretched,
O dumb tradition from what far darkness fetched:
Each little architect with its one design
Perpetual, fixed and right in stuff and line,
Each little ministrant who knows one thing,
One learnèd rite to celebrate the spring.
Whatever alters else on sea or shore,
These are unchanging: man must still explore.

J. C. SQUIRE from *The Birds*

I here recall an incident of my young days in a far land,
less civilized than ours. I had a neighbour in my home
for whom I had little love. He was a greedy rascal, a
petty rural magistrate with an itching palm, and if justice
was required at his hands it had to be bought with money
like any other commodity. One summer afternoon he
rode over to my home and asked me to go for a walk with

him by the river. It was a warm brilliant day in early autumn, and when we had walked about a couple of miles along the bank to a spot where the stream was about fifty yards wide, we sat down on the dry grass under a large red willow. A flock of birds was in the tree—a species of a most loquacious kind—but our approach had made them silent. Not the faintest chirp fell from the branches that had been full of their musical jangle a few minutes before. It was a species of troupial, a starling-like bird of social habits, only larger than our starling, with glossy olive-brown plumage and brilliant yellow breast. *Pecho amarillo* (yellow breast) is its vernacular name. Now as soon as we had settled comfortably on the grass the entire flock, of thirty or forty birds, sprang up into the air, going up out of the foliage like a fountain, then suddenly they all together dropped down, and sweeping by us over the water burst into a storm of loud ringing jubilant cries and liquid notes. My companion uttered a sudden strange harsh discordant laugh, and turning away his sharp dry fox-like face too late to hide the sudden moisture I had seen in his eyes, he exclaimed with savage emphasis on the first word—" *Curse* the little birds—how glad they are!"

W. H. HUDSON from *Adventures Among Birds*

A FAVOUR

The way a crow
  Shook down on me
The dust of snow
  From a hemlock tree

Has given my heart
A change of mood
And saved some part
Of a day I had rued.

ROBERT FROST

. . . deep in brambly hedges dank
The small birds nip about, and say:
" Brothers, the Spring is not so far away! "

FRANCES CORNFORD from *The Hills*

1146686

It was a clear, bracing day in early November, and the
broad, bare stubbles of central Essex stretched away
into the blue distance on all sides for miles and miles.
There was a keen wind blowing which made standing
about uncomfortable, and I had come many miles and
was feeling rather tired and dull. The professed object
of my pilgrimage was not birds at all, but the little priory
of Dunmow, which I was curious, if not particularly
eager, to see. As I passed through the miles of wide,
clean autumn country I must confess to some vacuity
of mind. It was one of those days when the fields seem
to hold no secrets, showing their uninteresting emptiness
unashamedly—when Rooks and Wood-pigeons, Chaffinches and Yellow Hammers must form the bird watcher's
staple diet. I was slightly bored.

As I opened the little gate which leads from a neighbouring field into the old churchyard, a flash of red
caught my eye, and the next moment I was looking, for

the first time in my life, at a Black Redstart. Instantly my whole outlook was enlivened and enlightened, and like an excited schoolboy I could hardly restrain my enthusiasm and excitement.

To anyone who has not experienced such a feeling it naturally seems silly that one should be sent into transports of joy by a little dark-grey bird with a red-brown tail. And from the scientist, who has neither time nor use for such meaningless satisfactions, a confession as I have just made, will probably excite nothing but contempt: for, according to his own professions, all birds are as one to him. He has put away childish things.

But as I watched this restless, exhilarating little creature flashing about the ancient walls of the old building, now flirting its brilliant tail before me over the dark ground, here doubling back suddenly and disappearing, now flicking Wheatear-like among the plough-furrows for insects, or examining the churchyard wall for minutiae, I could not help philosophizing a little over the very real pleasure that one gets from seeing new birds. It is the problem of the charm of birds in a nutshell.

For many years I have been bird-watching, never a week passing without some kind of field-day, and here for the first time was a Black Redstart. There was, to begin with, a pleasure in something hoped for turning up after a long period of waiting and hoping. Perhaps every English ornithologist with any imagination at all hopes to see nearly all the birds on the British List. It is a fond hope, certainly—childish but very natural. Unlike the old gentleman in the song, who had never seen a jaguar nor yet an armadillo, the ornithologist never relapses into supposing that he never will see the rarest species. Whether he is willing to admit it or not (and sometimes he isn't), there lurks somewhere in his mind some fond hope that he will one day be able to report a Great Bustard, that on some idyllic summer's afternoon he will see shining Bee-eaters skimming among English trees, or that (before his time comes) he will yet see Spoonbills and Avocets stalking about some gleaming, mysterious mudflat.

W. K. RICHMOND from *Quests for Birds*

A short while ago I saw, within the space of one week, two species under circumstances which showed me quite clearly that the pleasures I experience in watching birds, particularly new birds, has really not changed in the slightest from that which I felt as a boy. As the years go by, the ornithologist in England necessarily finds that the occasions when he meets new species grow more infrequent. Perhaps the experience becomes even more precious on that account—at any rate both incidents convinced me that a purely scientific attitude to birds is neither possible nor to be desired. In both cases I was much surprised by the actual reality of the birds—having come, through reading about them and looking at illustrations, to expect something quite different.

The first occasion was in Norfolk. A friend and I set out shortly before dawn in mid-October to row across Hickling Broad in search of Bearded Tits, which, we had been told, were most easily observed at such an hour. It was a strange, misty-pearly light in which we began, the fresh, icy morning breeze sending the waves clapping noisily, and even violently, against the boatside. Not a soul was moving on the great water. A few gulls came leisurely flying in from the sea. From the posts which mark the channel over this, the largest of the Broads, we disturbed a silent Heron and two or three Cormorants, but there did not seem to be a great deal about on the grey waters. The glass revealed Coots in all directions, a Great Crested Grebe eyeing us uneasily at a distance, and a few ducks, nearly all of them Mallard. Slowly we made our way across to a large yellow reed-bed which seemed to us to be a likely spot for the birds we were looking for. A Water-Rail squealed as we drew near, but otherwise everything, apart from the low whispering of the reeds, seemed as silent as a deserted graveyard. As some of these reed-beds are several miles long and almost a mile wide from the edge of the water, we had not been very optimistic about seeing the birds at the first attempt, but before we had driven our boat into the reeds we heard at a distance the unmistakable ringing note (so often and so badly described) of the Bearded Tit. A moment later we saw two or three of the birds trooping over the feathery tops of the reeds, and watched them descend once more and disappear amongst them. Desperately we pushed the boat through thick sedge, not caring whether we got beached or not, and to our relief came out on the other side in a long channel of water, hemmed in on all sides by the reeds. Along this we slowly quanted, and approached the hidden birds quite closely, hearing all the time a number of Coal-Tit-like notes from the birds as they flew excitedly about. At this distance the curious " ching-ching-ching " notes, so suppressed and mysterious, seemed even more curious than they did at a distance. The black streak of the moustache of these cinnamon-coloured birds could be seen on the cocks when they flew, but most striking of all was the large brilliant red tail, as they darted up and over the tops of the reeds. Try as we might, we could not see the birds properly at rest. They were constantly darting about, uttering their strange, restless cries, never still for a moment, and always just on the wrong side of the reeds. This activity gave the impression that there

Bearded Tit

was quite a number of birds, but at length three birds, disturbed by the boat, flew up to a fair height, and with strong steady dropping flight disappeared into the distance. We had expected from the books some delicate, fairy-like birds, scarcely able to support themselves in the struggle of life, but here were creatures brimming over with life and vitality, even more fascinating and unusual than we had dared to hope. Long did we quant up and down the passages and shallow lagoons of this huge reed-bed, into which small boats very rarely venture, but we saw no more of the charming " Reed Pheasant," and at length pushed back on to the open broad, to row back to a well-earned breakfast with a sense of exhilaration and satisfaction such as Man not frequently attains to.

The other occasion was as unlooked for as that in which the Black Redstart figured so pleasantly. I had been watching on a certain sewage farm for several weeks, not without some success. It was now the very end of October, however, and the migrating waders seemed to have all passed on. In the drear light of the late afternoon Lapwings were calling plaintively from the flats, and now and then a Snipe rose with harsh grating calls. The light was bad; there was a white mist rising over the water, and there seemed to be nothing interesting about in the way of birds. Sewage farms are not particularly edifying places even at the best of times, but at such times as this they are the most depressing surroundings imaginable. I was just packing away the telescope I had with me, and was about to turn away disappointed, when I saw something moving several hundreds of yards away on one of the large settling tanks or " meres " of the farm. My mind first registered the possibility of ducks, then, as the definition of the glass grew clearer, I thought of Black-headed Gulls, then of Black Terns (which I had just recently seen on this same piece of water). But these two birds, which I could see only "through a glass darkly," were unaccountably unlike anything I had ever seen previously. They kept moving about on the water in a haphazard, jerky fashion, bobbing about from side to side. When, after two or three seconds of adjusting the glass,

Grey Phalaropes

I got the lens clear, I saw to my delight that the birds were Grey Phalaropes. Immediately I threw off all caution and walked right up to the birds, which were very tame and allowed me to approach within a few feet. Anything so strange I had never seen before. Here were two little birds, smaller than thrushes, swimming about like ducks; their heads jerking forward and backwards quickly all the time, and yet their bodies gliding smoothly forward through the water. They held their necks high out of the water, and every moment were snatching insects or vegetable matter from the surface with forward and sideways movements. A diagram of the directions of their path would look most inconsequential; every moment they were changing direction, doubling backwards, and always moving with a jerky, delicate zigzag motion which gave a perfect impression of nervous energy.

One of the birds was in transitional plumage, its wings and back still in summer feathers and its neck still suffused with the rosy colour which makes the Grey Phalarope a distinctly red bird throughout the breeding season. The other was already in grey and white winter dress. All the time I watched them they kept darting about over the water, snatching at invisible things and always swimming hastily away in the opposite direction just as if they were afraid of their own shadows. Although they had come together it was evident that they had no ties. They swam away from each other, each foraging on its own, now and then giving a shrill, metallic " tlip-tlip-tlip " note, as if to keep in touch with each other. I threw small stones at them, just to see how tame they were. At this they rose nimbly out of the water, uttering their metallic notes rapidly, and either came down within a yard or two, or flew round and round and then returned to the same spot from which they flew up. I watched these birds which chance had suddenly placed before me until darkness rendered them almost invisible. The next morning only one remained, and I could not help ruminating a little at having been present, as it were, at the parting of two such birds, which possibly had travelled several thousand of miles together.

Both these experiences had one thing in common, the strange sense of the reality and the nervous vitality of the birds. Both of them were so much more intensely and dynamically alive than I had ever imagined they could be. It is this realization of vivid, intense life which is the thrilling thing about seeing a new bird—the root, in fact, of all bird-watching. The commoner birds, which we see nearly every day, have grown familiar to us—we no longer see them as they really are, and it is sometimes necessary for an occasionally uncommon bird to remind us what kind of creatures they are which we seek after. Any biologist will tell us the cold facts of bird anatomy; the temperature of its blood, the possible workings of its brain; any text-book will tell us all about its habits, its plumage, almost anything we want to know. But I doubt whether the bird *itself* can be known except in rare flashes of insight such as have been described.

W. K. RICHMOND from *Quest for Birds*

Oft have I seen in fields the little birds
    Go in between a bullock's legs to eat;
But what gives me most joy is when I see
    Snow on my doorstep, printed by their feet.

W. H. DAVIES from *Birds*

Feb. 19, 1770. Your observation that " the cuckoo does not deposit its egg indiscriminately in the nest of the first bird that comes in its way, but probably looks out a nurse in some degree congenerous, with whom to entrust its young," is perfectly new to me; and struck me so forcibly, that I naturally fell into a train of thought that led me to consider whether the fact was so, and what reason there was for it. When I came to recollect and inquire, I could not find that my cuckoo had ever been seen in these parts, except in the nest of the wagtail, the hedge-sparow, the titlark, the white-throat, and the red-breast, all soft-billed insectivorous birds. The excellent Mr. Willughby, mentions the nest of the *palumbus* (ring-dove), and of the *fringilla* (chaffinch), birds that subsist on acorns and grains, and such hard food: but then he does not mention them as of his own knowledge; but says afterwards that he saw himself a wagtail feeding a cuckoo. It appears hardly possible that a soft-billed bird should subsist on the same food with the hard-billed: for the former have thin membranaceous stomachs suited to their soft food; while the latter, the granivorous tribe, have strong muscular gizzards, which, like mills, grind, by the help of small gravels and pebbles, what is swallowed. This proceeding of the cuckoo, of dropping its eggs as it were by chance, is such a monstrous outrage on maternal affection, one of the first great dictates of nature; and such a violence on instinct; that, had it only been related of a bird in the Brazils, or Peru, it would never have merited our belief. But yet, should it farther appear that this simple bird, when divested of that natural στοργή that seems to raise the kind in general above themselves, and inspire them with extraordinary degrees of cunning and address, may be still endured with a more enlarged faculty of discerning what species are suitable and congenerous nursing-mothers for its disregarded eggs and young, and may deposit them only under their care, this would be adding wonder to wonder, and instancing in a fresh manner that the methods of Providence are not subjected to any mode or rule, but astonish us in new lights, and in various and changeable appearances.

What was said by a very ancient and sublime writer concerning the defect of natural affection in the ostrich, may be well applied to the bird we are talking of:

" *She is hardened against her young ones, as though they were not hers* :

" *Because God hath deprived her of wisdom, neither hath he imparted to her understanding.*" [1]

Query.—Does each female cuckoo lay but one egg in a season, or does she drop several in different nests according as opportunity offers?

GILBERT WHITE from *Selborne*

Feb. 19, 1770. You wonder, with good reason, that the hedge-sparrows, etc., can be induced to sit at all on the egg of the cuckoo without being scandalized at the vast disproportioned size of the supposititious egg.

GILBERT WHITE from *Selborne*

Third Season (1920) Record.
The laying of the Fourteenth Egg. June 8.
The third nest of No. 6 pair, which was the only one available to-day, had still only one egg at 9.30 a.m. on the 7th. This morning it had two, not three as there

[1] *Job xxxix*, 16, 17

ordinarily should have been. And yet it is extremely
unlikely that an egg had been removed as the fostered
ultimately laid a full clutch of five. Meadow Pipit " sixes "
are unknown in this district, and indeed, extremely rare
anywhere in England.

A party of four, we reached the common at 1 p.m.
The Cuckoo—soon in evidence—was distinguished from
her mates by her silence except when " bubbling." From
the attention paid to her by the No. 6. Pipits it was evident
that they expected favours from the Cuckoo.

From about 3 p.m. onwards the Cuckoo, after having
spent a certain amount of time watching the male Pipit
of No. 8 pair (which pair, by the way, acted as fosterers
four days later), showed evident intentions of fulfilling
our expectations of the victimization of No. 6 pair. Twice
she flew to a large divided pear tree (G) in an orchard
on the east side of the common, hopping up to her
invariable perch whence she could command a view of
the nest, just as she had done when watching on May 29
the former nest, 6^2, of the same pair, where, on May 31,
she laid her tenth egg.

Passers-by disturbed her at 4 p.m., when it was evident
that she was anxious to lay. She flew across, right over
my head, to the centre orchard, accompanied by two
male Cuckoos, all three afterwards wheeling over to the
north end of the common. Unaccompanied she then flew
to an isolated oak tree (F) which borders the area on the
south-east side, but owing to the thickness of the foliage
it was impossible to see her.

Between 4.30 and 4.45 the Cuckoo made four floating
glides down to the nest, scarcely alighting and immediately
returning to the same tree. But on the last occasion she

stayed at the nest for rather over a minute, and during the whole of this time I could clearly see one of the Pipits, although both were at the nest, fluttering and tumbling around the gorse near the Cuckoo, which was mainly concealed by the herbage. The male Pipit had been in constance attendance on her during the preceding half-hour, accompanying her backwards and forwards on her flights to the nest.

In a little more than sixty seconds the Cuckoo had laid her egg. As she left the nest and flew across to the " east orchard" I got a perfect view of an egg between her mandibles. So short had been her stay at the nest that I yet feared that this egg she was so carrying might be her own, and so I did not hurry to the nest. But five minutes later all of us assembled there and found it to contain the Cuckoo's fourteenth egg, and one only of the Pipit's, the former being still quite warm.

EDGAR CHANCE from *The Cuckoo's Secret*

After spending most of the morning in a hide near the thick crab-apple tree (a favourite Cuckoo observation post) hoping to get some film of the female Cuckoo in the tree, P. B. Smyth came across to tell me that a Cuckoo was moving about on the ground in a neighbouring field. We carried the hide and my gear across and fixed up the hide near the place to which she had been gliding. Smyth placed a dummy nest in a line with the hide and the Cuckoo's tree so that I could get her glide. I settled down inside the hide to await the blowing of the whistle which was to be the signal that she had started. The whistle blew, but as I had seen her start from the tree I was already turning the handle. The Cuckoo glided down but unfortunately alighted to the left of the hide. As she was out of the picture I left off turning and watched her instead. She walked about evidently searching for a nest and all the time two, sometimes three, Pipits were pecking

Cuckoo at Meadow Pipit's Nest

at her, flying on to her, and pulling feathers out of her back; she really did very little to stop them, only emitting a curious noise, a sort of grunt, apparently in defiance or as a warning. For some minutes she continued to search and then flew away.

Some minutes later she again glided from her tree and alighted in the same place as before. Practically the same things happened as previously, and, after a few minutes of unsuccessful search, she again flew away. Smyth then came across to me, and we decided to move the dummy nest to a spot near to where she alighted on the two previous occasions; the nest, containing three eggs, was placed in a most open spot where from the hide I had an entirely uninterrupted view. The whistle blew and I started to turn the handle of the camera, but soon stopped as the Cuckoo alighted just outside the area covered by the lens. She pottered about, still heckled by the Pipits. At one time I noticed a Pipit with its beak full of Cuckoo's feathers, distinctly proving its antipathy to Cuckoos prowling around its neighbourhood. The Cuckoo continued to search, at one time going quite fifteen yards away from me. Eventually she came towards me again, Smyth having walked round into her view and slightly frightened her so that she took a short flight of ten yards. She still searched, until at last she saw the nest. She ran to it, dived her head into it and then pushed herself forward until she lay right on the nest, her tail being towards me and her head practically in the heather at the back of the nest. For eight to ten seconds she lay perfectly still, looking for all the world like a pigeon. I am not sure what the Pipits were doing at this time for I was concentrating on the Cuckoo. She then flew right off the nest and disappeared from my sight. Smyth came across and found that she had laid her egg and taken one of the three eggs of the Pipit away with her.

EDGAR CHANCE from *The Cuckoo's Secret*

DB

When first hatched the Cuckoo is naked, blind, and an ugly squat-shaped little creature of fleshy hue. It is distinctly large for the size of the egg, which by the way is very thick-shelled.

The young Cuckoo, produced from an egg which we watched in 1921 for the purposes of the film, will well serve to illustrate the earlier salient points, as we had the youngster under close observation. On the evening of June 9 a Meadow Pipit's nest contained three eggs and one of a Cuckoo. On the afternoon of June 20 the Cuckoo and two Pipits had hatched—it turned out that the Pipit's third egg was addled. Early on the morning of the 21st we found that the young Cuckoo was getting energetic and had already ejected the addled egg. Hawkins and I got into the hide and watched the Pipits brooding and feeding the restless young Cuckoo and its two nest-mates. It was very pretty to watch the male Pipit bring food whilst the female was brooding; she raised herself up and distinctly directed the distribution by the male of his burden of food. We were within four feet of the nest. We left at 4 p.m., and in our absence the young Cuckoo ejected his two nest-mates, which upon our return at 9.30 p.m. we found dying and stiff. I took them in my hands, breathed on them, and they gradually relaxed and came to life. One I risked by slipping it at dusk into the nest of a Meadow Pipit sitting on four eggs; the other was placed in flannel in a basket in an open oven. In the very early morning of June 22 they were both alive. We put them in with the young Cuckoo, and after Hawkins had taken several good pictures of the young parasite again ejecting them I transferred them to another nest which contained some newly hatched nestling of their own species.

EDGAR CHANCE from *The Cuckoo's Secret*

The incubation of birds must be considered as correspondent to the gestation of quadrupeds. Nature has imparted to the females of the accipitres a larger size and greater vigour than to the males, from the necessity of providing living prey for the young. The females of the gallinacea, on each of whom singly devolves the care of a very numerous offspring, could not provide for it, if their chicks were not endowed with the instinct of seeking food for themselves. We find that it is towards the period of the birth of the young that the mothers put in requisition all the resources of their instinct. So much tenderness and trouble lavished without compensation; such a sublime and generous self-devotion in the most urgent dangers, proves that this natural and amiable sentiment is not the result of any mechanical connexion of ideas and sensations, but of a law altogether divine. The swallow, precipitating itself into an edifice in flames to rescue its young; the hen, which hesitates not to brave death in defence of her chickens; the timid lark presenting herself to the fowler, to divert him from her nest; the little colibris, which prefer an eternal slavery with their offspring to liberty without them;—in fine, all these touching evidences of affection for the helpless, in animals so light and volatile, clearly indicate the sacred impulse communicated to all that breathe by the Mighty Being, who has willed the perpetuity and support of every species. Here, indeed, we recognize the workmanship of the Divinity in all its admirable wisdom and surpassing benevolence: *digitus Dei est hic!*

We also find the birds deserving of the most attentive observation in the education of their young. The assiduity with which they bring them food; the care which they take

to adapt it to their tender stomachs; the degrees by which
they teach them to fly, calculating with such accuracy the
proportion of their growing strength; all these, and many
other points of a similar nature, are subjects of the highest
interest to the contemplative lover of Nature.

BARON CUVIER from *The Class Aves*, 1829

Tues., Dec. 14, 1824. A copple-crowned crane shot at
Billings's pond in the Green. 'Twas four foot high from
the toes to the bill. On the breast and rump was a thick,
shaggy down full of powder, which seemed to be a sort
of pounce-box to the bird, to dress its feathers with to
keep out the wet. Its neck and breast were beautifully
stained with streaks of watery brown. Its back was slate-
grey. The down on its head was of the same colour.

JOHN CLARE from his *Diary*

The sinking sun is taking leave,
And sweetly gilds the edge of Eve,
While huddling clouds of purple dye
Gloomy hang the western sky.
Crows crowd croaking overhead,
Hastening to the woods to bed.
Cooing sits the lonely dove,
Calling home her absent love.
With " Kirchup! Kirchup! " 'mong the wheats
Partridge distant partridge greets;
Beckoning hints to those that roam,
That guide the squandered covey home.

Swallows check their winding flight,
And twittering on the chimney light.
Round the pond the martins flirt,
Their snowy breasts bedaubed with dirt,
While the mason, 'neath the slates,
Each mortar-bearing bird awaits:
By art untaught, each labouring spouse
Curious daubs his hanging house.

JOHN CLARE from *Summer Evening*

What it is that the crows talk about is a secret from most of us. One fancies that many of them are jokers much given to pulling other crows' legs. Seldom are they settled in a field for long when one of them suddenly gives warning, like a boy crying " Cave! " and startles the whole crowd of them into circles of flight. They settle down again, a whirl of them coming to rest, and again a rook gives the alarm. Off they are, the more nervous of them, on short circling flights, and, if you watch them for an hour, you will not often see them at rest for more than a few seconds at a time. It may be that you can fool all the crows some of the time and some of the crows all the time, but that you cannot fool all the crows all the time. One cannot tell. What seems probable, however, is that many of the crows enjoy being jostled into fear. They want an excuse for movement: that is apparently the origin of most games. To keep perpetually moving is a Law of Nature with them as it is with flies and planets. The ability to move at will is the chief thing that distinguishes a living creature from a stone. Hence living creatures abhor stillness and stagnation as properties of the dead. Children, birds and fish are seldom still. They must circulate at all costs— not for any purpose, save that circulation is a good thing in itself.   ROBERT LYND from *Solomon in All His Glory*

Virgil, as a familiar occurrence, by way of simile, describes a dove haunting the cavern of a rock in such engaging numbers, that I cannot refrain from quoting the passage: and John Dryden has rendered it so happily in our language, that without farther excuse I shall add his translation also:—

" Qualis speluncâ subitò commota Columba,
    Cui domus, et dulces latebrosò in pumice nidi,
    Fertur in arva volans, plausumque exterrita pennis
    Dat tecto ingentem—mox aere lapsa quieto,
    Radit iter liquidum, celeres neque commovet alas."

" As when a dove her rocky hold forsakes,
    Rous'd, in her fright her sounding wings she shakes;
    The cavern rings with clattering:—out she flies,
    And leaves her callow care, and cleaves the skies:
    At first she flutters:—but at length she springs
    To smoother flight, and shoots upon her wings."

GILBERT WHITE from *Selborne*

When feeding, without any doubt, upon living prey, eider-ducks are accustomed to dive, going right to the bottom, and often coming up with what they find there

—a crab or other kind of shell-fish—to dispose of it on
the surface at their leisure. The chick can dive as easily
as the grown bird, but one may watch these family excursions for a long time without once seeing either of them
do so. Instead, they now merely duck to get the seaweed,
which almost reaches the surface. The chicks, however,
are often raised by the swell of the sea beyond the height
at which they can nibble it comfortably, and it is then
funny to see the hinder portion of their little bodies sticking up in the air, with their legs violently kicking, as they
hold on with might and main top revent being floated off on
the wave. Sometimes a brisk one bids fair to tilt them right
over, but they always ride it in the most buoyant manner.

EDMUND SELOUS from *The Bird Watcher in the Shetlands*

The most attractive animal I have seen in London was
a duck. I was standing on the edge of the Round Pond
in Kensington Gardens. It was one of those blowy days
on which the Round Pond is a tumultuous ocean, whipped
by the storm into huge rollers three inches high. As the
little model yachts ploughed their way across the pond,
many of them heeled over till their mainsails dipped into
the tide. Two of them had their sails so heavily weighted
with water that they were unable to right themselves and
lay helpless and drifting on their sides. Had I been the
owner of a model yacht, I should have been timid of
racing in such foaming seas. The English are a race of
seamen, however, and, even with the spectacle of the
wreckage spread out before them as a warning, the yachts-
men loosed their green and their blue and their white

boats into the wind as though they had not a fear. There are no other yacht races to compare in excitement with those on the Round Pond. Cowes is dull compared to it. Each race takes exactly the right time—two to three minutes—and the spectators can follow it from start to finish. But it was not in appreciation of yacht-racing that I began to write. Man is a spirit, not an animal, in battling with circumstances such as wind and tide. Nor do animals organize games in this serious fashion. The animal that delighted me, as I have said, was a duck. Superficially, it was like all the other ducks on the pond. If all the ducks in Kensington Gardens were marshalled before me for purposes of identification, I could not pick this one out. Yet there must have been something different about it. The ordinary duck, when it sees a yacht bearing down on it, scuttles out of the way as human beings do when getting out of the way of a motor bus. Never but once have I seen a duck showing any interest in a yacht except for the purpose of not being run down by it. This duck, however, I repeat, was different. A beautiful green yacht with bellying white sails bore down on it while it was not looking, and the duck, on turning its head round after a vigorous preening of its breast feathers, suddenly beheld the deck leaning over towards it and almost touching its tail, as though inviting it to step aboard. Whether it was startled into its next action I do not know, but, quick as a cat, it wheeled round and, to the amazement of the assembled spectators, scrambled on to the deck and took up its position at the tiller. The yacht wobbled for a moment under the unexpected weight, but the duck wobbled too, and so kept its place. In so heavy a sea a heavy duck was an advantage to the yacht,

which no longer lay over at a dangerous angle, but began
to move in stately speed across the pond. For a time the
duck looked about it as though a little puzzled by the
motion and by the seascape that swept past it at so incredible a speed. If the boat lurched under a sudden squall
the duck gave a frightened lurch also. But, as it kept its
footing on its magnificently flat feet, its self-confidence
seemed to grow, and it gazed round at the other ducks
with an air of boastfulness. At last, as though to suggest
that it had been accustomed to sailing for years, it ceased
even to look round at the others and began to nibble
vigorously at its breast feathers like a duck on dry land.
By the time the yacht was drawing near to the opposite
shore the duck appeared to be settling down to sleep,
but, on looking up, it saw a crowd of men, women and
children laughing uproariously at it, whereupon it slid
hastily off into the water and floated off towards the
middle of the pond with a ruffled air of contempt for so
ill mannered a race. . . . That, I think, is the most
exciting event that has happened in Kensington Gardens in
recent years.   ROBERT LYND from *Solomon in All His Glory*

Then there are the ducks. The countryman may boast
of his nightingales, his larks, his woodpeckers, his kingfishers, his jays. But, after all, the ducks on the Serpentine
have points of superiority to any of these birds. They,
too, will repay you if you take your courage in both hands
and go out boldly with bread in a paper bag. How nobly
they ride the ripples of the stormy pond, awaiting the
bread-giver! How, on catching a distant sight of him, they

hasten like a fleet of small motor boats to his neighbourhood! How exquisitely the blue feather shines out of the
drab in the wing even of the dullest duck! How gorgeously
the drake's head gleams with shifting blue and green
lights! How lordlily his tail curls! Was ever pig's tail
prettier? Then there are the tufted ducks, each with its
straight black hair blowing about in the wind like the
straight black hair of a quack dentist, or a piano-tuner,
or an elocution master. Each of them, too, has a little
round eye as yellow as bright sunshine, and each of them
has the gift of standing on its head and performing feats
as dexterous as the cart-wheels of a street arab. I saw a
small ragged boy in Hyde Park last week amusing a baby
in a perambulator extemporized out of a sugar-box by
throwing small stones among the tufted ducks. I dislike
the habit of throwing stones at ducks, and, though none
of them seemed to be hitting the birds, I felt nervous
for their little daffodil eyes. I spoke my mind about it—
not to the small boy, for I am always afraid that if I
reprove people my pulpit blood may assert itself—but in
an aside to a lady. She went across to him, and instead of
treating him as a brand to be plucked from the burning,
as I should have done, she spoke to him almost as a
fellow-sinner. " You're taking care not to hit any of them,
aren't you? " she said, smiling. He turned up an enthusiastic face on which there was a large smudge on each
cheek and a large smudge on his small nose. He was just
big enough to be able to walk and talk without accident.
He beamed good nature and said in a series of gasps of
excitement: " You throw things at 'em, and they stands
on their 'eads." It was certainly true. The tufted ducks
were standing on their heads, peering after the sunk

Tufted Drakes

pebbles in the hope that they were bread, till they must have been giddy. As I watched·them my attitude to the youngster changed. I, too, had rather see a duck standing on its head than almost any other sort of acrobat. I love to see the uneasy equilibrium, and the kicking legs with the joints going up and down like piston-rods. Besides, it amused the baby. Was it virtuous? I do not know. If one of the ducks had been hit, my attitude would probably have changed back again to the normal, and I should have spoken my mind angrily—to the lady. But no harm was done beyond giving the ducks headaches. . . .

But the subjects of ducks is endless. Have you ever seen a teal? Why, a teal alone is the beginning of a story as long as *The Arabian Nights.*

ROBERT LYND from *Solomon in All His Glory*

Petersfield, Friday Evening, Nov. 11, 1825. We started, therefore, this morning, coming through the Duke of Buckingham's park, at Avington, which is close by Easton, and on the same side of the Itchen. This is a very beautiful place. The house is close down at the edge of the meadow land; there is a lawn before it, and a pond supplied by the Itchen, at the end of the lawn, and bounded by the park on the other side. The high road, through the park, goes very near to this water; and we saw thousands of wild-ducks in the pond, or sitting round on the green edges of it. . . . To see so many *wild*-fowl, in a situation where everything is in the *parterre*-order, has a most pleasant effect on the mind.

WILLIAM COBBETT from *Rural Rides*

On the face of this expanse of waters, and perfectly secure from fowlers, lie all day long, in the winter season, vast flocks of ducks, teals, and widgeons, of various denominations; where they preen and solace, and rest themselves, till towards sunset, when they issue forth in little parties (for in their natural state they are all birds of the night) to feed in the brooks and meadows; returning again with the dawn of the morning.

GILBERT WHITE from *Selborne*

Widgeon

The fly-catcher is of all our summer birds the most mute and the most familiar: it also appears the last of any. It builds in a vine, or a sweetbriar, against the wall of a house, or in the hole of a wall, or on the end of a beam or plate, and often close to the post of a door where people are going in and out all day long. This bird does not make the least pretension to song, but uses a little inward wailing note when it thinks its young in danger from cats or other annoyances: it breeds but once, and retires early.

GILBERT WHITE from *Selborne*

March 26, 1773. The flycatcher of the *Zoology* (the *stoparola* of Ray), builds every year in the vines that grow on the walls of my house. A pair of these little birds had one year inadvertently placed their nest on a naked bough, perhaps in a shady time, not being aware of the inconvenience that followed. But an hot sunny season coming on before the brood was half fledged, the reflection of the wall became insupportable, and must inevitably have destroyed the tender young, had not affection suggested an expedient, and prompted the parent-birds to hover over the nest all the hotter hours, while with wings expanded, and mouths gaping for breath, they screened off the heat from their suffering offspring.

A further instance I once saw of notable sagacity in a willow-wren, which had built in a bank in my fields. This bird a friend and myself had observed as she sat in her nest; but were particularly careful not to disturb her, though we saw she eyed us with some degree of jealousy. Some days after as we passed that way we were desirous of remarking how this brood went on; but no nest could be found, till I happened to take up a large bundle of long green moss, as it were, carelessly thrown over the nest, in order to dodge the eye of any impertinent intruder.

GILBERT WHITE from *Selborne*

Sometimes goldfinches one by one will drop
From low hung branches; little space they stop;
But sip, and twitter, and their feathers sleek;
Then off at once, as in a wanton freak:
Or perhaps, to show their black and golden wings,
Pausing upon their yellow flutterings.

JOHN KEATS

Tuesday Forenoon, Sept. 12, 1826. I saw again, this morning, large flocks of *goldfinches* feeding on the thistle-seed on the roadside. The French call this bird by a name derived from the thistle, so notorious has it always been that they live upon this seed. *Thistle* is, in French, *chardon;* and the French call this beautiful little bird *chardonaret.* I never could have supposed that such flocks of these birds would ever be seen in England. But it is a great year for all the feathered race, whether wild or tame: naturally so, indeed; for every one knows that it is the *wet*, and not the *cold*, that is injurious to the breeding of birds of all sorts, whether land-birds or water-birds. They say that there are, this year, double the usual quantity of ducks and geese: and, really, they do seem to swarm in the farm-yards, wherever I go.

WILLIAM COBBETT from *Rural Rides*

Sept., 1826. From Sharncut I came through a very long and straggling village, called Somerford, another called Ocksey, and another called Crudwell. Between Somerford and Ocksey I saw, on the side of the road, more *goldfinches* than I had ever seen together; I think fifty times as many as I had ever seen at one time in my life. The favourite food of the goldfinch is the seed of the *thistle*. This seed is just now dead ripe. The thistles are all cut and carried away from the fields by the harvest; but they grow alongside the roads; and, in this place, in great quantities. So that the goldfinches were got here in flocks, and, as they continued to fly along before me, for nearly half a mile, and still sticking to the road and the banks, I do believe I had, at least, a flock of ten thousand flying before me. *Birds* of every kind including patridges and pheasants and all sorts of poultry, are most abundant this year.

WILLIAM COBBETT from *Rural Rides*

And now I suppose I shall always like Thomas à Becket better because he once lived near Worthing, where I myself have in all my life spent only one brief week-end. And, indeed, if you read the guide-book, you will discover some surprisingly interesting things about him. You will discover that he was connected with the Abbey of Fécamp in Normandy, and that, probably or possibly, he was the first man to introduce his favourite flower, the lily of the valley, from France to England. You will also discover, as further evidence of the ancient connection between the hinterland of Worthing and the Abbey of Fécamp, that there is a little Continental bird that migrates every year to this part of England alone in order to eat the figs in Thomas à Becket's garden. It is called the beccafico, or fig-eater. I confess this discovery gave me almost as great a surprise as the shooting of the landlady. It is a delightful notion that a little foreign bird should cross the sea every year for hundreds of years and select the figs in one tiny neighbourhood as though they were the

Goldfinches

best of all possible figs. Were there not figs at Steyning? How I should have made any little foreign bird welcome to the plumpest of them! Why, this hereditary taste for the Archbishop's figs is little short of a miracle. " It can't be true," I said, as I read it, hoping that it was. On returning to London, I took down from the shelves an entirely cold-blooded work, *The Handbook of British Birds*, and turned up " Fig-eater " in the index. The index, alas!

Garden Warbler

referred me to " Garden Warbler," and under " Garden Warbler " I read:

" This is the *pettychaps*, *beccafico* or *fig-eater* of Willughby and Ray (*Orn.*, pp. 216, 217). Jesse was assured by a resident at Worthing ' that a *beccafico* annually visits the fig orchard near that place,' and he supposed (erroneously) that it was found in no other part of England (*Gleanings*, iii., p. 78)."

That, I am afraid, is law-court evidence, and, when a man is able to quote things in brackets, the finest story in the world vanishes—for me, at least—into thin air.

ROBERT LYND from *Solomon in All His Glory*

Nov. 20, 1773. A few house martins begin to appear about the sixteenth of April; usually some few days later than the swallow. For some time after they appear the *hirundines* in general pay no attention to the business of nidification, but play and sport about either to recruit from the fatigue of their journey, if they do migrate at all, or else that their blood may recover its true tone and texture after it has been so long benumbed by the severities of winter. About the middle of May, if the weather be fine, the martin begins to think in earnest of providing a mansion for its family. The crust or shell of this nest seems to be formed of such dirt or loam as comes most readily to hand, and is tempered and wrought together with little bits of broken straws to render it tough and tenacious. As this bird often builds againt a perpendicular wall without any projecting ledge under, it requires its utmost efforts to get the first foundation firmly fixed, so that it may safely carry the super-structure. On this occasion the bird not only clings with its claws, but partly supports itself by strongly inclining its tail against the wall, making that a fulcrum; and thus steadied it works and plasters the materials into the face of the brick or stone. But then, that this work may not, while it is soft and green, pull itself down by its own weight, the provident architect has prudence and forbearance enough not to advance her work too fast;

but by building only in the morning, and by dedicating
the rest of the day to food and amusement, gives it sufficient
time to dry and harden. About half an inch seems to be
a sufficient layer for a day. Thus careful workmen when
they build mud-walls (informed at first perhaps by this
little bird) raise but a moderate layer at a time, and then
desist; lest the work should become top-heavy, and so

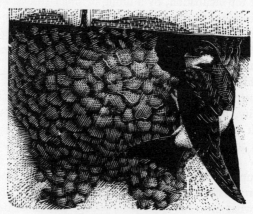

House Martin

be ruined by its own weight. By this method in about
ten or twelve days is formed an hemispheric nest with
a small aperture towards the top, strong, compact, and
warm; and perfectly fitted for all purposes for which it
was intended. But then nothing is more common than
for the house-sparrow, as soon as the shell is finished, to
seize on it as its own, eject the owner, and to line it after
its own manner.

After so much labour is bestowed in erecting a mansion, as nature seldom works in vain, martins will breed on for several years together in the same nest, where it happens to be well sheltered and secure from the injuries of weather. The shell or crust of the nest is a sort of rustic work full of knobs and protuberances on the outside: nor is the inside of those that I have examined smoothed with any exactness at all; but is rendered soft and warm, and fit for incubation, by a lining of small straws, grasses, and feathers; and sometimes by a bed of moss interwoven with wool. In the nest they tread, or engender, frequently during the time of building; and the hen lays from three to five white eggs.

At first when the young are hatched, and are in a naked and helpless condition, the parent birds, with tender assiduity, carry out what comes away from their young. Was it not for this affectionate cleanliness the nestlings would soon be burnt up, and destroyed in so deep and hollow a nest, by their own caustic excrement. In the quadruped creation the same neat precaution is made use of; particularly among dogs and cats, where the dams lick away what proceeds from their young. But in birds there seems to be a particular provision, that the dung of nestlings is enveloped into a tough kind of jelly, and therefore is the easier conveyed off without soiling or daubing. Yet, as nature is cleanly in all her ways, the young perform this office for themselves in a little time by thrusting their tails out at the aperture of their nest. As the young of small birds presently arrive at their full growth, they soon become impatient of confinement, and sit all day with their heads out at the orifice, where the dams, by clinging to the nest, supply them with food from morning

to night. For a time the young are fed on the wing by
their parents; but the feat is done by so quick and almost
imperceptible a sleight, that a person must have attended
very exactly to their motions before he would be able
to perceive it. As soon as the young are able to shift for
themselves, the dams immediately turn their thoughts
to the business of a second brood; while the first flight,
shaken off and rejected by their nurses, congregate in
great flocks, and are the birds that are seen clustering and
hovering on sunny mornings and evenings round towers
and steeples, and on the roofs of churches and houses.
These congregatings usually begin to take place about the
first week in August; and therefore we may conclude that
by that time the first flight is pretty well over. . . .
Those which breed in a ready finished house get the
start in hatching of those that build new by ten days or
a fortnight. These industrious artificers are at their labours
in the long days before four in the morning: when they
fix their materials they plaster them on with their chins,
moving their heads with a quick vibratory motion. They
dip and wash as they fly sometimes in very hot weather,
but not so frequently as swallows. It has been observed
that martins usually build to a north-east or north-west
aspect, that the heat of the sun may not crack and destroy
their nests: but instances are also remembered where
they bred for many years in vast abundance in a hot
stifled inn-yard, against a wall facing to the south. . . .
Martins love to frequent towns, especially if there are
great lakes and rivers at hand; nay, they even affect the
close air of London. And I have not only seen them
nesting in the Borough, but even in the Strand and Fleet
Street; but then it was obvious from the dinginess of their

aspect that their feathers partook of the filth of that sooty atmosphere. . . .

As the summer declines the congregating flocks increase in numbers daily by the constant accession of the second broods; till at last they swarm in myriads upon myriads round the villages on the Thames, darkening the face of the sky as they frequent the aits of that river, where they roost. They retire, the bulk of them I mean, in vast flocks together about the beginning of October: but have appeared of late years in a considerable flight in this neighbourhood, for one day or two, as late as November the third or sixth, after they were supposed to have been gone for more than a fortnight. . . .

House martins are distinguished from their congeners by having their legs covered with soft downy feathers down to their toes. They are no songsters; but twitter in a pretty inward soft manner in their nests. During the time of breeding they are often greatly molested with fleas.

GILBERT WHITE from *Selborne*

On the estate where I am now employed the keeper shot a female sparrow-hawk. Afterwards her nest was found with screaming youngsters in it. I pleaded for their lives and kept it under observation. It was too late in the season for the male to get another mate, but I saw him making repeated visits to the nest with food. On the second day the whining noise of the young hawks was much less noticeable, and on the third day it died down altogether. We climbed up to the nest and found three dead birds scarcely a week old in it. The weather was fine and I do not think exposure was the cause of death, but starvation in the midst of plenty. A whole plucked chaffinch, a partially plucked hedge-sparrow, some nestlings, and a portion of what might have been a rabbit, were lying around them. The old hawk had certainly done his best to provide food, but having done so he thought that he had fulfilled all that was required of him. The duties of getting the food ready for the table, dividing it up, and feeding the family were beyond him. That had always been the mother's function. He had simply brought the food to an old stump and uttered a low call, whereupon she had flown down from the nest and taken it away to feed the family.   J. W. SEIGNE from *Woodcock and Snipe*

THE WATER OUSEL

A shadow by the water's edge,—
A flash across the mossy ledge,
  That stems the roaring race.
Dark were his plumes as dim twilight,
The crescent on his throat gleamed white,
  The breeze was in his face.

I follow, but he flies before,
And when I gain the sandy shore
  Close, close, methinks, behind:—
His tiny footprints speck the beach,
He fleets to some sequestered reach,
  A shadow on the wind.

Love flies me as that dusky bird,
I too have marked his flight, and heard

The rustle of his wings.
He leads me with divine deceit,
To trace the print of vanished feet,
Not where he nests and sings.

A. C. BENSON

Dipper

July 8, 1773. We have had, ever since I can remember,
a pair of white owls that constantly breed under the eaves
of this church. As I have paid good attention to the manner
of life of these birds during their season of breeding,
which lasts the summer through, the following remarks
may not perhaps be unacceptable:—About an hour before
sunset (for then the mice begin to run) they sally forth in
quest of prey, and hunt all round the hedges of meadows
and small enclosures for them, which seem to be their
only food. In this irregular country we can stand on a
eminence and see them beat the fields over like a setting-
dog, and often drop down in the grass or corn. I have

minuted these birds with my watch for an hour together, and have found that they return to their nests, the one or the other of them, about once in five minutes; reflecting at the same time on the adroitness that every animal is

Barn Owl

possessed of as regards the well-being of itself and off-spring. But a piece of address, which they show when they return loaded, should not, I think, be passed over in silence.—As they take their prey with their claws, so they carry it in their claws to their nest: but, as the feet are necessary in their ascent under the tiles, they constantly perch first on the roof of the chancel, and shift the mouse from their claws to their bill, that the feet may be at liberty to take hold of the plate on the wall as they are rising under the eaves.

White owls seem not (but in this I am not positive) to hoot at all: all that clamorous hooting appears to me to come from the wood kinds. The white owl does indeed snore and hiss in a tremendous manner; and these menaces well answer the intention of intimidating: for I have known a whole village up in arms on such an occasion, imagining the church-yard to be full of goblins and spectres. White owls also often scream horribly as they fly along; from this screaming probably arose the common people's imaginary species of screech-owl, which they superstitiously think attends the windows of dying persons. The plumage of the remiges of the wings of every species of owl that I have yet examined is remarkably soft and pliant. Perhaps it may be necessary that the wings of these birds should not make much resistance or rushing, that they may be enabled to steal through the air unheard upon a nimble and watchful quarry.

GILBERT WHITE from *Selborne*

Too-hoo

When blanching winter stark and clear
Silvers the mind with silence white
Till gaudy eye and noisy ear
  Have second hearing, second sight;
When trees are numb as graveyard stones,
And the hard hush nips my narrow-bones,

I listen the crisp and tinkling tune
Of water crystalling under the moon,—
    The frigid, death-voiced moon.
While cold and sharp and shining sheer
Orion's dagger pricks my ear,
Under an old fir's grizzled cowl,
    Big with his drowsy wide surprise
Wakens the hunched and pawky owl
    And blinks his big moon-marvellous eyes:
Over and over and round and round
His slow wits turn and make no sound.
And I, goose-fleshed, and still as he,
    While thoughts but twit my birdlike mind,
Stare upward through a skeleton tree
    Toward truth all star-entwined,
And send, as song-touched poets do
To silence when no words come through,
When raptured sage is toper too,
    An owl's too-hooo.

                                JAMES A. MACKERETH

There are two little owls' nests in the paddock. One of
them is in a hollow pear-tree to the east; and the other
is in a hollow apple-tree to the west. The little owl is
not a nightbird to anything like the same extent as the
other owls. It flies furtively from tree to tree, wicked in
the full blaze of the sun. It has a guilty conscience and
glides down in the shadow of the trees on noiseless wings
at the slightest movement. Before dipping into the hole
of the tree that is its house, it takes up a position in the
crook of a low branch and looks round to see if it is being

observed. It sits infamously still, and, standing in the darkness of a barn door, you can see the yellow of its eyes twenty yards away. At intervals it jerks nervously round, like a criminal expecting the hand of a detective on its shoulder. Should it see you, and should you not move, it begins to bob its body up and down at you, as though to say, " If you are alive, go away! " There is a scene in *The Kid* in which Charlie Chaplin bobs his body

Little Owl

up and down in the same threatening way every time his runaway enemy looks round. His every gesture was an intimation that he would be after the fellow if he did not clear off in double-quick time. But everybody knew that Charlie himself would have run for his life if the man had but turned and come towards him. The owl was like that. A little girl in a blue overall said to me: " Let us bob at him and see what he will do." She bobbed in imitation of him. He bobbed again. She bobbed in answer.

He did not wait for any more of it, but fled like a guilty soul right out of the paddock. We went over to look into his nest where three little white downy creatures sleep, blissful and innocent as tiny pigs. You could see them either by looking down into the hollow stem of the tree from above, or by looking through the small hole in the side out of which the owl swept the garbage of beetles' wing-cases and other uneatable things, as down a rubbish-chute. There were no other comforts or conveniences in the home. Near the three little pigs lay the dried skin of a mouse, eaten long before the nestlings were out of the shell. As for the nestlings themselves, innocent though they at first appeared, each had already the Roman nose of its father and mother; and one wondered whether, in fairness to the other birds, they ought ever to have been allowed to leave the shell. One egg still lay in the nest unhatched. It was a nice case of conscience whether to take it away or leave it to its small chance of bursting into a bird of prey. If you have heard the other birds clamouring over the safety of their infants when an owl is watching them from a tree, you do not want to see too many owls—not, at least, too many little owls, who are but predatory aliens—in the world.

ROBERT LYND from *Solomon in All His Glory*

Happening to make a visit to my neighbour's peacocks, I could not help observing that the trains of those magnificent birds appear by no means to be their tails; those long feathers growing not from their *uropygium*, but all up their backs. A range of short brown stiff feathers,

about six inches long, fixed in the *uropygium*, is the real
tail, and serves as the fulcrum to prop the train, which
is long and top-heavy, when set on end. When the train
is up, nothing appears of the bird before but its head
and neck; but this would not be the case were those long
feathers fixed only in the rump, as may be seen by the
turkey-cock when in a strutting attitude. By a strong
muscular vibration these birds can make the shafts of
their long feathers clatter like the swords of a sword-
dancer; they then trample very quick with their feet, and
run backwards towards the females.

GILBERT WHITE from *Selborne*

Jan 9, 1665. I went to St. James's Park, where I saw
various animals, and examined the throat of the *onocrotalus*,
or pelican, a fowl between a stork and a swan; a melancholy water-fowl, brought from Astracan by the Russian
Ambassador; it was diverting to see how he would toss
up and turn a flat fish, plaice, or flounder, to get it right
into his gullet at its lower beak, which, being filmy,
stretches to a prodigious wideness when it devours a
great fish. Here was also a small water-fowl, not bigger
than a moorhen, that went almost quite erect, like the
penguin of America; it would eat as much fish as its
whole body weighed; I never saw so insatiable a devourer,
yet the body did not appear to swell the bigger. The Solan
geese here are also great devourers, and are said soon to
exhaust all the fish in a pond. Here was a curious sort of
poultry not much exceeding the size of a tame pigeon,
with legs so short as their crops seemed to touch the

earth; a milk-white raven; a stork, which was a rarity
at this season, seeing he was loose, and could fly loftily;
two Balearian cranes, one of which having had one of
his legs broken and cut off above the knee, had a wooden
or boxen leg and thigh, with a joint so accurately made
that the creature could walk and use it as well as if it
had been natural; it was made by a soldier. The park was
at this time stored with numerous flocks of several sorts
of ordinary and extraordinary wild fowl, breeding about
the Decoy, which for being near so great city, and among
such a concourse of soldiers and people, is a singular and
diverting thing.   JOHN EVELYN from *The Diary*

In the centre of this grove there stood an oak, which,
though shapely and tall on the whole, bulged out into
a large excrescence about the middle of the stem. On this
a pair of ravens had fixed their residence for such a series
of years, that the oak was distinguished by the title of the
Raven-tree. Many were the attempts of the neighbouring
youths to get at this eyry: the difficulty whetted their
inclinations, and each was ambitious of surmounting the
arduous task. But, when they arrived at the swelling, it
jutted out so in their way, and was so far beyond their
grasp, that the most daring lads were awed, and acknow-
ledged the undertaking to be too hazardous. So the ravens
built on, nest upon nest, in perfect security, till the fatal
day arrived in which the wood was to be levelled. It was
in the month of February, when those birds usually sit.
The saw was applied to the butt, the wedges were inserted
into the opening, the woods echoed to the heavy blows

of the beetle or mallet, the tree nodded to its fall; but
still the dam sat on. At last, when it gave way, the bird
was flung from her nest; and, though her parental affection deserved a better fate, was whipped down by the
twigs, which brought her dead to the ground.

GILBERT WHITE from *Selborne*

Seawards I had for horizon the low ridge of the sand-
hills overgrown with coarse grey-green grass, and when
on the ridge itself I looked over a vast stretch of yellowish-
brown sand; for it was low tide, with the sea visible as
a white line of foam and the gleam of water more than
a mile away. Here on the sandy ridge there is an old
sea-ruined coastguard station, and, coming to it, I sat
down on a pile of brushwood at the side of the half-
fallen buildings, and after I had been there two or three
minutes a bird fluttered up from the grass close to my
feet and perched on the wood three or four yards from
me. A redwing! A tired traveller from the north, he had
no doubt arrived at that spot during the night, and was
waiting to recover from his great fatigue before continuing his journey inland. He must have been very tired to
remain by himself in such beautiful weather at that spot,
when, close by on the farther side of the salt grey marsh,
the green wooded country, blue in the haze, was so plainly
visible. For the redwing is a most sociable bird, and so
long as his wings can bear him up he cannot endure to
be left behind. Furthermore, he is exceedingly shy of the
human form, especially when he first arrives on our shores;
yet here was this shy bird, alone and sitting very quietly,

FB

within three or four yards of me! Still, it was evident that he was a little troubled at my presence, a little suspicious, from the way he eyed me, flirting his tail and wings; and once or twice, opening wide his beak, he uttered his alarm-note, a sound closely resembling the harsh, prolonged cry of the familiar missel-thrush. But these little signs of alarm were soon over, and he grew quiet, only continuing to emit his low musical chirp a dozen or more times a minute.

W. H. HUDSON from *Adventures Among Birds*

. . . he once more attempted to fly, but settled again on a stick not twenty yards away, and there he appeared disposed to stay, his head well drawn in, the beak raised, his bright eyes commanding a view of the wide sky above. He would be able to see a flock of passing redwings and call to them, and if the feeble sound reached them it would perhaps bring them down to have speech with and cheer him in his loneliness. He would also be able to catch sight of a prowling crow coming his way; for he feared the crow, knowing it for an enemy of the weak and ailing, and would have time to hide himself in the long grass.

There I left him, going away along the shore, but an hour or two later I returned to the same spot, coming over the wide sands, and lo! where I had left one redwing there were now two. One flew wildly away at my approach to a distance of eighty or a hundred yards before alighting again; the other remained, and when I drew near it again moved on its perch, a little alarmed as at first, flirting its wings and tail and once uttering its call-note; and then, recovering from its fear, it began uttering little chirps as before. Those tender little musical sounds, reminiscent of vanished days in distant lands, were somewhat sad, as if the bird complained at being left alone. But his mate had not forsaken him after all, or perhaps she had gone on with the others and then returned to look for him at the last roosting-place.

Having found my bird, I determined to make the most of our second meeting. I had never had an opportunity of looking at a redwing so closely before in such a favourable light, and, seeing it in that way, I found it a more beautiful bird than I had thought it. Perched at a height of above five feet, it was seen against the pale sky in that soft sunlight, pale but crystal clear, and its eyes and every delicate shade in its colouring were distinctly visible. The upper parts were olive-brown, as in the throstle, but the cream-coloured band over the large dark eye made it very unlike that bird; the dark spotted under-parts were cream-white tinged with buff, the flanks bright chestnut red.

W. H. HUDSON from *Adventures Among Birds*

The evening proceedings and manoeuvres of the rooks are curious and amusing in the Autumn. Just before dusk they return in long strings from the foraging of the day, and rendezvous by thousands over Selborne-down, where they wheel round in the air, and sport and dive in a playful manner, all the while exerting their voices, and make a loud cawing, which, being blended and softened by the distance that we at the village are below them, becomes a confused noise or chiding; or rather a pleasing murmur, very engaging to the imagination, and not unlike the cry of a pack of hounds in hollow, echoing woods, or the rushing of the wind in tall trees, or the tumbling of the tide upon a pebbly shore. When this ceremony is over, with the last gleam of day, they retire for the night to the deep beechen woods of Tisted and Ropley.

GILBERT WHITE from *Selborne*

March 17, 1927. I spent some hours this afternoon in watching rooks at their nests. Properly to see and to understand, one ought to have an observatory amidst and overlooking the actual tree-tops, so as to be able to look directly down into the nests and to note what goes on there with absolute accuracy. This, I think, would be quite possible to make during the winter, for one might have a narrow spiral staircase ending in a small railed platform, masked all the way up with timber having the bark on, and with a further screen of branches at the top. The work could proceed gradually during any hour of the day between breakfast and not long after lunch, so as not to interfere with the visits of the birds which take place, usually, soon after daybreak and again towards the latter part of the afternoon. This or some other kind of concealment (but I can think of none better) would be necessary, so that one might go up at any time in the nesting period without disturbing the birds. How easy would this, and things like this, be for a rich man—and how delightful they ought to be! But it is far otherwise, for the end here is not slaughter, but observation. Were the relative strength and distribution of these two impulses reversed, how great—at least how much greater—would be our knowledge of the intimate life habits of the whole animal kingdom! But for such high conquests we care not, but march continually under the black ugly banner of death.

EDMUND SELOUS from *Realities of Bird Life*

1934. Observed in flight or from afar, the rook is a plain black bird. But that does scanty justice to the beautiful colours in his plumage, for so far from being plain black there are four distinct shades of colouring in the bird. His beak and " face " are white, while the crown of his head is a very deep purple-blue, especially deep in the ear-coverts. The feathers on his back are strongly tinted with mauve and bronze, and his tail is dull, almost slate-blue. So far, indeed, is he from being black that every feather seems to be glossed, and as he turns in the sun now this view gives a picture of shot bronzes and mauves, now that reveals the deep richness of the blue that makes up his plumage. He is, indeed, a very beautiful bird, and as he stands perched in the sun against the delicate tracery of the deep green fir-needles he makes a picture to live in the mind for all time and to banish all the old impressions of the bird before he was seen at close quarters.

G. K. YEATES from *The Life of the Rook*

Let me try to give the whole performance in as great detail as possible.[1] The male is sitting on a tall twig in

[1] The following behaviour takes place upon the ground, in the fields around the rookery as well as in the tree-tops.

the next tree to that in which the nest is slowly growing. *"Caw, caw"*—down goes his head, neck outstretched and bill agape, his tail fanned out to each caw. He recovers his dignity—*"Caw, caw"*—the performance is repeated.

Rook Displaying

A little beneath him in a lower bough there sits another rook—the lady of his choice. To her the eager male above flies. The position is now changed. His proximity seems to stir the female's latent desires, and in her turn she takes on the role of the solicitous one. With neck stretched out till her beak touches his, she lowers her body upon the bough and with rapidly quivering wings demands something. But what is this desire of hers? Mating? I think not—at least, not as the dominant thought, not as the direct stimulus to her present behaviour. Fundamentally, of course, her desire is to mate, but at this point her requirement is, I am convinced, nothing greater than the worldly one of food. For around the gift of food lies the centre of the rook's courtship.

But this is anticipating. When the male has given her the food, however little it may be—and sometimes it looks as though he only makes play at giving it—the female flies to the nest. The male follows—and there, and there only, does the sacred rite of mating take place. With the rook the nest is the marriage couch. Although the introductory actions may take place away from the nest, on it alone do the birds bring their courtship to its fulfilment.

G. K. YEATES from *The Life of the Rook*

When the eggs lie in the nest, however, the more carefree days of early March are passed, and to each of the sexes new duties fall and more particular tasks are allotted. The part of each sex, then, during the incubation period must be our first consideration. To take the female first. Her primary task is, of course, that of incubating the eggs.

.   .   .   .   .

The primary duty of the male, not only during this period but throughout the whole nesting-time, lies in the production of food.

.   .   .   .   .

To be fed by her mate is the cause of very great excitement to the female. It is clearly a performance from which she gets the greatest pleasure. Just as before when courtship was in progress, conjugal feeding was characterized by ecstatic wing-flapping and gestures, so, too, now it is the same. How much the female looks forward to this interlude may be gathered from the way in which she cocks her eye at every passing bird, and the great distances at which she will recognize her partner returning home with a pouch-load of food. In this connection I particularly remember watching a pair feeding in another part of the rookery, particularly well suited to observation from the ground by reason of the sharp rise of the land giving the observer a viewpoint on a level with the nests in the high elms. My attention was attracted by the wild flapping and ecstatic caws from a single bird incubating on one of the nests near at hand. She had spotted her mate when he was but a speck in the distance and his very appearance had stirred her to these gestures. It seemed strange for the moment to think that the bird had been capable of identifying its mate at so great a distance, but that, I suppose, is due to the limitations of human eyesight. Why should a bird not be able to tell its mate's wing beats just as we can recognize from afar the walk and bearing of a person beloved?

G. K. YEATES from *The Life of the Rook*

The actual moment of hatching brings intense excitement to the female. I have once been fortunate enough to be in the hide at the time of its occurrence, while my friend

Southern was later also to witness the same event at
another nest. The female stood up over her eggs, wondering, it seemed, what was happening beneath her. She
stood there a moment or so, and then with a low and
excited burst of cawing flew off, to return a moment later
with the male. Both alighted at the nest, looked down
at the latest arrival in the cup beneath them, and then
at each other. It was perhaps the most human scene I
have ever beheld in the bird world.

G. K. YEATES from *The Life of the Rook*

Both yesterday and this morning some of the rooks here
walked about on the lawn, collecting leaves. They picked
these up with perfect facility whilst holding others in
the bill, so that they flew away, each time, with a little
bundle of them. Yet this is a hard, horny bill, not a human
hand with fine, flexible jointed fingers, each with its soft
fleshy " cushion." Would we not, were we to see said
fingers performing this office at the will of some " neat-
handed Phyllis "—would we not, I say, knowing nothing
of these matters and never having thought about rooks,
be inclined to dilate on the delicacy and nice sense of
touch of this human hand, on its unapproached excellent
as an implement, on the crudeness and clumsiness of all
other such implements in nature compared with it—the
impossibility, for instance, of a beak or a claw doing what
said hand was doing now, and so on and so forth? To be
sure we would—or might—for we have already and it
has got into print. The same reflection has occurred to
me on seeing a heron *bill* fish, including eels, which he
does with a deftness and nicety—an inevitability—which

the human hand could not emulate; or a melodious warbler carrying a long chain of flies which he has in some way entangled together so that it depends like a necklace. EDMUND SELOUS from *Realities of Bird Life*

There are three creatures, the squirrel, the field-mouse, and the bird called the nut-hatch which live much on hazel nuts; and yet they open them each in a different way. The first, after rasping off the small end, splits the shell in two with his long fore-teeth, as a man does with his knife; the second, nibbles a hole with his teeth, so regular as if drilled with a wimble, and yet so small that one would wonder how the kernel can be extracted through it; while the last picks an irregular ragged hole with its bill: but as this artist has no paws to hold the nut firm while he pierces it, like an adroit workman, he fixes it, as it were in a vice, in some cleft of a tree, or in some crevice; when, standing over it, he perforates the stubborn shell. GILBERT WHITE from *Selborne*

The seagull, however, seems to me to be a more interesting London bird than the sparrow. The seagull is a bird that can spy a piece of bread almost as far as a vulture can spy a corpse. It is impossible to enter one of the London parks with a piece of dry bread in your pocket without every seagull knowing it for a mile around. I was standing by the Round Pond the other day, when a small girl came up with a paper bag full of bread to feed the ducks. She opened the bag and, taking out a slice that had seen better days, said to me gravely, " Would *you* like a bit? " I felt

Rooks

it would be ungracious to refuse, and no sooner had she passed me the slice of bread than a cloud of gulls came falling down out of the sky, each gull with a different-sized brown patch on its head. They whirled about us with such clamour that there was nothing to be done but begin to feed them. I have never before thrown bread at seagulls, but I found it extraordinarily satisfying. It was like watching the most brilliant possible fielding at cricket.

ROBERT LYND from *Solomon in All His Glory*

Black-Headed Gulls

A Visit from the Sea

Far from the loud sea beaches
  Where he goes fishing and crying,
Here in the inland garden
  Why is the sea-gull flying?

Here are no fish to dive for;
  Here is the corn and lea;
Here are the green trees rustling,
  Hie away home to sea!

Fresh is the river water
  And quiet among the rushes;
This is no home for the sea-gull
  But for the rooks and thrushes.

Pity the bird that has wandered!
  Pity the sailor ashore!
Hurry him home to the ocean,
  Let him come here no more!

High on the sea-cliff ledges
  The white gulls are trooping and crying,
Here among rooks and roses,
  Why is the sea-gull flying?

ROBERT LOUIS STEVENSON

Mist—mist—brown mist; but a sense in the air of
    snow flakes!
  I stand where the ripples die,
Lift up an arm and wait, till my lost ones know me,
  Wheel overhead, and cry.

Salt in the eyes, and the seagulls, mewing and
    swooping,
Snatching the bread from my hand;
Brushing my hand with their breasts, in swift caresses
To show that they understand.

Oh, why are you so afraid? We are all of us exiles!
Wheel back in your clamorous rings!
We have all of us lost the sea, and we all remember.
But you—have wings.

ALFRED NOYES from Seagulls on the Serpentine

We passed, whilst exploring one of these caverns, just
beneath a ledge of rock, where a shag sat brooding over
two tiny little things, but just hatched, perfectly naked,
and jet black all over. This poor bird showed an anxiety
which could hardly have been overpassed in the most
devoted of human mothers, and I almost believe her
sufferings were as great—for surely all extremities are
equal. Her hoarse, bellowing cries reverberated through
all the place, and helped, with the gloom, the murky
light flung by our candles, the lurid colouring, and the
deep, gurgling noises of the sea, to make a weird, Tar-
tarean picture, difficult to excel. But it was not in sound
alone that she vented her displeasure, for she was angry
as well as alarmed. As the boat passed, she rose on the
nest, and, in a frenzy of apprehension, snapped her bill,
and alternately advanced and retreated her long, snake-
like and darkly iridescent green neck. Though my head
was but a foot or two away from her, she kept her place

on the nest, and becoming more and more beside herself, behaved, at last, in such a manner as it is difficult to describe, but which upon the human plane and amongst the lower classes, is called "taking on."

EDMUND SELOUS from *The Bird Watcher in the Shetlands*

It was with the main object of discovering the incubation- and fledgling-periods that I marked a number of nests of the Manx Shearwater (*Puffinus p. puffinus*) on the island where I live. Skokholm lies off the far south-west of Pembrokeshire and comprises about 250 acres of rough grazing, heather, bracken and thrift. It is entirely rock-bound and the height of the land varies between 50 and 150 feet above sea-level. It was formerly under cultivation and farmed, but has been idle and overrun by rabbits since the end of the last century. Some of the points noted below were observed during 1928, my study of the bird covering two years. The nests were marked in the year 1929.

In 1928 the first Shearwater was heard and seen on February 9th and by the 26th they were numerous. In 1929 they were even earlier. I heard the first bird on February 2nd. On February 15th severe frost and snow set in and the Shearwaters were not heard again until the 26th, after which date they gradually began to return. By the middle of March of both years the Shearwaters were to be found all over the island, occupying their nesting-holes in full force.

Throughout the day they lie quiescent in the farthest recesses of the burrows. I have found them sitting singly, but in March and April more often in pairs. The experiments given below have helped me to discover that the birds visit their nesting holes each night with great regularity, but the circumstances that govern their presence or absence by day have not been revealed. The facts are that sometimes one bird will be present, sometimes the pair, and sometimes neither during the day. The attendances are very irregular during the day and very regular at night in that part of the season before the egg is laid.

The depth of the burrow varies according to the depth of the soil. Where the rabbit has penetrated, no matter how far, where the soil is soft and deep, there the Shearwater goes. When I was looking for nests I traced the birds by ear and nose. By imitating the call-note, it is often possible to get a sitting bird to respond from its burrow. By putting one's nose close to a burrow, the unmistakable and not quite pleasant smell of a Shearwater can often be detected. Many of the nests were too deep to get at. With spade, crowbar and guiding stick I followed the tortuous windings of the rabbit-burrows, making borings from three to six feet deep, but in vain. The cackle of the birds from far below would sound derisively to my ear. On the other hand, where the soil is thin over the bare bedrock, the burrows are shallow and more easily traced to the end recess. Most of these shallower holes are occupied by the Puffin (*Fratercula arctica grabae*), which does not, as far as I have yet noticed, descend so deep as the Shearwater into the more labyrinthine burrows. The shortest burrow I have a record of is an arm's length, curved, and not quite three feet long.

The marked nests were all in shallow burrows. The method of watching was to trace the burrow to the end, and to cut very carefully a large sod immediately over the nest. This sod then served as a very convenient observation door, which could be lifted up for the purpose of inspecting the nest at any time.

Nest A. Burrow four feet long, in peaty, shallow soil on a rocky knoll eleven yards from my house. Materials, a little dried grass and six or seven chicken feathers. This nest was watched from April 26th onward. One bird or a pair was present almost regularly by day. On May 6th there were no birds present. On May 7th there was one bird sitting on a fresh white egg. This bird was immediately marked and later ringed with a B.B. ring, the last two figures of which were 81. On the 8th and 9th, 81 still sat alone during the day. It was visited at night by another bird, presumably its mate, and there was on each occasion a great deal of cackling in the burrow. I was not able to discover whether the sitting bird was, or was not, fed by its mate. I can only suppose so, in view of the length of time spent by one bird incubating the egg.

At about 10.15 p.m. G.M.T. on May 8th and about 10.30 p.m. G.M.T. on May 9th, when the whole island was resounding with the screams of the Shearwaters, the mate of 81 arrived suddenly out of the sky, screaming loudly, and falling with an audible thump upon the turf a few inches from the mouth of the burrow. At intervals since dusk, and rarely during the day, 81 had been cackling from the nest and from 9 p.m. onwards the cackling had become more and more frequent. About me, as I sat on an outcrop of rock, Shearwaters were calling from underground. 81 answered its mate as soon as the latter touched

GB

the ground. With a barely perceptible pause, the incoming bird shuffled into the burrow. It is impossible to describe the unearthly cackling and cooing which now ensued. I waited an hour, during which the birds gradually became less noisy, with increasing intervals of several minutes' silence. With my ear to the ground immediately above the nesting-recess I was able to hear frequent shuffling and movement going on, with o ccasional faint squeaks, and often the deafening uproar of the pair cackling in duet. I confess my patience wore out after midnight and I left the pair to their connubial bliss. From May 15th to 19th the mate, which I ringed as 82, sat alone; from the 20th to the 25th, 81 sat; from the 26th to the 28th, 82 sat; from the 29th to the 31st, 81 sat; from June 1st to the 4th, 82 sat. The birds were now becoming shy. I visited them once a day only, at sunset. My main object was to find out the incubation-period, and I was very anxious to disturb the sitting birds as little as possible lest they should desert. Upon my lifting the sod from above the hole, the sitting bird was now more timid and would move off the egg and shuffle out of sight along the burrow. After the 4th I did not try to capture the bird, but merely contented myself with one quick look daily at the egg. On June 18th I found *both* birds on the nest.

On June 26th the egg was pipped in one place. On the 27th the young bird had hatched, but was still wet, thus having taken fifty-two days to hatch. On the 28th the nestling was dry and downy. The youngster was daily brooded up to July 3rd, when it was left alone during the day until the 7th, when I found one parent sitting beside the growing, downy youngster. The parents did not again stay in the burrow by day. The first down is pushed out by the second down as the nestling grows. It is difficult to gauge the actual time of sprouting of the second down, as the first down remains attached to the second, but this occurred about the 16th day. On August 1st, the 35th day, the double down of the bird was nearly two inches long, and the nestling resembled an enormous grey powder-puff. The colour of the down is accurately described in the *Practical Handbook*. Signs of feathers were now evident: on the 42nd day the quills and tail-feathers appeared from their sheaths. On the 62nd day the young bird was completely feathered, but some down still showed on the nape, lower belly and thighs.

From this day, until it disappeared, the nearly fledged youngster was not fed or in any way attended by its parents. I already suspected that the bird had been deserted, but to make sure I placed a small sod at the mouth of the hole in such a position that it would be pushed in by a bird seeking ingress and out by a bird seeking egress. A Shearwater, I knew, is capable of pushing almost any object aside if it wishes to enter a burrow. This was on August 28th. The sod was left untouched until September 3rd, this proving to me that the nestling had fasted for six days and stayed a voluntary prisoner in its hole. On September 3rd the sod had been pushed out and there was quite a lot of the nestling's down adhering to it, giving plain evidence of the young bird's activity. On September 4th I spent the night out of doors watching the bird. At about 10.15 p.m. G.M.T. it suddenly shuffled out of its burrow and it remained the whole night almost in the same position on a slight rise at the mouth of the burrow. Once or twice it shook its wings as if trying them. About 2 a.m. it silently returned to its burrow.

This procedure it adopted up to September 8th. I went out each night at about 11 p.m. to note this specially. On the 6th it fluttered away from me six yards into some nettles, but the next morning I found it safe in its burrow. On September 8th it had gone altogether, after a period of seventy-three days from hatching to final departure.

.   .   .   .   .

The time the adults return to the burrows from the sea depends on the time of sunset and the state of the moon. They fly inland at about two hours after sunset as a rule, and this is a fairly regular time throughout the season. Thus, in March, they are screaming over my house from 8 p.m. onwards. On moonless or cloudy nights they arrive early or punctually, but on clear moonlit evenings they may be as much as an hour late. In June, then, the time of arrival is usually just about or after 10 p.m. G.M.T. Throughout the season the time of departure, or rather cessation of activity on land, is punctually at about 2.30 a.m. G.M.T. By 3 a.m. the last Shearwater has hurried to its burrow or to the sea.

Moonlight also affects the volume of the noise made by the island colony. When the moon is shining the uproar is reduced to the calling, within earshot, of perhaps a dozen birds at one time. On cloudy moonless nights the uproar is so continuous that only the individual notes of those birds passing close to the observer are distinguishable from the general bedlam. The characteristic note, used both as a call-note and an alarm, is variously rendered by observers, but I can find nothing that renders it as well as

cuck-cuck-oo, or cuck-cuck-cuck-oo,

usually repeated three, sometimes four, and rarely five times in quick succession. The incoming birds begin calling before they reach land. I have heard them calling at a distance of at least one hundred yards from the cliff, over the sea. Each bird has a distinctive variation in tone or pitch of note, some high, some low, some very harsh, and some fairly soft. At a distance the note distinctly resembles the early crowing of an immature chicken, but is, of course, higher and quicker.

      .   .   .   .   .

At about the 60th day (in Nest A the 62nd and in Nest C the 59th) the adults entirely desert the nestling. The young bird remains in its burrow, fasting, and no doubt drawing upon its reserve of fat. It finishes growing its juvenile plumage, and loses most of its down, which falls in a circle about the nest, together with the dried scale of the growing feathers, the whole forming quite a rampart about the bird! There is very little excreta in the burrow at this time, at least visible, and the nestling is always dry, clean, and has no offensive smell when handled.

After waiting a few days in the nest for the parental visit, the nestling at last makes its way to the mouth of the burrow at the usual time in the evening. It sits at the mouth of the burrow for most of the night, occasionally moving its wings, but otherwise still and silent. These young, nearly fledged birds, sitting at the mouths of the burrows, are a feature of the island bird-life at night in early September.

      .   .   .   .   .

It takes the nestling five or six days to pluck up courage to leave its burrow altogether. During this period it comes

out each evening to the mouth of the burrow, retiring again
at about 2.30 a.m.

. . . . .

Left to itself, the young Shearwater, fully feathered
and generally with varying amounts of down still clinging
to its head and underparts, at last, perhaps driven by hunger
as well as instinct, makes a bid for liberty. If the wind is
strong, almost to gale force, the chances are that it will,
in exposed places, be able to fly straight from its nesting-
hole, and be held by the wind long enough to enable it
to obtain a proper impetus to fly out to the sea. I have
thrown young Shearwaters, some still very fat and with
much down still showing, up into a strong wind and
watched them fly steadily upwards and onwards to the
sea. These birds had never flown a yard before, but on
attaining a proper impetus, they flew with a wonderful
strength and grace.

The story is very different, however, on calmer nights.
The Shearwater starts off from its hole with a sudden and
bold flutter of its wings, but of course barely rises in the
air at all. If the ground is level and clear of vegetation it
attains what may be described as a flying walk, i.e., it
patters along the ground with its feet, sustaining itself
with quickly-beating wings. The slightest unevenness of
the ground upsets this progress, which in any case exhausts
the bird after a few yards. On very uneven ground the
young bird advances on all fours, pushing with its feet
and partly outstretched wings. To surmount a high
object it uses its beak just as some other young birds do,
as a hook to pull up with.

The young bird seems to know the shortest way to the
sea. After several days of calm, on September 14th, 1929,

a night with little wind, I found young birds making their way to the sea over or through every natural obstacle. They scrambled through the densest bracken and over heather, clumps of thrift, bog-grass and rocks. Their progress was spasmodic and it would seem that they were compelled to rest in order to recover from the exertion. One bird presented a pitiful sight. It was emaciated, no doubt because of an extra long fast, and painfully light to handle, yet the urge to reach the sea was so strong that it literally staggered along, falling after each effort into the most extraordinary and helpless attitudes upon its back. It progressed very slowly and at 3 a.m. was lying on its back in some bracken, having failed to reach the sea. Later it died, and on the scales weighed 10·25 ozs.

The birds which reached the cliffs blundered straight over them, and catching the slight updraft of air, flapped and glided downwards into the darkness over the sea. About one bird in ten was completely free of down.

The young birds hatched in burrows in the centre of the island have a long way to travel on calm nights and many do not reach the cliffs in one night. Dawn finds them in every place and position, and those that are near the cover of holes, bracken and heather are fortunate. Gulls, Buzzards and Crows are early abroad seeking the birds which have not found cover for the day.

R. M. LOCKLEY from article *On the Breeding-habits of the Manx Shearwater, with Special Reference to its Incubation and Fledging-periods*

These Arctic skuas bathe together very prettily. They sit high and light on the water, duck their heads under it, and throw it over them with their wings. Between their ablutions they often sport in the air, swooping at and chasing one another. Their motions are such as one might imagine those of elemental spirits to be, and their wild cry adds to this imaginary resemblance. Oh, that cry, that wild, wild cry, that music of the winds, the clouds, the drifting rain and mist—like them, free as them, voicing their freedom, making their spirit articulate! Who can describe it, or put down into poor, paltry syllables the glory that lives in it? Let none try. Let no clumsy imitation disfigure it, but let it live for ever in the memory of him who sat on the great ness-side, on the dividing-line of sea and sky, and heard it pealing so clearly, so cheerly, so gladly wild, so wildly, madly glad. So let it come to him again in his own soul's music, scudding with the clouds, driving with the driving mists, ringing out like "the wild bells to the wild sky." And never let that sky be blue that it rings to, unless in pale, moist patches, drowning amidst watery clouds; and never let there be a sun, to be called one, but only a glint and a gleaming, a storming of stormy light, a wet beam flung on a rain-cloud.

EDMUND SELOUS from *The Bird Watcher in the Shetlands*

It was a fortunate coincidence which brought two experienced bird observers to St. James's Park on September 18th and placed them at the right moment in the most suitable position to witness the arrival of an Arctic Skua. This bird, attracted by the large number of Gulls, swept in from the river about 2 p.m. The Gulls immediately recognized their tormentor and made off in a body. For a few moments the Skua characteristically pursued one of them, then gave up the chase and alighted on the water, where both observers had a good view of it. It was one of the dark plumaged variety. The novelty and peacefulness of the situation and a superabundance of white bread, however, offered no temptation to this rollicking pirate and, after a short tour of inspection, it set a course for more promising hunting grounds and disappeared.

C. S. BAYNE from an article in the Report of the Committee
on *Bird Sanctuaries in Royal Parks (England)*, 1935

The baby snipe is, I think, the most delightful creature I know. A ball of dark brown fluff, the ends of which are tipped with white, it looks rather like a huge hairy caterpillar in the grass. The back is streaked with darker brown and black so that the protective colouring is almost more perfect than that of its parents. The bill at first is very short and soft and not much use for the purpose of worm finding, so for some time the chick is fed by the parents. The instinct of self-preservation asserts itself when the chick is only a few hours old, and it will crouch in the grass so perfectly still that it is almost impossible to see. When picked up in the hand it still remains motionless, but the little black eyes are full of apprehension; for the little mite, even in its first day in this world, knows that there is something wrong with this proceeding.

E. C. KEITH from *Woodcock and Snipe*

The most intimate meeting I have ever had with a snipe was once in May when I was sitting on the side of a river waiting for a rise of fish. This snipe had been flying round me for some time continually uttering the usual *jick jack* notes when eventually it came to ground about twenty yards away. There was nothing unusual in this, for I was in a favourite snipe nesting place, but as I idly watched its movements I was struck by the peculiar attraction which I seemed to have for the bird. It walked very slowly and sedately in my direction, quietly *jick jacking* as it came, and all the time eyeing me very carefully. I sat perfectly still, wondering how far the bird would dare to come and what its purpose might be; for the nearer it came the more deliberate was the approach and the quieter the notes. When within no more than four yards it halted, and we steadily regarded each other for perhaps half a minute, with a strange friendly interest.

By this time I had decided that it was a hen bird and that I was sitting very close to her nest; but she evinced no sign of alarm and merely stared at me with the curiosity which a child might show at seeing some unusually grotesque animal at the Zoo. Her gaze was perfectly steady, and I could not help wondering what was going on in the tiny brain behind that black penetrating eye. It was a direct challenge, almost a duel of will-power, but at last she was satisfied that for once I meant no harm, and quietly flew away. I have often watched snipe at close range but never before have I been watched as well, so deliberately and thoughtfully. That this wild and cunning bird of the winter should now fearlessly approach me to within a few yards seemed almost uncanny. It was a good illustration of the complete change which comes over our snipe

in the spring, a change which affords us a golden opportunity to get to know our bird and its ways and habits.
No longer does it rise with a defiant challenging screech
to disappear as rapidly as possible, but rather welcomes
our company provided we do not become too inquisitive.

Even the harsh *scape* of the winter is discarded for the
rather ugly monotonous *jick jack* love song of the spring,

Snipe

and this is frequently repeated from the air and the ground. Both birds utter these notes and I think that both birds drum, but as the sexes are exactly alike in size and plumage, it is a difficult matter to tell definitely which bird is the performer. It is of course usually the cock which we hear drumming during the day, as the hen is spending most of her time at the nest. When sitting, she takes early morning exercise in the air and again at night where she probably drums. All birds have definite love songs although some are only noises. That of the snipe is the *jick jack*, and drumming is merely an expression of feelings and high spirits, a kind of *joie de vivre*.

. . . . .

The bird first rises steeply and usually silently to a considerable height, perhaps almost out of sight, and then dives towards the ground at an angle of 45 degrees or rather less.

The drumming starts with the downward swoop and ends with it. Assuming that the bird is well up in the air when the dive starts, there will be several periods of drumming in the downward flight, for after each swoop the snipe rises again by means of its own impetus and repeats the dive. The drumming lasts only for about three seconds, but the important point is that it starts and ends simultaneously with the dive.

If one is reasonably near the performer during the latter stage of the descent, it is quite easy to see, by means of a pair of good field glasses, each movement and to arrive at our own conclusions as to the cause of the sound. It will be seen that when the downward swoop starts, the tail is spread fan-shaped to the limit and the two outside tail feathers stand apart from the rest, almost at right angles to the bird. The wings are half-closed, forming two funnels for the air to pass through, and they are quivering. The swoop is always, so far as I have seen, against the wind, and there is never any other noise produced during the period of drumming. I have often watched carefully to see whether the bill was closed, and, so far as I could tell, it was; but this is a difficult matter about which to be too positive.

E. C. KEITH from *Woodcock and Snipe*

The alarm note of the Snipe is a harsh " Scape, scape " uttered as it rises and while on the wing. The creaking call-note is uttered most frequently when the bird descends, and also when it stands on some hillock or perches on a post or branch. When I was moored near Hoveton Broad in May, 1904, a Snipe perched on the dead branches of an old willow tree near the yacht every evening at sunset and creaked vigorously, keeping a sharp look-out meanwhile, and occasionally preening its feathers.

During the summer of 1911 a post on my island was the favourite resting-place of a Snipe which drummed overhead most of the day. When tired of that amusement, he would descend with almost motionless wings (like a Pipit), creaking loudly, drop on to the post and continue calling, moving both mandibles of his bill as he did this.

In 1907, when I was hidden beneath a heap of reeds photographing the Reeve, a Snipe frequently settled on my shoulder, and expressed his emotions in the usual creaking manner. As he was close to my ear the effect was thrilling. For some seconds before the actual sound escaped, a wheezing noise, like the whirr of machinery, went on inside the bird; then suddenly the harsh sound was emitted, and simply shouted—all unconsciously—into my ears. Once or twice I felt the slender bill gently prodding my cheek all over, and once it was thrust into my ear. As there seemed to be a platonic friendship existing between the Snipe and the Reeve, I often enjoyed this unwonted sensation. The rubbish-heap method of photography was absolutely exhausting, but it had lively compensations.

E. L. TURNER from *Broadland Birds*

Many people speak ill of sparrows. I can understand dislike of them in the country, but I cannot understand it in the town. In the country they are invaders, driving out of the neighbourhood better birds than themselves. Other birds apparently regard them as low, and will not consort in the same garden with them. They will not, at least, make friends, and they have a happier air when the sparrows are gone. In town, on the other hand, the sparrow is at home. He does not keep the other birds away, for they would not come in any case. He has no music for the traffic to drown—no bright plumage for the smoke to blacken. He is a little parasite, who can pick up a living where a more sensitive bird would starve. He is cheeky, Cockney, insuppressible. He is, in a sense, vicious. He will go through a bed of crocuses and break their necks with as little compunction as a fox destroying geese. It would not be so bad if he really wanted to eat the crocuses, but it is as though he actually enjoyed wasting them. He leaves them lying, yellow and purple and white, like a battle-field of flowers. No cat was ever more cruel. But, apart from this, I do not see what can be said against him by the townsman. How charming a little dancer he is as he hops in scores and in fifties round a Londoner who has bread—hops backwards and forwards like a marionette or like someone whose feet have been tied together for fun, or like a small child hopping up and down in sheer excitement. He may not, as an individual, be so confiding as the robin. But the robins do not come dancing round a human being in families like the family of the old woman who lived in a shoe.

ROBERT LYND from *Solomon in All His Glory*

The sparrow is an unfeeling enemy to these birds (the house-martins) and when their nest is nearly finished they will take it by storm and make use of it themselves. In these emergencies the martins will both occupy the nest and keep in for days together, while the besieging robbers sit as patiently on the thatch above, watching the opportunity to enter. When the martins are pined out and forced to leave their nest for food the cock-sparrow seizes the chance immediately, and the poor martins find on their return a determined occupant who resists their every effort to regain the lawful possession of their houses. Sometimes they return the insult afterwards by an odd revenge; when the old sparrows leave the nest for food, and they will do when they have been in quiet possession of it awhile, they instantly sally to the nest, where others of their companions, as I have often seen, join helping hand and block up the entrance till the hole is too small for the sparrows to enter; who, on their return, fancy(ing) some strategy is laid to entrap them, leave it with little or no hesitation; for I have observed that the sparrow cannot get into the hole of a finished nest, who always watches to seize possession before (they) have finished the entrance, adding the lining of straw and feathers themselves. And one of these can easily be known by straw hanging out of the hole, as they use more straw than the martin.

JOHN CLARE from his *Diary*

Now from the roost, or from the neighbouring pale,
Where, diligent to catch the first faint gleam
Of smiling day, they gossip'd side by side,
Come trooping at the housewife's well-known call
The feather'd tribes domestic. Half on wing,
And half on foot, they brush the fleecy flood,
Conscious and fearful of too deep a plunge.
The sparrows peep, and quit the sheltering eaves,
To seize the fair occasion; well they eye
The scatter'd grain, and thievishly resolved
To escape the impending famine, often scared
As oft return, a pert voracious kind.
Clean riddance quickly made, one only care
Remains to each, the search of sunny nook,
Or shed impervious to the blast.

WILLIAM COWPER from the *Winter Morning Walk*

SPARROWS SELF DOMESTICATED IN TRINITY COLLEGE, CAMBRIDGE

None ever shar'd the social feast,
Or as an inmate, or a guest,
Beneath the celebrated dome,
Where once Sir Isaac had his home,
Who saw not (and with some delight
Perhaps he view'd the novel sight)
How num'rous, at the tables there,
The sparrows beg their daily fare.
For there, in ev'ry nook, and cell,
Where such a family may dwell,
Sure as the vernal season comes
Their nests they weave in hope of crumbs,
Which kindly giv'n, may serve with food
Convenient their unfeather'd brood;
And oft as with its summons clear
The warning bell salutes their ear,
Sagacious list'ners to the sound,
They flock from all the fields around,
To reach the hospitable hall,
None more attentive to the call.
Arriv'd, the pensionary band,
Hopping and chirping, close at hand,
Solicit what they soon receive,
The sprinkled, plenteous donative.
Thus is a multitude, though large,
Supported at a trivial charge;
A single doit would overpay
Th' expenditure of ev'ry day,

HB

And who can grudge so small a grace
To suppliants, natives of the place?

WILLIAM COWPER

To Sparrows Fighting

Stop, feathered bullies!
    Peace, angry birds;
You common Sparrows that,
    For a few words,
Roll fighting in wet mud,
To shed each other's blood.

Look at those Linnets, they
    Like ladies sing;
See how those Swallows, too,
    Play on the wing;
All other birds close by
Are gentle, clean and shy.

And yet maybe your life's
    As sweet as theirs;
The common poor that fight
    Live not for years
In one long frozen state
Of anger, like the great.

W. H. DAVIES

Selborne, Jan. 29, 1774. All the summer long is the swallow
a most instructive pattern of unwearied industry and affection; for, from morning to night, while there is a family
to be supported, she spends the whole day in skimming

Swallows in Osiers

close to the ground, and exerting the most sudden turns and quick evolutions. Avenues, and long walks under hedges, and pasture-fields, and mown meadows where cattle graze, are her delight, especially if there are trees interspersed; because in such spots insects most abound. When a fly is taken a smart snap from her bill is heard, resembling the noise at the shutting of a watch-case; but the motions of the mandibles are too quick for the eye. . . .

The swallow is a delicate songster, and in soft sunny weather sings both perching and flying; on trees in a kind of concert, and on chimney-tops.

GILBERT WHITE from *Selborne*

Sept. 28, 1774. Swifts are no songsters, and have only one harsh screaming note; yet there are ears to which it is not displeasing, from an agreeable association of ideas, since that note never occurs but in the most lovely summer weather.

They never settle on the ground but through accident; and when down can hardly rise, on account of the shortness of their legs and the length of their wings: neither can they walk, but only crawl; but they have a strong grasp with their feet, by which they cling to walls. Their bodies being flat they can enter a very narrow crevice; and where they cannot pass on their bellies they will turn up edgewise. GILBERT WHITE from *Selborne*

Sept. 28, 1774. As I have regarded these amusive birds with no small attention, if I should advance something new and peculiar with respect to them, and different from all other birds, I might perhaps be credited; especially as my assertion is the result of many years' exact observation. The fact that I would advance is, that swifts tread, or copulate, on the wing; and I would wish any nice observer, that is startled at this supposition, to use his own eyes, and I think he will soon be convinced. In another class of animals, viz., the insect, nothing is so common as to see the different species of many genera in conjunction as they fly. The swift is almost continually on the wing; and as it never settles on the ground, on trees, or roofs, would seldom find opportunity for amorous rites, was it not enabled to indulge them in the air. If any person would watch these birds of a fine morning in May, as they are sailing round at a great height from the ground, he would see, every now and then, one drop on the back of another, and both of them sink down together for many fathoms with a loud piercing shriek. This I take to be the juncture when the business of generation is carrying on.   GILBERT WHITE from *Selborne*

Swifts

On the fifth of July, 1775, I again untiled part of a roof over the nest of a swift. The dam sat in the nest; but so strongly was she affected by natural στοργή for her brood, which she supposed to be in danger, that, regardless of her own safety, she would not stir, but lay sullenly by them, permitting herself to be taken in hand. The squab young we brought down and placed on the grass-plot, where they tumbled about, and were as helpless as a new-born child. While we contemplated their naked bodies, their unwieldy disproportioned *abdomina*, and their heads, too heavy for their necks to support, we could not but wonder when we reflected that these shiftless beings in a little more than a fortnight would be able to dash through the air almost with the inconceivable swiftness of a meteor; and perhaps, in their emigration must traverse vast continents and oceans as distant as the equator.   GILBERT WHITE from *Selborne*

When I did wake this morn from sleep,
It seemed I heard birds in a dream;
Then I arose to take the air—
The lovely air that made birds scream;

WILLIAM H. DAVIES from *Early Morn*

I was staying for Whitsun one year at a little inn on the Upper Thames. Under the eaves a number of house-martins were building their mud nests. I was interested to find out something of their courtship, but there had

been no courting in evidence during the Saturday afternoon
and evening. So, knowing that such activities are often
most pronounced in the early morning, I got up before
dawn on the Sunday. To my surprise, there were no
martins to be seen—none in or by their nests, none
flying round. I walked round the place, and up and down
the towpath, along which spread a faint mist from the
river, and still saw nothing of my birds. Then from the barn
came a single swallow, and flew steeply up into the sky.
I followed its flight with my eyes, and suddenly saw
why I had failed to find the martins. They were all up
there in the blue, circling round in company with some
barn-swallows and chimney-swifts, from which I could
just distinguish them at the height they were flying.
The sun had not yet risen where I stood on the solid
earth; but he already reached the birds high above my
head. And as the earth spun and the sun's rays approached
its surface, the birds sank with them, twittering all
the time; until finally the light struck the inn and
flooded the meadows, and the birds dispersed to the
duties of the day.

JULIAN HUXLEY from *Bird-Watching and Bird Behaviour*

SOMEHOW THIS WORLD IS WONDERFUL

Somehow this world is wonderful at times,
As it has been from early morn in May;
Since first I heard the cock-a-doodle-doo—
Timekeeper on green farms—at break of day.

Soon after that I heard ten thousand birds,
Which made me think an angel brought a tin
Of golden grain, and none was scattered yet—
To rouse those birds to make that merry din.

I could not sleep again for such wild cries,
And went out early into their green world;
And then I saw what set their little tongues
To scream for joy—they saw the East in gold.

W. H. DAVIES

The history of the stone curlew, *charadrius oedicnemus*, is as follows. It lays its eggs, usually two, never more than three, on the bare ground, without any nest, in the field; so that the countryman, in stirring his fallows, often destroys them. The young run immediately from the egg like partridges, etc., and are withdrawn to some flinty field by their dam, where they skulk among the stones, which are their best security; for their feathers are so exactly of the colour of our grey spotted flints, that the most exact observer, unless he catches the eye of the young bird, may be eluded. The eggs are short and round: of a dirty white, spotted with dark bloody patches. Though I might not be able, just when I pleased, to procure you a bird, yet I could show you them almost any day; and any evening you may hear them round the village, for they make a clamour which may be heard a mile. *Oedicnemus* is a most apt and expressive name for them, since their legs seem swoln like those of a gouty man. After harvest I have shot them before the pointers in turnip-fields. GILBERT WHITE from *Selborne*

A troupe of long-tailed tits crosses from plantation to plantation, swimming through the air like a shoal of fishes, or rather like a procession of fishes, one waiting to start until the other has arrived; each of them rising and falling in a flight like the curve of a wave. Having arrived in the tops of the beeches, they become acrobats, flinging themselves from peril to peril in an endless trapeze act, encouraging each other in voices as tiny as the voice of a coal-tit, as tiny almost as the voice of the goldcrest.   ROBERT LYND from *Solomon in All His Glory*

I had the good fortune this year to find a nest just begun, low down in the fork, of a small birch, in such an open position that one could stand or sit within ten feet and see clearly every action of the birds—and they took no notice of me at all. The nest on this date, March 23, was a small shallow cup. The arrival of the two birds was heralded by their thin " tsee, tsee," and an occasional " tchup." They each brought stuff for the nest, and while one waited, the other went into the nest, sat in it and put its mouthful on to the rim. Then it pulled up a thin piece of stuff from the edge of the nest and bent it over the rim, carefully poking in the end. This it did in three or four places, turning round in the nest to reach different points here and there. All this was done very rapidly, and when the bird left the nest its mate immediately went in and repeated the performance. I could see no difference at all in the actions of the two birds. The stuff brought to the nest was often so small that one could not see it without binoculars. This applied chiefly to pieces of lichen and fine thread-like material which was probably cobweb; pieces of moss were generally bigger, though still very small.

After many spells of watching I found that certain actions were regularly performed. From beginning to end no building was ever done except when the bird was sitting in the nest, and as it sat the long tail was cocked up over the back. Both birds always entered the nest from exactly the same point, though as the nest grew this point of course rose with it and eventually it was here that the entrance hole became automatically fixed. The new material was always added to the rim of the nest, and the operation of pulling stuff over the rim and tucking it in was part of the regular routine. This was usually done from the outside to the inside but occasionally the reverse. The birds always seemed able to pull up a thready piece of stuff for this purpose. Sometimes this was certainly moss, but often it was fine yellowish brown vegetable fibre, and sometimes what was evidently cobweb.

Another regular habit which began as soon as the nest had grown to a comfortable cup was for the bird to wriggle about as it sat in the nest. Obviously this was to shape it, and was often so vigorously done as to shake the whole structure; but the nest was resilient and strong and no harm was ever done.

A week after I had begun to watch, and perhaps nine days after the nest was started, doming over began. The same building routine as already described continued, but now no material was added to the rim at the point of entry and for a short distance on each side of it. As the rim of the nest grew higher on the far side the bird

stretched up and pulled material over towards it and
tucked it in. A good deal more effort was required
because the birds had to stretch out and pull over, and
in doing this they often had some difficulty, but never

Long-tailed Tits

attempted to do anything to the nest when they were outside it.

The shaping of the nest at this stage was an amusing sight. The bird would put its head under the dome and keep pushing it up and wriggling from side to side so that the whole nest looked alive. Then out would come its head from the entry side, and it would stretch over the top and pull it down, then in again and push it up. The fashioning of the dome was evidently a ticklish business, but very gradually it grew over and round until at last the point at which the birds had always come into the nest had become a little entrance hole near the top of a perfect egg-shaped nest.

Even now there was much to be done, and for the next two days there was a great deal of pushing up from the inside, for the dome was inclined to sag, and often it was a struggle to get out. Moss was taken and pushed up from inside into the dome. Soon, however, the main business was the lining of feathers. Even at the very beginning I saw one feather put into the nest and occasionally an odd one was brought afterwards, but when the dome was over feathers were frequently used. As pigeons and crows roost in this wood and a sparrow hawk lives there, feathers were plentiful, and often several were brought in one beakful, and sometimes a whole bunch from some little heap where the hawk had plucked its prey.

Though they frequently collected material quite near the nest, these tits, like other birds, often went quite a long way off, and my friends and I have traced them back from a measured distance of 197 yards. When feathers are scarce they have been known to go much farther.

The first egg was laid on April 7, fifteen days after I had first seen the nest, which thus took seventeen days to build. Even then the lining was not complete, and feathers were still being carried a week later when it contained seven or eight eggs.

H. F. WITHERBY from an article *The Secret of the Long-Tailed Tit's Architecture*

Every species of titmouse winters with us; they have what I call a kind of intermediate bill between the hard and the soft, between the Linnæan genera of *fringilla* and *motacilla*. One species alone spends its whole time in the woods and fields, never retreating for succour in the severest seasons to houses and neighbourhoods; and that is the delicate long-tailed titmouse, which is almost as minute as the golden-crowned wren: but the blue titmouse, or nun (*parus caeruleus*), the cole-mouse (*parus ater*), the great black-headed titmouse (*fringillago*), and the marsh titmouse (*parus palustris*), all resort, at times, to buildings; and in hard weather particularly. The great titmouse, driven by stress of weather, much frequents houses, and, in deep snows, I have seen this bird, while it hung with its back downwards (to my no small delight and admiration), draw straw lengthwise from out the eaves of thatched houses, in order to pull out the flies that were concealed between them, and that in such numbers that they quite defaced the thatch, and gave it a ragged appearance.

The blue titmouse, or nun, is a great frequenter of houses, and a general devourer. Beside insects, it is very fond of flesh; for it frequently picks bones on dung-hills: it is a vast admirer of suet, and haunts butchers' shops. When a boy, I have known twenty in a morning caught with snap mousetraps, baited with tallow or suet. It

Woodcock Chicks

will also pick holes in apples left on the ground, and be well entertained with the seeds on the head of a sunflower. The blue, marsh, and great titmice will, in very severe weather, carry away barley and oat straws from the sides of ricks.   GILBERT WHITE from *Selborne*

There, in a very secluded and shaded spot, under a spreading white-pine, there was yet a clean firm sward to sit on.

Thither the woodcock led her brood, to probe the mud for worms, flying but a foot above them down the bank, while they ran in a troop beneath; but at last, spying me, she would leave her young and circle round and round me, nearer and nearer till within four or five feet, pretending broken wings and legs, to attract my attention, and get off her young, who would already have taken up their march, with faint wiry peep, single file through the swamp, as she directed. Or I heard the peep of the young when I could not see the parent bird. There too the turtle-doves sat over the spring, or fluttered from bough to bough of the soft white-pines over my head.

H. D. THOREAU from *Walden*

A woodcock on the nest is perhaps one of the most charming sights in all nature. The beautifully mottled plumage, the dark velvet bands on the head, and the varying shades of brown and grey on the back, match the surroundings whether of dead leaves or bracken perfectly. The bill itself looks like a dead twig. Only the eyes, those large expressive eyes, black as night, betray the bird to a close observer.

J. W. SEIGNE from *Woodcock and Snipe*

After seeing a number of woodcocks' nests one is left with the impression that these birds must pay the closest attention to the surroundings before the site is chosen.

Even when their nests are right out on bare and open ground they are hard enough to find. I remember one under an avenue of beeches where there was no under-cover whatsoever. For two weeks the woodcock squatted there every day in the open with no pretence at any concealment. Twenty-five yards away a path in regular use led up to the house, yet the nest would have remained undiscovered but for the keeper's dog. The sitting bird was almost invisible, so marvellously did the ground pattern of beech leaves blend with her plumage.

The nests are invariably made on very dry ground well above any boggy patch or hollow, which is seldom far away. Woodcock need water, too, even if it be only a puddle; for, like snipe, they are thirsty birds and cannot feed without frequently washing the mud off their bills.

The whole aim of a woodcock seems to be to make the nest as simple and unpretentious as possible so as to be at one with the surroundings. Often it is merely an impression of the breast made by the bird squatting in the moss and turning round and round while it arranges with the bill any stray bits of brambles or ferns which are not quite to its liking. If lined at all, it is only a matter of a few leaves or pine needles or fronds of fern—whatever happens to be handy.

The usual number of eggs is four; but three is quite common and I have once found five. Their brown markings on a pale buff or creamy background make these eggs quite inconspicuous and they are sometimes slightly pyro-form, but nothing like a snipe's.

A very favourite site is at the foot of a spruce or other tree. I have found nests too, under a holly bush in an open glade of bracken, near a solitary oak in the middle

of a fir wood, and in a gorse brake in a common marked
by a stunted larch.

All these nests were in or near favourite " pitches "
for woodcock in winter as well as summer. I call these
" woodcock residences "; that is to say spots where at
most times you can be pretty certain of finding one or
more 'cock at home.

It may be pure coincidence but time after time I have
noticed that these residences are marked by some dis-
tinguishing feature. Something which would be clearly

Woodcock

IB

visible to a bird in flight. Where two rides meet in a wood, for instance, a clearing with a conspicuous mark such as a solitary fir or a fallen tree; a clump of dark firs standing out against a background of larches or other trees, and so on. It is all guess-work, of course; but I have come to think that such features correspond to our signposts and that they not only help resident birds in their daily comings and goings but play a part in bringing migrants back again.

J. W. SEIGNE from *Woodcock and Snipe*

One evil March day I was taking shelter behind a ditch from a hailstorm when a woodcock pitched under a fir tree quite near and quite unaware of my presence. In a few seconds another one landed on the moss in front and immediately started to strut about in the most exaggerated and comical way, with the neck feathers fluffed out, tail fully expanded and wings drooping. Every now and then this bird would pause and tilt the body forward, almost overbalancing in a frenzy of passion not very poetically expressed by sharp grunts or croaks which were clearly audible.

J. W. SEIGNE from *Woodcock and Snipe*

One of the things which I wanted to find out about woodcock was whether both birds took a turn on the nest, although there is little doubt that most of the incubation is done by the female. I usually visited the nest just before sunset, when birds like woodcock and snipe like to fly round their homes and have a bite of supper. It took several evenings of patient watching before I succeeded. I was lying in the bracken as usual watching the sitting bird, which I will call the hen, although again it is only possible to guess. Suddenly her mate flew over and landed near her. She rose slowly from the nest and walked over to meet him, whereupon he laid his bill slantways along hers. Both birds remained motionless in this position for nearly a minute. They looked exactly like two swordsmen about to engage.

When both birds were satisfied that the proper etiquette prescribed for the occasion had been observed, and the proper compliments paid, the new arrival took the place of the sitting bird on the eggs. She rose immediately and flew away into the setting sun. In its own way this little ceremony was quite as impressive as the changing of the guard.

In the home life of birds there is nothing more charming to watch than these little interchanges of courtesies and compliments. While their immense capacity for emotion may lead them into extravagances of passion and love-making, it is the quieter side of their lives, when passion has been sated, which is so interesting to observe. The careful and punctilious observance of these little courtesies and attentions makes it possible to understand something of that affection and consideration for each other which in the case of many birds lasts through life. It is not merely a phase which passes with courtship and nesting. I have seen it in the depth of winter in the sharing of food and tit-bits often hard enough to come by.

J. W. SEIGNE from *Woodcock and Snipe*

I was sitting on a mossy bank when suddenly a woodcock flew past and alighted about thirty yards away. On looking closely at the spot I saw a young woodcock on the ground beside her. Both birds ran about for a few minutes; then the parent suddenly rose with the young one. Owing to the distance away I could not see how she was carrying it. When about ten feet in the air, to my surprise the woodcock hovered for a second with rapid wing beats and let the chick drop. After a violent fluttering the little fellow landed head first on the soft moss. My impression at the time was that the mother was giving her offspring a lesson in confidence and flying. She again alighted beside it and both started running about in the prettiest way imaginable. By this time they were quite near me and the old bird must have become aware of my presence, for she uttered a low croaking note and the chick immediately ran underneath her. She gave it a few light taps with her bill as if to make sure it was properly in position, then rose without difficulty, passing over my head and carrying the young one between the thighs, pressed close to the breast, and clasped firmly in the claws. When it passed me the bird, which was a particularly large one, was flying well and did not seem at all embarrassed by the extra weight it was carrying. The head was held in the normal flying position and the whole bill was visible pointing straight downwards. It took no part in the actual carrying and the chick's bill was just visible protruding from the parent's breast.

J. W. SEIGNE from *Woodcock and Snipe*

A woodcock's ear is situated in front of the eye, and this very forward position may even help it more than a snipe, where the ear is directly below the eye. It is, however, seldom necessary for them to listen; for there are plenty of worms in the soft oozy bogland where they love to feed, and all they have to do is to probe away industriously.

A woodcock's bill is very similar to that of a snipe only a little larger and thicker, and even more swollen at the top. It is extremely sensitive and pitted with nerve cells. If sunk in the ground it can probably detect any movement or vibration and flash to the brain the exact whereabouts of its prey.

Once after listening like this the woodcock in question plunged its bill deep into the soil, turned it this way and that with savage jerks, then dragged out, bit by bit, a large worm. It was rather like a thrush or blackbird on the lawn. In order to exert more leverage the woodcock had to lean backwards, almost overbalancing at times. The head was then thrown well back and the worm started its downward journey, the bird's whole attitude being suggestive of deep satisfaction.

Unfortunately at this interesting moment I made a grave mistake. I tried to creep a little closer to get a better view, and the bird flew away in a great fluster. With its broad wing-spread it is extraordinary what a noise a woodcock sometimes makes rising out of cover, especially when frightened. I was doubly annoyed, for besides the rare experience of seeing a woodcock like this in a good light, the method of feeding was in itself unusual. As a rule both woodcock and snipe can swallow all their food without withdrawing their bills from the soil.

J. W. SEIGNE from *Woodcock and Snipe*

And God said, Let the waters bring forth abundantly
the moving creature that hath life, and fowl that may
fly above the earth in the open firmament of heaven.

And God created great whales, and every living
creature that moveth, which the waters brought forth
abundantly, after their kind, and every winged fowl
after his kind: and God saw that it was good.

And God blessed them, saying, Be fruitful and multiply,
and fill the waters in the seas, and let fowl multiply in
the earth. And the evening and the morning were the
fifth day.

Genesis i, 20–23.

When that the monethe of May
Is comen and that I hear the foules synge,
And that the floures gynnen for to sprynge.
Fairewel my boke and my devocion.

CHAUCER

VESPERS

O blackbird, what a boy you are!
How you do go it
Blowing your bugle to that one sweet star—
How you do blow it!

And does she hear you, blackbird boy, so far?
Or is it wasted breath?
" Good Lord! she is so bright
To-night! "
The blackbird saith.

T. E. BROWN

His own shrill matin joined the various notes
Of Nature's music, from a thousand throats:
The blackbird strove with emulation sweet.
And Echo answered from her close retreat;
The sporting white-throat, on some twig's end borne,
Poured hymns to freedom and the rising morn;
Stopt in her song, perchance the starting thrush
Shook a white shower from the black-thorn bush,
Where dew-drops thick as early blossoms hung,
And trembled as the minstrel sweetly sung.

ROBERT BLOOMFIELD from *Daybreak*

Blackbird

The Blackbird

His notes come through the apple-tree
Flowing with a leisurely
Cool and suave limpidity;

Deliberately they glide and swing,
As if he had not only Spring
But centuries in which to sing.

He'll pause between each tune as though
Knowing so many made him slow
To choose which next shall shine and flow.

And the golden globes, the dancing spots
Of light through leaves' opaquer blots,
Seem the bodies of those golden notes.

CAMILLA DOYLE

Birds sing on earth all day among the flowers,
Taking no thought of any other thing
But their own hearts, for out of them they sing:
Their songs are kindred to the blossom heads,
Faint as the petals which the blackthorn sheds,
And like the earth—not alien songs as ours.
To them this greenness and this island peace
Are life and death and happiness in one;
Nor are they separate from the white sun,
Or those warm winds which nightly wash the deep,
Or starlight in the valleys, or new sleep;
And from these things they ask for no release.

FREDEGOND SHOVE from The World

And to those who are nerved and sinewed for the task, the habitation of the bittern is well worthy of a visit, not merely as it teaches us how much we owe to the successive parent generations that subdued those dismal places, and gradually brought the country to that state of richness and beauty in which we found it, but also on account of the extreme on contrast, and the discovery of that singular charm and enchantment with which nature is, in all cases, so thoroughly imbued and invested; so that where man cannot inhabit, he must still admire; and even there, he can trace the plan, adore the power, and bless the goodness, of that Being, in whose sight all the works of creation are equally good.

On a fine clear day in the early part of the season, when the winds of March have dried the heath, and the dark surface, obedient to the action of the sun, becomes soon warm and turns the exhalations which steal from the marsh upward, so that they are dissipated in the higher atmosphere, and cross not that boundary to injure the more fertile and cultivated places,—even the sterile heath and the stagnant pool, though adverse to our cultivation, have their uses in wild nature; and but for these, in a climate like ours, and in the absence of culture, the chain of life would speedily be broken.

Upon such a day, it is not unpleasant to ramble towards the abode of the bittern; and, to those especially who dwell where all around is art, and where the tremulous motion of the ever-trundling wheel of society dizzies the understanding, till one fancies that the stable laws of nature turn round in concert with the minor revolutions of our pursuits, it is far from being unprofitable. Man, so circumstanced, is apt to descend in intellect, as low, or even lower than those unclad men of the woods whom he despises; and there is no better way of enabling him to win back his birthright as a rational and reflective being, than a taste of the cup of wild nature, even though its acerbity should make him writhe at the time. That is the genuine medicine of the mind, far better than all the opiates of the library; and the bounding pulse of glowing and glorious thought, returns all the sooner for its being a little drastic.

The dry height is silent, save the chirp of the grass-hopper, or the hum of some stray bee which the heat of the day has tempted out, to see if there are any honeyed blooms among the heath; but, by and by, you hear the warning whistle of the plover, sounded perhaps within a few yards of your feet, but so singularly inward and ventriloque, that you fancy it comes from miles off; the lapwing soon comes at the call, playing and wailing around your head, and quits you not till you are so near the marshy expanse that your footing is heavy, and the ground quakes and vibrates under your feet. That is not much to be heeded, if you keep the line of the rushes, for a thick tuft of these sturdy plants makes a safe foot-fall in any bog. You may now, perhaps, start the twite, but it will utter its peevish chirp, and jerk off; and if there is a stream with banks of some consistency, you may see the more lively wagtail, which will jerk and run, and flirt about, as if showing off for your especial amuse-ment. If there is a wide portion of clear water, you may perhaps see the wild duck with her young brood sailing out of the reeds, like a vessel of war leading the fleet which she protects; or if the pool is smaller, you may see the brown and yellow of the snipe gliding through the herbage on the margin, as if it were a snake in the grass. Not a wing will stir, however, or a creature take much heed of your presence, after the lapwing wails her farewell.

In the tuft of tall and close herbage, not very far from the firm ground, but yet so placed near or rather in the water that you cannot very easily reach it, the bittern may be close all the time, wakeful, noting you well, and holding herself prepared to " keep her castle "; but you cannot raise her by shouting, or even by throwing stones, the last of which is treason against nature, in a place solely under Nature's dominion. Wait till the sun is down, and the last glimmer of the twilight has got westward of the zenith, and then return to the place where you expect the bird.

The reeds begin to rustle with the little winds, in which the day settles account with the night; but there is a shorter and a sharper rustle, accompanied by the brush of rather a powerful wing. You look round the dim horizon, but there is no bird: another rustle of the wing, and another, still weaker and weaker, but not a moving thing between you and the sky around. You feel rather disappointed—foolish, if you are daring; fearful, if you are timid. Anon, a burst of uncouth and savage laughter breaks over you, piercingly, or rather gratingly loud, and so unwonted and odd, that it sounds as if the voices of a bull and a horse were combined, the former breaking down his bellow to suit the neigh of the latter, in mocking you from the sky.

That is the love-song of the bittern, with which he serenades his mate; and uncouth and harsh as it sounds to you, that mate hears it with far more pleasure than

she would the sweetest chorus of the grove; and when
the surprise with which you are at first taken is over,
you begin to discover that there is a sort of modulation
in the singular sound. As the bird utters it he wheels
in a spiral, expanding his voice as the loops widen, and
sinking it as they close; and though you can just dimly

Bittern

discover him between you and the zenith, it is worth
while to lie down on your back, and watch the style of
his flight, which is as fine as it is peculiar. The sound
comes better out, too, when you are in that position;
and there is an echo, and, as you would readily imagine,
a shaking of the ground; not that, according to the tale
of the poets, the bird thrusts his bill into the marsh, and

shakes that with his booming, though (familiar as I once was for years with the sound, and all the observable habits of bitterns) some kindly critic, on a former occasion, laboured to convert me from that heresy. A quagmire would be but a sorry instrument, even for a bittern's music; but when the bittern booms and bleats overhead, one certainly feels as if the earth were shaking; but it is probably nothing more than the general affection of the sentient system by the jarring upon the ear—an affection which we more or less feel in the case of all harsh and grating sounds, more especially when they are new to us.

ROBERT MUDIE from *The Feathered Tribes of the British Isles*, 1841

The black-cap has in common a full, sweet, deep, loud and wild pipe; yet that strain is of short continuance, and his motions are desultory; but when that bird sits calmly and engages in song in earnest, he pours forth very sweet, but inward melody, and expresses great variety of soft and gentle modulations, superior perhaps to those of any of our warblers, the nightingales excepted.

Black-caps mostly haunt orchards and gardens; while they warble their throats are wonderfully distended.

GILBERT WHITE from *Selborne*

THE BOBOLINK

Black bird scudding
Under the rainy sky,
How wet your wings must be!
And your small head how sleek and cold with water.

Oh, Bobolink, 'tis you!
Over the buffeted orchard in the summer draught,
Chuckling and singing, charging the rainy cloud,
A little bird gone daft,
A little bird with a secret.

Only the bobolink on the rainy
Rhubarb blossom,
Knows my heart.
For whom adversity has not a word to say that can be
    heard
Above the din of summer.
The rain has taught us nothing. And the hooves of cattle,
    and the cat in the grass
Have taught us nothing.
The hawk that motionless above the hill
In the pure sky
Stands like a blackened planet
Has taught us nothing,—seeing him shut his wings and
    fall
Has taught us nothing at all.
In the shadow of the hawk we feather our nests.

Bobolink, you and I, an airy fool and an earthy,
Chuckling under the rain!

I shall never be sad again.
I shall never be sad again.

Ah, sweet, absurd,
Belovèd, bedraggled bird!

EDNA ST. VINCENT MILLAY

The bobolinks rallied them up from the dell,
The orioles whistled them out of the wood;
And all of their saying was, "Earth, it is well!"
And all of their dancing was, "Life, thou art good!"

BLISS CARMAN from *The Daisies*

The morning air was quite glittering with bird song. I heard the first chewinks of the year, and song-sparrows were practising all their different tunes. The bluebird throated his warm warble. And from the edge of the prairies the meadow-larks sang out clear and loud, all wistfulness gone from their voices. On the edge of the slough I stopped, very still in my tracks, to watch two diminutive greenish birds at war in a thorn-apple tree. I was not conscious that there was anything else living close beside me except a slim brown bush just out of reach, and I watched the birds, puzzled for an instant over their identity, when suddenly they both told it to me. A tiny crest of red fury was erected upon each head, proclaiming the ruby-crowned kinglet. They teetered and swung at each other, scolding on a note as high and thin as an insect's. It was laughable to see such display of gallantry in the two smallest cock birds in all the woods.

I laughed, and the low brown bush plucked itself out of the marsh, and with dangling legs and outstretched neck became a bittern that departed, uttering its disgusted cry of "Faugh! Faugh!"

DONALD CULROSS PEATTIE from *Singing in the Wilderness*

To the Cuckoo

O blithe new-comer! I have heard,
I hear thee and rejoice:
O Cuckoo! shall I call thee bird,
Or but a wandering voice?

While I am lying on the grass,
Thy loud note smites my ear!
From hill to hill it seems to pass,
At once far off and near!

I hear thee babbling to the vale
Of sunshine and of flowers;
And unto me thou bring'st a tale
Of visionary hours.

Thrice welcome, darling of the spring!
Even yet thou art to me
No bird, but an invisible thing,
A voice, a mystery.

The same whom in my school-boy days
I listen'd to; that cry
Which made me look a thousand ways
In bush, and tree, and sky.

To see thee did I often rove
Through woods and on the green:
And thou wert still a hope, a love;
Still long'd for, never seen!

And I can listen to thee yet;
Can lie upon the plain
And listen, till I do beget
That golden time again.

Oh blessed bird! the earth we pace
Again appears to be
An unsubstantial, fairy place;
That is fit home for thee!

WILLIAM WORDSWORTH

He rises and begins to round,
He drops the silver chain of sound,
Of many links without a break,
In chirrup, whistle, slur and shake,
All intervolved and spreading wide,
Like water-dimples down a tide
Where ripple ripple overcurls
And eddy into eddy whirls;
A press of hurried notes that run
So fleet they scarce are more than one,
Yet changingly the trills repeat
And linger ringing while they fleet.

.   .   .   .   .

Unthinking save that he may give
His voice the outlet, there to live
Renewed in endless notes of glee,
So thirsty of his voice is he,
For all to hear and all to know
That he is joy, awake, aglow,

KB

The tumult of the heart to hear
Through pureness filtered crystal-clear,
And know the pleasure sprinkled bright
By simple singing of delight,
Shrill, irreflective, unrestrained,
Rapt, ringing, on the jet sustained
Without a break, without a fall,
Sweet-silvery, sheer lyrical,
Perennial, quavering up the chord
Like myriad dews of sunny sward
That trembling into fulness shine,
And sparkle dropping argentine;

GEORGE MEREDITH from *The Lark Ascending*

Nay more; the very birds of the air, those that be not Hawks, are both so many and so useful and pleasant to mankind, that I must not let them pass without some observations. They both feed and refresh him; feed him with their choice bodies, and refresh him with their heavenly voices: I will not undertake to mention the several kinds of Fowl by which this is done: and his curious palate pleased by day, and which with their very excrements afford him a soft lodging at night:—These I will pass by, but not those little nimble musicians of the air, that warble forth their curious ditties with which nature hath furnished them to the shame of art.

At first the Lark, when she means to rejoice, to cheer herself and those that hear her; she then quits the earth, and sings as she ascends higher into the air, and having ended her heavenly employment, grows then mute, and sad, to think she must descend to the dull earth, which she would not touch, but for necessity.

How do the Blackbird and Thrassel with their melodious voices bid welcome to the cheerful Spring, and in their fixed months warble forth such ditties as no art or instrument can reach to!

Nay, the smaller birds also do the like in their particular seasons, as namely the Laverock, the Tit-lark, the little Linnet, and the honest Robin that loves mankind both alive and dead.

But the Nightingale, another of my airy creatures, breathes such sweet loud music out of her little instrumental throat, that it might make mankind to think miracles are not ceased. He that at midnight, when the very labourer sleeps securely, should hear, as I have very often, the clear airs, the sweet descants, the natural rising and falling, the doubling and redoubling of her voice, might well be lifted above earth, and say, " Lord what music hast thou provided for the Saints in heaven, when thou affordest bad men such music on Earth! "

IZAAK WALTON from *The Compleat Angler*

The opening of the birch leaves is the signal for the pheasant to begin to crow, for the blackbird to whistle, and the thrush to sing; and just when the oak-buds begin to look reddish, and not a day before, the whole tribe of finches burst forth in songs from every bough, while the lark, imitating them all, carries the joyous sounds to the sky.   WILLIAM COBBETT from *Rural Rides*

On First Having Heard the Skylark

Not knowing he rose from earth, not having seen him
 rise,
Not knowing the fallow furrow was his home,
And that high wing, untouchable, untainted,
A wing of earth, with the warm loam
Closely acquainted,
I shuddered at his cry and caught my heart.
Relentless out of heaven his sweet crying like a crystal dart
Was launched against me. Scanning the empty sky
I stood with thrown-back head until the world reeled.
Still, still he sped his unappeasable shafts against my
 breast without a shield.
He cried forever from his unseen throat
Between me and the sun.
He would not end his singing, he would not have done.
" Serene and pitiless note, whence, whence are you? "
I cried. " Alas, these arrows, how fast they fall!

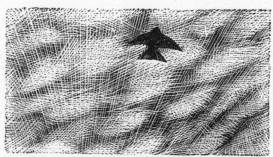

Skylark

Ay, me, beset by angels in unequal fight,
Alone high on the shaven down surprised, and not a
    tree in sight! "
Even as I spoke he was revealed
Above me in the bright air,
A dark articulate atom in the mute enormous blue,
A mortal bird, flying and singing in the morning there.
Even as I spoke I spied him, and I knew,
And called him by his name;
" Blithe Spirit! " I cried. Transfixed by more than mortal
    spears
I fell; I lay among the foreign daisies pink and small,
And wept, staining their innocent faces with fast-flowing
    tears.   EDNA ST. VINCENT MILLAY

SONG

Pack, clouds, away, and welcome day,
    With night we banish sorrow;
Sweet air, blow soft, mount, larks, aloft
    To give my Love good-morrow!
Wings from the wind to please her mind,
    Notes from the lark I'll borrow;
Bird, prune thy wing, nightingale, sing,
    To give my Love good-morrow;
        To give my Love good-morrow
    Notes from them both I'll borrow.

Wake from thy nest, robin red-breast,
    Sing, birds, in every furrow;

And from each hill, let music shrill
Give my fair Love good-morrow!
Blackbird and thrush in every bush,
Stare, linnet, and cock-sparrow!
You pretty elves, amongst yourselves
Sing my fair Love good-morrow;
To give my Love good-morrow
Sing, birds, in every furrow!

THOMAS HEYWOOD

The lark, that tirra-lyra chants.

SHAKESPEARE

The merry Lark his matins sings aloft;
The Thrush replies; the Mavis descant plays;
The Ouzel shrills; the Ruddock warbles soft.

SPENSER

Hark, hark! the lark at heaven's gate sings.

SHAKESPEARE

. . . the lark at break of day arising
From sullen earth, sings hymns at heaven's gate.

SHAKESPEARE

THE HORNBILL

Out in the solemn wilderness alone,
Where ghosts of ages sleep,
And shadows creep,
From mossy bole to bole, from stone to stone,

Just as they crept a thousand years before;
Where you may hear the wind arise and moan,
Whisper and sigh, and sink to rest once more,
In that dim place,
I heard a sudden hollow laughter peal,
The merriment of some inhuman race,
Who seemed to steal,
On velvet padded feet from shade to shade,
Watching me, mocking me, just out of sight;
For when I turned to look, they laughed again,
Though nothing stirred, except the secret flight
Of one large bird,
Who disappeared among the deeper trees.
Then, from afar, re-echoed down the breeze
That wicked demon laughter I had heard.

JOHN STILL

STORMCOCK IN ELDER

In my dark hermitage, aloof
From the world's sight and the world's sound,
By the small door where the old roof
Hangs but five feet above the ground,
I groped along the shelf for bread
But found celestial food instead:

For suddenly close at my ear,
Loud, loud and wild, with wintry glee,
The old unfailing chorister
Burst out in pride of poetry;
And through the broken roof I spied
Him by his singing glorified.

Scarcely an arm's-length from the eye,
Myself unseen, I saw him there;
The throbbing throat that made the cry,
The breast dewed from the misty air,
The polished bill that opened wide
And showed the pointed tongue inside:

The large eye, ringed with many a ray
Of minion feathers, finely laid;
The feet that grasped the elder-spray;
How strongly used, how subtly made,
The scale, the sinew, and the claw,
Plain through the broken roof I saw;

The flight-feathers in tail and wing,
The shorter coverts, and the white
Merged into russet, marrying
The bright breast to the pinions bright,
Gold sequins, spots of chestnut, shower
Of silver, like a brindled flower.
Soldier of fortune, north-west Jack,
Old hard-times' braggart, there you blow!
But tell me ere your bagpipes crack
How you can make so brave a show,
Full-fed in February, and dressed
Like a rich merchant at a feast.

One-half the world, or so they say,
Knows not how half the world may live;
So sing your song and go your way,
And still in February contrive
As bright as Gabriel to smile
On elder-spray by broken tile.

RUTH PITTER

Missel Thrush

THE NIGHTINGALE NEAR THE HOUSE

Here is the soundless cypress on the lawn:
It listens, listens. Taller trees beyond
Listen. The moon at the unruffled pond
   Stares. And you sing, you sing.

The star-enchanted song falls through the air
From lawn to lawn down terraces of sound,
Darts in white arrows on the shadowed ground;
   And all the night you sing.

My dreams are flowers to which you are a bee
As all night long I listen, and my brain
Receives your song, then loses it again
   In moonlight on the lawn.

Now is your voice a marble high and white,
Then like a mist on fields of paradise,
Now is a raging fire, then is like ice,
   Then breaks, and it is dawn.

HAROLD MONRO

'Tis the merry nightingale
That crowds, and hurries, and precipitates
With fast thick warble his delicious notes,
As he were fearful that an April night
Would be too short for him to utter forth
His love-chant, and disburthen his full soul
Of all its music!

          And I know a grove
Of large extent, hard by a castle huge,
Which the great lord inhabits not; and so
This grove is wild with tangling underwood,
And the trim walks are broken up, and grass,
Thin grass and kingcups grow within the paths.
But never elsewhere in one place I knew
So many nightingales; and far and near,
In wood and thicket, over the wide grove,
They answer and provoke each other's song,
With skirmish and capricious passagings,
And murmurs musical and swift jug jug,
And one low piping sound more sweet than all—
Stirring the air with such an harmony,
That should you close your eyes, you might almost
Forget it was not day! On moonlight bushes,
Whose dewy leaflets are but half-disclosed,
You may perchance behold them on the twigs,
Their bright, bright eyes, their eyes both bright and full,
Glistening, while many a glow-worm in the shade
Lights up her love-torch.

          A most gentle maid,
Who dwelleth in her hospitable home
Hard by the castle, and at latest eve
(Even like a lady vowed and dedicate
To something more than Nature in the grove)
Glides through the pathways; she knows all their notes,
That gentle maid! and oft, a moment's space,
What time the moon was lost behind a cloud,
Hath heard a pause of silence; till the moon
Emerging, hath awakened earth and sky

With one sensation, and these wakeful birds
Have all burst forth in choral minstrelsy,
As if some sudden gale had swept at once
An hundred airy harps.

SAMUEL TAYLOR COLERIDGE from *The Nightingale*

Hark! ah, the Nightingale!
  The tawny-throated!
Hark! from that moonlit cedar what a burst!
What triumph! hark!—what pain!

O Wanderer from a Grecian shore,
Still, after many years, in distant lands,
Still nourishing in thy bewilder'd brain
That wild, unquench'd, deep-sunken, old-world pain—
  Say, will it never heal?
And can this fragrant lawn
With its cool trees, and night,
And the sweet, tranquil Thames,
And moonshine, and the dew,
To thy rack'd heart and brain
  Afford no balm?

  Dost thou to-night behold
Here, through the moonlight on the English grass,
The unfriendly palace in the Thracian wilds?
  Dost thou again peruse
With hot cheeks and sear'd eyes
The too clear web, and thy dumb Sister's shame?
  Dost thou once more assay

Thy flight, and feel come over thee,
Poor Fugitive, the feathery change
Once more, and once more seem to make resound
With love and hate, triumph and agony,
Lone Daulis, and the high Cephissian vale?
 Listen, Eugenia—
How thick the bursts come crowding through the leaves!
 Again—thou hearest!
Eternal Passion!
Eternal Pain!

     MATTHEW ARNOLD from *Philomela*

Nightingale

What bird so sings, yet so does wail?
O! 'tis the ravished nightingale.
" Jug, jug, jug, jug, tereu! " she cries,
And still her woes at midnight rise.
Brave prick-song! who is't now we hear?
None but the lark so shrill and clear;
Now at heaven's gates she claps her wings,
The morn not waking till she sings.
Hark, hark, with what a pretty throat
Poor robin redbreast tunes his note!
Hark how the jolly cuckoos sing,
" Cuckoo," to welcome in the spring!
" Cuckoo," to welcome in the spring!

LYLY

To the Nightingale which the Author heard sing on New Year's Day, 1792

Whence is it, that amaz'd I hear
   From yonder wither'd spray,
The foremost morn of all the year,
   The melody of May?

And why, since thousands would be proud
   Of such a favour shewn,
Am I selected from the crowd,
   To witness it alone?

Sing'st thou, sweet Philomel, to me,
   For that I also long
Have practis'd in the groves like thee,
   Though not like thee in song?

Or sing'st thou rather under force
    Of some divine command,
Commission'd to presage a course
    Of happier days at hand?

Thrice welcome then! for many a long
    And joyless year have I,
As though to-day, put forth my song
    Beneath a wintry sky.

But thee no wintry skies can harm,
    Who only need'st to sing,
To make ev'n January charm,
    And ev'ry season Spring.

WILLIAM COWPER

There is no bird, I believe, whose manners I have studied
more than that of the *caprimulgus* (the goat-sucker), as it
is a wonderful and curious creature: but I have always
found that though sometimes it may chatter as it flies,
as I know it does, yet in general it utters its jarring note
sitting on a bough; and I have for many an half hour
watched it as it sat with its under mandible quivering,
and particularly this summer. It perches usually on a
bare twig, with its head lower than its tail, in an attitude
well expressed by your draughtsman in the folio *British
Zoology*. This bird is most punctual in beginning its song
exactly at the close of day; so exactly that I have known
it strike up more than once or twice just at the report
of the Portsmouth evening gun, which we can hear when
the weather is still. It appears to me past all doubt that

its notes are formed by organic impulse, by the powers of the parts of its windpipe, formed for sound, just as cats purr. You will credit me, I hope, when I tell you that, as my neighbours were assembled in an hermitage on the side of a steep hill where we drink tea, one of these church-owls came and settled on the cross of that little straw edifice and began to chatter, and continued his note for many minutes: and we were all struck with wonder to find that the organs of that little animal, when put in motion, gave a sensible vibration to the whole building! This bird also sometimes makes a small squeak, repeated four or five times; and I have observed that to happen when the cock has been pursuing the hen in a toying way through the boughs of a tree.

GILBERT WHITE from *Selborne*

Let not the Screech-Owl, nor the Stork, be heard;
Nor the night Raven, that still deadly yells;

SPENSER

Then nightly sings the staring owl,
   Tu-whit;

SHAKESPEARE

Sweet Suffolk owl, so trimly dight
With feathers like a lady bright,
Thou sing'st alone, sitting by night,
  Te whit, te whoo!

Tawny Owl

LB

Thy note, that forth so freely rolls,
With shrill command the mouse controls,
And sings a dirge for dying souls,
   Te whit, te whoo!

ANON

PRID-KAL-OCT

O Asian birds, that round me in the gloom
Patter and peck unseen, or with loud stroke
Soar to the covert of some branching oak,—
To-morrow comes the destined hecatomb.

Shout once again your strident orisons,
   Thanks for the dewy morning, for the food
   By hands unseen at woodland corners strewed,
For water cool, that through the thicket runs.

To-morrow comes the end:—the wood astir
   With patient tramping figures, and the noise
   Of tree-trunks tapped, the cry of eager boys,
   The startled rush, and battling as you rise
Above the copse, beyond the topmost fir,
   Death, lightning death, amid the echoing skies.

A. C. BENSON

The redbreast warbles still, but is content
With slender notes, and more than half suppress'd;
Pleased with his solitude, and flitting light

From spray to spray, where'er he rests he shakes
From many a twig the pendent drops of ice,
That tinkle in the wither'd leaves below.
Stillness, accompanied with sounds so soft,
Charms more than silence.

WILLIAM COWPER from *The Winter Walk at Noon*

September Tenth. In autumn some of the sweetness of spring steals back again. There are the blessed rains, the sharp nights, the mornings smelling of wet loam and winy air as if blown from the mountains. The woods are filling up with clouds of asters. And best of all, the birds return. Few are the voices of the forest, but the robin has taken to singing again his old " Cheer up, cheery, Wake up, weary! " The grackles gather in the wet woods just as they do in March, and from the fields comes a slender, wistful whistling of the meadow-larks, of all songs I know the most poignant except the farewell whistling of the white-throat sparrow. But there is something sad about these songs, something that merely reminds us of a happiness we once knew, that is gone.

DONALD CULROSS PEATTIE from *An Almanac for Moderns*

I remember that once, when riding late one afternoon in a lonely place on the pampas, I pulled up my horse again and again to listen to that mysterious noise which is like no other sound on earth. A sound that was like the thin blue summer or dry fog, which partially veils or dims and appears to pervade the entire landscape, producing the appearance of a heaven and earth mingled or interfused; a sound that was everywhere in earth and air and sky, but changing in power; at intervals loud as the summer humming of insects, then decreasing and at last so faint as to be scarcely audible, so that listening you almost came to think it an imaginary sound.

Doubtless the sound came to me from a great distance, as no male or other rhea was visible to me at the time, although when emitting its call the bird stands erect, a tall conspicuous object on the wide level plain, his long neck inflated and the pinions with their white plumes spread open. There had been an ostrich hunt that day, and the sounds I listened to probably came from two or three birds calling from widely separated points.

.   .   .   .   .

I remember that in my home on the pampas, when I was a boy, we used to stand out of doors on those exceptionally still, clear mornings when all distant objects seemed near, and when all sounds appeared to travel twice as far as at ordinary times. We would listen with delight on such mornings, which were usually in the winter, to the calls and cries of the great water-fowl in three or four rush- and sedge-grown lagoons situated at different points and at various distances from our home, from something over a mile to two miles and a half. From all of them we could distinctly hear certain species; the alarm cry and song-like performance of the crested screamer; the short, rapidly reiterated call of the great blue ibis, a sound as of hammer-strokes on an anvil, only more aerial, more musical; the frenzied shrieks of the large ypecaha rail, several birds shrieking in chorus, and the prolonged sad wailing cries of the courlan, the " crazy widow " of the natives; but other big loud-voiced birds were inaudible at that distance—the scream of the great heron, for example, and the trumpeting of the

Crested Screamer

Coscoroba swan, their notes being without the shrill quality of the others. A human being with a voice, proportionate to his size, of the character of the bird voices I have described, would be audible seven or eight miles away in a still atmosphere. As it is, small as the big birds are compared with the big great-voiced beasts, their voices carry much further, and the call of an ibis will outdistance the roaring of stags and lions, braying of asses and neighing of horses, bellowing of cattle, howlings of " old man " araguatos, monkeys and wolves, and screaming of hyaenas.

W. H. HUDSON from *A Hind in Richmond Park*

After the starlings had flown
Over the plain and were gone,
There was one of them stayed on alone
In the trees; it chattered on high,
Lifting its bill to the sky,
Distending its throat,
Crooning harsh note after note,
In soliloquy,
Sitting alone.
And after a hush
It gurgled as gurgles a well,
Warbled as warbles a thrush,
Had a try at the sound of a bell
And mimicked a jay. . . .

FORD MADOX HUEFFER from *The Starling*

THE DYING SWAN

The plain was grassy, wild and bare,
Wide, wild and open to the air,
Which had built up everywhere

An under-roof of doleful gray.
With an inner voice the river ran,
Adown it floated a dying swan,
And loudly did lament.
   It was the middle of the day
Ever the weary wind went on,
   And took the reed-tops as it went.

Some blue peaks in the distance rose,
And white against the cold-white sky,
Shone out their crowning snows.
   One willow over the river wept,
And shook the wave as the wind did sigh;
Above in the wind was the swallow,
   Chasing itself at its own wild will,
   And far thro' the marish green and still
   The tangled water-courses slept,
Shot over with purple, and green, and yellow.

The wild swan's death-hymn took the soul
Of that waste place with joy
Hidden in sorrow: at first to the ear
The warble was low, and full and clear;
And floating about the under-sky,
Prevailing in weakness, the coronach stole
Sometimes afar, and sometimes anear;
But anon her awful jubilant voice,
With a music strange and manifold,
Flow'd forth on a carol free and bold;
As when a mighty people rejoice
With shawms, and with cymbals, and harps of gold,
And the tumult of their acclaim is roll'd

Thro' the open gates of the city afar,
To the shepherd who watcheth the evening star.
And the creeping mosses and clambering weeds,
And the willow-branches hoar and dank,
And the wavy swell of the soughing reeds,
And the wave-worn horns of the echoing bank,
And the silvery marish-flowers that throng
The desolate creeks and pools among,
Were flooded over with eddying song.

ALFRED, LORD TENNYSON

HOME THOUGHTS FROM ABROAD

Oh, to be in England
  Now that April's there,
And whoever wakes in England
Sees, some morning, unaware,
That the lowest boughs and the brush-wood sheaf
Round the elm-tree bole are in tiny leaf,
While the chaffinch sings on the orchard bough
In England—now!

And after April, when May follows,
And the whitethroat builds, and all the swallows!
Hark, where my blossomed pear-tree in the hedge
Leans to the field and scatters on the clover
Blossoms and dewdrops—at the bent spray's edge—
That's the wise thrush; he sings each song twice over,
Lest you should think he never could recapture
The first fine careless rapture!

ROBERT BROWNING from *Home Thoughts from Abroad*

THE THRUSH'S NEST

Within a thick and spreading hawthorn bush
That overhung a molehill large and round,
I heard from morn to morn a merry thrush
Sing hymns of rapture, while I drank the sound
With joy—and oft, an unintruding guest,
I watched her secret toils from day to day;
How true she warped the moss to form her nest,
And modelled it within with wood and clay.
And by and by, like heath-bells gilt with dew,
There lay her shining eggs as bright as flowers,
Ink-spotted over, shells of green and blue:
And there I witnessed in the summer hours
A brood of nature's minstrels chirp and fly,
Glad as the sunshine and the laughing sky.

JOHN CLARE

THRUSHES

Tossed on the glittering air they soar and skim
Whose voices make the emptiness of light
A windy palace. Quavering from the brim
Of dawn, and bold with song at edge of night,
They clutch their leafy pinnacles and sing
Scornful of man, and from his toils aloof
Whose heart's a haunted woodland whispering;
Whose thoughts return on tempest-baffled wing;
Who hears the cry of God in everything,
And storms the gate of nothingness for proof.

SIEGFRIED SASSOON

In the hedge round the paddock a whitethroat is noisy all day. He is a delightful little creature, with a song like a signature scribbled with a quill pen. He keeps out of sight most of the time, but he cannot resist the temptation of an occasional upward dive into the air, as though he were playing at being a lark. He even attempts to imitate

Song Thrush

the lark's profuseness of speech when on the wing, as he jerks and scrambles and sideslips among the air above the trees. Then suddenly he becomes frightened and precipitates himself downwards in a series of desperate dives till he has reached the safety of the hedge or his post in an ash-tree again.

ROBERT LYND from *Solomon in All His Glory*

Amid the drearness of dell and thornbush, the song of the wren hidden in the wet branches seems all the more triumphant. It is a song brilliant as a rainbow in a wet sky—brilliant as a dance of rainbows. There is a shameless optimism in it that clothes the bare hedges with something better than leaves. There is no other resident bird so incapable of melancholy. The robin is often pensive, and sings to us and looks down at us from the apple-tree as though he sympathized with us. But the wren never sings except to say that it is the best of all possible worlds. His must have been the voice that first sounded immediately after God saw that it was all very good. The wren is the incarnate Amen of creation. He has moods of anger, it is true, when his grating voice can be heard in the hedge, and he has moments of mild fear, when his little brown form scurries ahead of one, five yards at a time, among the thorns of the lane. But, when the danger is past, he recovers his spirits and raises his song with an exaggerated boastfulness. " The wren, the wren, the king of all birds," an old country rhyme begins. He certainly swells into a king in his song. If Noah had put his cock wren out on the roof of the Ark, the flood would no longer have seemed a barren waste, but would have scintillated for him as the thing his imagination had desired.   ROBERT LYND from *Solomon in All His Glory*

November Second. You will awaken one of these autumn mornings to the sound of a long sweet whistle blowing from the fields. I chanced to hear it this day because I was listening, in the early morning, for a bird of quite another sort—the first call-notes of my youngest boy, who is now at the stage when joy begins at five in the morning. But he chanced to sleep longer, and so I heard the white-throat sing.

I heard it last spring, in rain. Now, under a faultless blue sky, very high and light, it utters a few notes, in reverie, a silvery attenuation of the bridal song. Perhaps we might think the white-throat is saying farewell to us; but he is in truth only just arrived from his northern breeding grounds, and now, in company with winter wrens and siskins and brown creepers, he will pass the inclement season here, as well he may.

For the ducks, the owls and falcons, and a few small passerine birds, wintering in this countryside represents a sojourn in the south. Our latitude would appear to be low enough for their needs. For the gulls and ducks all winter long there may be found some open water here; for the creatures of prey there are small mammals that do not hibernate; and for the little song birds the weed seeds still rise above the casual drifts, and there is foraging about the generous unthrifty American barns. So modest are the requirements of this dun and humble company.

DONALD CULROSS PEATTIE from *An Almanac for Moderns*

Aug. 7, 1778. A good ornithologist should be able to distinguish birds by their air as well as by their colours and shape; on the ground as well as on the wing, and in the bush as well as in the hand. For, though it must not be said that every species of birds has a manner peculiar to itself, yet there is somewhat in most genera at least, that at first sight discriminates them, and enables a judicious observer to pronounce upon them with some certainty. Put a bird in motion

. . . " Et vera incessu patuit." . . .

Thus kites and buzzards sail round in circles with wings expanded and motionless; and it is from their gliding manner that the former are still called in the north of England gleads, from the Saxon verb *glidan* to glide. The kestrel, or wind-hover, has a peculiar mode of hanging in the air in one place, his wings all the while being briskly agitated. Hen-harriers fly low over heaths or fields of corn, and beat the ground regularly like a pointer or setting-dog. Owls move in a buoyant manner, as if lighter than the air; they seem to want ballast. There is a peculiarity belonging to ravens that must draw the attention even of the most incurious—they spend all their leisure time in striking and cuffing each other on the wing in a kind of playful skirmish; and, when they move from one place to another, frequently turn on their backs with a loud croak, and seem to be falling to the ground. When this odd gesture betides them, they are scratching themselves with one foot, and thus lose the centre of gravity. Rooks sometimes dive and tumble in a frolicsome manner; crows and daws swagger in their walk; wood-peckers fly *volatu undoso*, opening and closing their wings at every stroke, and so are always rising or falling in curves. All of this genus use their tails, which incline downward, as a support while they run up trees. Parrots, like all other hook-clawed birds, walk awkwardly, and make use of their bill as a third foot, climbing and ascending with ridiculous caution. All the *gallinæ* parade and walk gracefully, and run nimbly; but fly with difficulty, with an impetuous whirring, and in a straight line. Magpies and jays flutter with powerless

Coot Taking Off

wings, and make no dispatch; herons seem incumbered with too much sail for their light bodies; but these vast hollow wings are necessary in carrying burdens, such as large fishes, and the like; pigeons, and particularly the sort called smiters, have a way of clashing their wings the one against the other over their backs with a loud snap; another variety called tumblers turn themselves over in the air. Some birds have movements peculiar to the season of love: thus ring-doves, though strong and rapid at other times, yet in the spring hang about on the wing in a toy-ing and playful manner; thus the cock-snipe, while breed-ing, forgetting his former flight, fans the air like the wind-hover; and the green-finch in particular exhibits such languishing and faltering gestures as to appear like a wounded and dying bird; the king-fisher darts along like an arrow; fern-owls, or goat-suckers, glance in the dusk over the tops of trees like a meteor; starlings as it were swim along, while missel-thrushes use a wild and desultory flight; swallows sweep over the surface of the ground and water, and distinguish themselves by rapid turns and quick evolutions; swifts dash round in circles; and the bank-martin moves with frequent vacillations like a butterfly. Most of the small birds fly by jerks, rising and falling as they advance. Most small birds hop; but wagtails and larks walk, moving their legs alternately. Skylarks rise and fall perpendicularly as they sing: wood-larks hang poised in the air; and titlarks rise and fall in large curves, singing in their descent. The white-throat uses odd jerks and gesticulations over the tops of hedges and bushes. All the duck-kind waddle; divers and auks walk as if fettered, and stand erect on their tails: these are the *compedes* of Linnaeus. Geese and cranes, and most wild-fowls, move in figured flights, often changing their position. The secondary remiges of *tringae*, wild-ducks, and some others, are very long, and give their wings, when in motion, an hooked appearance. Dab-chicks, moor-hens, and coots, fly erect, with their legs hanging down, and hardly make any dispatch; the reason is plain, their wings are placed too forward out of the true centre of gravity: as the legs of auks and divers are situated too backward. GILBERT WHITE from *Selborne*

The way of an eagle in the air.

Proverbs xxx. 19

When evening came and the warm glow grew
    deeper,
And every tree that bordered the green meadows
And in the yellow cornfields every reaper
And every corn-shock stood above their shadows
Flung eastward from their feet in longer measure,

Golden Eagle

Serenely far there swam in the sunny height
A buzzard and his mate who took their pleasure
Swirling and poising idly in golden light.

On great pied motionless moth-wings borne along,
  So effortless and so strong,
Cutting each other's paths together they glided,
Then wheeled asunder till they soared divided

Mallard Alighting

MB

Two valleys' width (as though it were delight
To part like this, being sure they could unite
So swiftly in their empty, free dominion),
Curved headlong downward, towered up the sunny
    steep,
Then, with a sudden lift of the one great pinion,
Swung proudly to a curve, and from its height
Took half a mile of sunlight in one long sweep.

        MARTIN ARMSTRONG from *The Buzzards*

As a gleaming mallard alighting in a pool
Among marsh-marigolds and splashing wet
Green leaves and yellow blooms, like jewels set
In bright, black mud, with clear drops crystal-cool,
Bringing keen savours of the sea and stir
Of windy spaces where wild sunsets flame
To that dark inland dyke. . . .

        WILFRID WILSON GIBSON from *Wings*

THE HAWK

The hawk slipt out of the pine, and rose in the
    sunlit air:
Steady and still he poised; his shadow slept on
    the grass:
And the bird's song sickened and sank: she cowered
    with furtive stare
Dumb, till the quivering dimness should flicker
    and shift and pass.

Suddenly down he dropped: she heard the hiss of
    his wing,
Fled with a scream of terror; oh, would she had
    dared to rest!
For the hawk at eve was full, and there was no
    bird to sing,
And over the heather drifted the down from a
    bleeding breast.

A. C. BENSON

Buzzards

Thus conformed, and provided with this wonderful apparatus of wings and covering, the bird does not hesitate to shoot into the region of tempests, and proceed to most prodigious distances. Nothing is more wonderful to the contemplation of the natural philosopher, than this power of flight. Its mechanism is combined with such astonishing skill, and rests upon such powerful resources, that no machine, invented by the most able mechanician, has, as yet, been found capable of imparting such a faculty to man. All who, without the aid of a balloon (which is not flying, but a sort of sailing) have attempted to elevate themselves into the air, have shared the fate of Icarus.

We shall enrich our pages with a few of the reflections of the illustrious Buffon on this subject. " To give some idea of the duration and continuity of motion in birds, and likewise of the proportion of time and space which their courses occupy, we shall compare their swiftness with that of quadrupeds in their greatest progressions, whether natural or forced. The stag, the rein-deer, and the elk can go through forty leagues in a single day. The rein-deer, harnessed to a sledge, can make thirty, and continue this many days in succession. The camel can make three hundred leagues in eight days. The horse, educated for the race, and chosen from among the lightest and most vigorous, can perform a league in six to seven minutes; but his speed soon relaxes, and he would be incapable of supporting a longer career, with the spirit and celerity with which he commenced. We have cited the example of an Englishman who went seventy-two leagues in eleven hours and thirty-two minutes, having changed horse one-and-twenty times; thus the best horses can make no more than four leagues in an hour, nor more than thirty leagues in a day. But the swiftness of birds is considerably greater. In less than three minutes we lose sight of a large bird; of a kite, for example, which proceeds horizontally, or an eagle, vertically, and the diameter of whose extent in flying is more than four feet. From this we may infer, that the bird traverses more than a space of four thousand five hundred feet in a minute,

Falcon

and that he can proceed twenty leagues in an hour. He may then easily proceed at the rate of two hundred leagues a day, flying for only ten hours. This supposes many intervals in the day, and the entire night for repose. Swallows, and other birds of passage, may thus proceed from our climate to the Line in less than seven or eight days. M. Adamson has seen and caught, on the coast of Senegal, swallows which arrived there on the 9th of October, that is, eight or nine days after their departure from Europe. Pietro della Valle says that, in Persia, the carrier-pigeon makes greater way in one day than a man on foot can do in six. The story of the falcon of Henry II is well known, which, pursuing with eagerness a smaller bustard at Fontainbleau, was taken the following day at Malta, and recognised by the ring which she bore. A falcon from the Canary Islands, sent to the Duke of Lerma, returned from Andalusia to the Isle of Teneriffe in sixteen hours, which is a passage of two hundred and fifty leagues. Sir Hans Sloane assures us that, at Barbadoes, the sea-gulls proceed in flocks to a distance of more than two hundred miles, and return again the same day. A course like this, of more than one hundred and thirty leagues, sufficiently indicates the possibility of a voyage of two hundred; and I believe we may conclude, from the combination of all these facts, that a bird of elevated flight can traverse every day four or five times as much space as the agile quadruped."

BARON CUVIER from *The Class Aves*

THE EAGLE . FRAGMENT

He clasps the crag with crooked hands;
Close to the sun in lonely lands,
Ring'd with the azure world, he stands.
The wrinkled sea beneath him crawls;
He watches from his mountain walls,
And like a thunderbolt he falls.

ALFRED, LORD TENNYSON

An impression of awe is left on the mind, as one of these great white birds unfolds the vast expanse of its wings, and with the most consummate ease dives into space from the ledge near which you have been standing. Much of impetus there must be in that apparently effortless plunge, or is it merely the weight of its own body (6 lbs.) which is enough to carry the Solan Goose a quarter of a mile in one long stately curve, before it need use its wings again?

J. H. GURNEY from *The Gannet*

Gannet Plunging

It is difficult to name the maximum height of a Gannet's plunge, but the most reliable observations were those made by Mr. W. E. Clarke, when spending a month for migration study on Eddystone Lighthouse. Knowing the level of the lighthouse gallery, he was able to determine approximately the height of many plunges, and in his opinion none, out of many thousand, exceeded one hundred and forty feet. Norman Heathcote thought some reached one hundred and fifty feet.

J. H. GURNEY from *The Gannet*

With a view of ascertaining whether the particulars furnished to Thompson seventy-three years ago were still accepted as facts at Ballantrae, I made enquiries of various persons, and in particular of Mr. William Girvan, who, for many years with his brother netted the sea-fowl on Ailsa Craig, of which he is still the tenant. Mr. Girvan at once said that it was not at all an uncommon thing for Gannets to be caught in nets set at from sixty to seventy-two feet (ten to twelve fathoms)—which is the usual depth for them with the fishermen there—the nets being generally weighted with heavy stones to keep them down.

This, Mr. William Leckie of Ballantrae, an equally good witness, has since by letter corroborated, he having on different occasions seen Gannets, and also Cormorants, brought up in the fishermen's nets, which nets he could safely say were set at from sixty to ninety feet down, and the birds must have penetrated to that depth to get into

them. Mr. Leckie has also seen Guillemots brought up
in nets which were set at a depth of a hundred and twenty
feet, and of this I have confirmation from the Girvan-
town fishermen, through Mr. R. Tannahill, the harbour
master there, who believes that Guillemots have been
taken at even greater depths than that.

J. H. GURNEY from The Gannet

> Like to an Eagle, in his kingly pride
> Soring through his wide Empire of the aire,
> To weather his brode sailes, by chaunce hath
>   spide
> A Goshauke, which hath seized for her share
> Uppon some fowle that should her feast prepare;
> With dreadful force he flies at her bylive,
> That with his souce, which none enduren dare,
> Her from the quarrey he away doth drive,
> And from her griping pounce the greedy prey doth
>   rive.

EDMUND SPENSER

Lucanus made some experiments on the altitudes at
which different birds could be seen from the ground:
the figures arrived at may be quoted here as they may
perhaps serve as a guide to the rough estimation of altitudes when the observer has no means of measurement
available. Birds stuffed in the attitude of flight were
suspended from a captive balloon in such a way that they
could be seen from the ground against the sky. It was

found that the outline of a Sparrow-Hawk (*Accipiter nisus*) was distinguishable at about 800 feet, that the bird was clearly visible as a spot about 2,100 feet, and disappeared from view at about 2,800 feet. The corresponding figures for the Rook (*Corvus frugilegus*) were about 1,000, 2,600, and 3,300 feet.

A. LANDSBOROUGH THOMSON from *Problems of Bird Migration*

When day declining sheds a milder gleam,
What time the may-fly haunts the pool or stream;
When the still owl skims around the grassy mead,
What time the timorous hare limps forth to feed;
Then be the time to steal adown the vale,
And listen to the vagrant cuckoo's tale;
To hear the clamorous curlew call his mate,
Or the soft quail his tender pain relate;
To see the swallow sweep the dark'ning plain
Belated, to support her infant train;
To mark the swift in rapid giddy ring
Dash round the steeple, unsubdu'd of wing.

GILBERT WHITE from *Selborne*

. . . wayward as the swallow,
Swift as the swallow along the river's light
Circleting the surface to meet his mirrored winglets.

Lovely are the curves of the white owl sweeping
Wavy in the dusk lit by one large star.

Lone on the fir-branch, his rattle-note unvaried,
Brooding o'er the gloom, spins the brown eve-jar.

GEORGE MEREDITH from *Love in the Valley*

Meinertzhagen (1921) has also collected observations made
by pilots of the Royal Air Force who had observed the
speed indicators of their machines while keeping level
with the birds. Only two of these records refer definitely
to birds actually on migration: White Storks (*Ciconia
ciconia*) were encountered migrating at 48 m.p.h. at 4,200
feet, and Mallard (*Anas platyrhyncha*) migrating at 50
m.p.h. Other speeds recorded are as follows: Rook, 45;
Gannet (*Sula bassana*), 48; Geese, 55; and Lapwing,
40–45 m.p.h. Greater velocities were recorded in three
instances. Golden Plover (*Charadrius apricarius*) when
pressed by a pursuing aeroplane accomplished 60 m.p.h.;
Swifts (*Apus apus*) feeding at a height of 6,000 feet above
Mosul easily passed and circled round an aeroplane doing
68 m.p.h.; and a Lammergeier made 110 m.p.h. while
" nose-diving " to escape an aeroplane.

A. LANDSBOROUGH THOMSON from *Problems of Bird
Migration*

I too many and many a time cross'd the river of
    old,
Watched the Twelfth-month sea-gulls, saw them
        high in the air floating with motionless wings,
        oscillating their bodies,

Saw how the glistening yellow lit up parts of their
    bodies, and left the rest in strong shadow,
Saw the slow wheeling circles and the gradual
    edging toward the south,
Saw the reflection of the summer sky in the water.

            WALT WHITMAN from *Crossing Brooklyn Ferry*

    As when some hunter in the spring hath found
A breeding eagle sitting on her nest,
Upon the craggy isle of a hill-lake,
And pierced her with an arrow as she rose,
And follow'd her to find her where she fell
Far off;—anon her mate comes winging back
From hunting, and a great way off descries
His huddling young left sole; at that, he checks
His pinion, and with short uneasy sweeps
Circles above his eyrie, with loud screams

Young Herring Gull

Chiding his mate back to her nest; but she
Lies dying, with an arrow in her side,
In some far stony gorge out of his ken,
A heap of fluttering feathers—never more
Shall the lake glass her, flying over it;
Never the black and dripping precipices
Echo her stormy scream as she sails by.

MATTHEW ARNOLD from *Aohrab and Rustum*

My gentle-hearted Charles! When the last rook
Beat its straight path along the dusky air
Homewards, I blest it! deeming, its black wing
(Now a dim speck, now vanishing in light)
Had cross'd the mighty orb's dilated glory,
While thou stood'st gazing; or when all was still,
Flew creeking[1] o'er thy head, and had a charm
For thee, my gentle-hearted Charles, to whom
No sound is dissonant which tells of Life.

SAMUEL TAYLOR COLERIDGE from
This Lime-Tree Bower my Prison

[1] Some months after I had written this line, it gave me pleasure to observe that Bartram had observed the same circumstance of the Savanna crane. "When these birds move their wings in flight, their strokes are slow, moderate and regular; and even when at a considerable distance or high above us, we plainly hear the quill-feathers; their shafts and webs upon one another creak as the joints or workings of a vessel in a tempestuous sea."

Skirting the river road, (my forenoon walk, my rest,)
Skyward in air a sudden muffled sound, the dalliance
    of the eagles,
The rushing amorous contact high in space together,
The clinching interlocking claws, a living, fierce,
    gyrating wheel,
Four beating wings, two beaks, a swirling mass tight
    grappling,
In tumbling turning clustering loops, straight down-
    ward falling,
Till o'er the river pois'd, the twain yet one, a moment's
    lull,
A motionless still balance in the air, then parting,
    talons loosing,
Upward again on slow-firm pinions slanting, their
    separate diverse flight,
She hers, he his, pursuing.

WALT WHITMAN

Yea, the stork in the heaven knoweth
her appointed times; and the turtle and
the crane and the swallow observe the
time of their coming.

Jeremiah viii. 7

When migrating its cry was heard at all hours from
morning to night, from February till April: and again
at night, especially when there was a moon.

White Stork

Lying awake in bed, I would listen by the hour to the sound coming to me from the sky, mellowed and made beautiful by distance and the profound silence of the moonlit world, until it acquired a fascination for me above all sounds on earth, so that it lived ever after in me; and the image of it is as vivid in my mind at this moment as that of any bird call or cry, or any other striking sound heard yesterday or but an hour ago. It was the sense of mystery it conveyed which so attracted and impressed me—the mystery of that delicate, frail, beautiful thing, travelling in the sky, alone, day and night, crying aloud at intervals as if moved by some powerful emotion, beating the air with its wings, its beak pointing like the needle of the compass to the north, flying, speeding on its seven-thousand-mile flight to its nesting home in another hemisphere.

W. H. HUDSON from *A Hind in Richmond Park*

In Yarkand we have found one at least of the breeding haunts of numbers of our Indian winter visitants, whose nests and eggs have hitherto been vainly sought for in the Himalayas, and of which, though some few individuals doubtless bred there, the great mass went, as we knew, farther north in summer.

What became of the vast multitudes which during the cold season swarm over the whole face of the country, has always been a puzzle. We now find that Yarkand is one, at any rate, of their favourite summer retreats, and that a belt of absolute desert, more than 100 miles in width, having an elevation of over 15,000 feet, and intersected by numerous more or less snow-capped ridges, the lowest passes over which attain an altitude of 18,000 feet above the sea level, opposes no invincible obstacle to the periodical migration of even the tiniest and most feeble-winged of our songsters.

It is startling to think of birds like the *Phylloscopi*, ill-adapted as they seem for lengthened flights, and, when not migrating, rarely flying more than a few yards at a time, yearly travelling from Yarkand to Southern India and back again. How these butterfly-like mites brave in safety the vast stretches of almost Arctic deserts—absolutely devoid of vegetation, where the thermometer habitually varies 50° in twelve hours, and a breeze springing up sends the mercury down far below zero and freezes men, horses, and even yaks, it is alleged, in a few hours, is verily a mystery.

HENDERSON AND HUME from *Lahore to Yarkand*

The extraordinary power of the migrating impulse was brought vividly home to me by the presence of a solitary red-throated pipit feeding on the banks of the river some 1,400 miles south of Cairo. Less than a year before I had seen this bird in its breeding haunts beyond the arctic circle in Russian Lapland, and I knew that it only nested north of the tree-limit. When I recalled my own journeys by boat and rail round the North Cape and then again down to Khartoum, and looked at the lonely, delicate little bird before me, it was almost impossible to realize that those feeble wings would in a few weeks' time be transporting that tender little body beyond the arctic circle.

H. F. WITHERBY from *Bird Hunting on the White Nile*

NB

Another visitor, but a pleasing one, appeared in the day-time. This was a little bird—the lesser Whitethroat—a summer visitor to England, and exceedingly numerous during our winter and spring on the White Nile. The Whitethroat came to my tent for water, a bucket of which was kept near my bed. On the very first day of my illness this bird found out the water and came into the tent, perching on the bed or my arm. It stayed there most of the day, and whenever I splashed my hand in the water it would hop down my arm and suck the drops of water from my finger tips. The bird was always thirsty, and although the river was quite near it seemed to prefer to drink in this way, and so I was amused by this delightful little bird all through the heat of the day. I missed it much on moving from this camp.

H. F. WITHERBY from *Bird Hunting on the White Nile*

One autumn, when most of the emigrants to the Arctic breeding-grounds had already gone, I witnessed a great migration of this very species—this beautiful sandpiper with the habits of a plover. The birds appeared in flocks of about one to two or three hundred, flying low and very swiftly due north, flock succeeding flock at intervals of about ten to twelve minutes; and this migration continued for three days, or, at all events, three days from the first day I saw them, at a spot about two miles from my home. I was amazed at their numbers, and it was a puzzle to me then, and has been one ever since, that a species thinly distributed over the immense area

of the Argentine pampas and Patagonia could keep to that
one line of travel over that uniform green, sea-like country.
For, outside of that line, not one bird of the kind could
anywhere be seen; yet they kept so strictly to it that I
sat each day for hours on my horse watching them pass,
each flock first appearing as a faint buff-coloured blur or
cloud just above the southern horizon, rapidly approaching
then passing me, about on a level with my horse's head,
to fade out of sight in a couple of minutes in the north;
soon to be succeeded by another and yet other flocks in
endless succession, each appearing at the same point as
the one before, following the same line, as if a line invisible

Curlew

to all eyes except their own had been traced across the green world for their guidance. It gave one the idea that all the birds of this species, thinly distributed over tens of thousands of square miles of country, had formed the habit of assembling, previous to migration, at one starting-point, from which they set out in successive flocks of a medium size, in a disciplined order, on that marvellous journey to their Arctic breeding-grounds.

W. H. HUDSON from *A Hind in Richmond Park*

When, out on horseback in the morning in late March or in April, I encountered flocks of these belated travellers —plover, curlew and sandpiper—I often tried to force them to fly south. They appeared tired as if they had been travelling all night, and were hungry and seeking food in the short dew-wet grass, but always with their heads to the north. Not a bird would be seen to turn aside in any other direction. Riding to the north side of the flock, I would suddenly wheel round and charge at it, and up they would spring, almost vertically, and fly over my head to a distance of forty or fifty yards, then drop down and go on looking for something to eat, still walking north.

One can but infer that the attraction, the impelling force—the " pull of the north," as I have called it— increases until in the belated travellers it is an actual physical pain, a pain and a sense of extreme fear, which is intensified if the bird attempts to fly south.

W. H. HUDSON from *A Hind in Richmond Park*

So when inclement winters vex the plain
With piercing frosts, or thick-descending rain,
To warmer seas the cranes embodied fly,
With noise, and order, through the midway sky;

From *The Iliad of Homer*
Translated by Alexander Pope

Cranes

Going down the Nile to Kosti, we saw many large companies of cranes all on migration to the North. At Sennar, sleeping on the roof of Dr. Drew's house, I was awakened at dawn by cranes flying over. They were spread in a great V across the sky and were all honking as they flew. A glorious sight.

ANON from a letter (1937)

Feb. 12, 1771. Old Belon, two hundred years ago, gives a curious account of the incredible armies of hawks and kites which he saw in the spring-time traversing the Thracian Bosphorus from Asia to Europe. Besides the above-mentioned, he remarks that the procession is swelled by whole troops of eagles and vultures.

Now it is no wonder that birds residing in Africa should retreat before the sun as it advances, and retire to milder regions, and especially birds of prey, whose blood being heated with hot animal food, are more impatient of a sultry climate: but then I cannot help wondering why kites and hawks, and such hardy birds as are known to defy all the severity of England, and even of Sweden and all north Europe, should want to migrate from the south of Europe, and be dissatisfied with the winters of Andalusia.

It does not appear to me that much stress may be laid on the difficulty and hazard that birds must run in their migrations, by reason of vast oceans, cross winds, etc.; because, if we reflect, a bird may travel from England to the equator without launching out and exposing itself to boundless seas, and that by crossing the water at Dover, and again at Gibraltar. And I with the more confidence advance this obvious remark, because my brother has always found that some of his birds, and particularly the swallow kind, are very sparing at their pains in crossing the Mediterranean: for when arrived at Gibraltar, they do not

> . . . " rang'd in figure wedge their way,
> . . . and set forth
> Their airy caravan high over seas
> Flying, and over lands with mutual wing
> Easing their flight " . . . (MILTON)

but scout and hurry along in little detached parties of
six or seven in company; and sweeping low, just over the
surface of the land and water, direct their course to the
opposite continent at the narrowest passage they can
find. They usually slope across the bay to the south-west,
and so pass over opposite to Tangier, which, it seems, is
the narrowest space.

GILBERT WHITE from *Selborne*

April Tenth. After the long spell of bad weather the birds,
who were banked up, I fancy, somewhere in the Carolinas,
are coming through in a torrent. There are so many that
I can keep but the most delirious count of them. My
records are carried away in fluttering confusion, like
the wind gauge in a hurricane. Every time I approach the
marsh I hear the warning cries of the herons, like the
drop of an old chain on its owns coils, and from beyond
the cat-tail lances the snaky neck and archaic head of the
bittern is turned to look at me, with the astonished and
disapproving gaze that archaeopteryx might have turned
on an anachronistic human.

In the wet maple woods, where the skunk cabbage leaf
is expanding in its unabashed ugliness, the grackles are
already quieting, and in their place I hear, morning and
evening, the first sounds of mourning doves. Along the
runs and rills kingfishers are setting up their riparian
claims with loud cries, like the whirling of a boy's wooden
rattle. I have simply lost all count of the order of arrival
of the sparrow tribe, of the swallows, vireos and warblers
and wrens. There is no order; they all seemed to come

on the same day, and continued to arrive in increasing numbers every day.

Now is the moment when the novice at bird-gazing needs a friend. Flowers are best identified, if one is a neophyte, by one's self. The mere exercise of tracking them to their names will fix them in the memory. But with the birds, a guide, a friend by the side, to point out what you ought to have seen, to pass you the binoculars and whisper eagerly in your ear, is worth a shelf of books.

DONALD CULROSS PEATTIE from *An Almanac for Moderns*

May 13, 1778. Among the many singularities attending those amusing birds the swifts, I am now confirmed in the opinion that we have every year the same number of pairs invariably; at least the result of my enquiry has been exactly the same for a long time past. The swallows and martins are so numerous, and so widely distributed over the village, that it is hardly possible to recount them; while the swifts, though they do not all build in the church, yet so frequently haunt it, and play and rendezvous about it, that they are easily enumerated. The number that I constantly find are eight pairs; about half of which reside in the church, and the rest build in some of the lowest and meanest thatched cottages. Now as these eight pairs, allowance being made for accidents, breed yearly eight pairs more, what becomes annually of this increase; and what determines every spring which pairs shall visit us, and re-occupy their ancient haunts?

Ever since I have attended to the subject of ornithology, I have always supposed that that sudden reverse of affection,

that strange ἀντιστοργή, which immediately succeeds in
the feathered kind to the most passionate fondness, is
the occasion of an equal dispersion of birds over the face
of the earth. Without this provision one favourite district
would be crowded with inhabitants, while others would be
destitute and forsaken.   GILBERT WHITE from *Selborne*

Nov. 4, 1767. About ten years ago I used to spend some
weeks yearly at Sunbury, which is one of those pleasant
villages lying on the Thames, near Hampton-court. In
the autumn, I could not help being much amused with
those myriads of the swallow kind which assemble in
those parts. But what struck me most was, that, from the
time they began to congregate, forsaking the chimnies
and houses, they roosted every night in the osier-beds
of the aits of that river. Now this resorting towards that
element, at that season of the year, seems to give some
countenance to the northern opinion (strange as it is) of
their retiring under water. A Swedish naturalist is so
much persuaded of that fact, that he talks, in his calendar
of *Flora*, as familiarly of the swallows going under water
in the beginning of September, as he would of his poultry
going to roost a little before sunset.

GILBERT WHITE from *Selborne*

.   .   .   .   .

As to the short-winged soft-billed birds, which come
trooping in such numbers in the spring, I am at a loss
even what to suspect about them. I watched them narrowly
this year, and saw them abound till about Michaelmas,

when they appeared no longer. Subsist they cannot openly among us, and yet elude the eyes of the inquisitive: and, as to their hiding, no man pretends to have found any of them in a torpid state in the winter. But with regard to their migration, what difficulties attend that supposition! that such feeble bad fliers (who the summer long never flit but from hedge to hedge) should be able to traverse vast seas and continents in order to enjoy milder seasons amidst the regions of Africa! GILBERT WHITE from *Selborne*

One early morning towards the close of last year, I was lying in bed, just awake, on the shores of the Victoria Nyanza, close on the equator in Central Africa. From my window, I could see the fronds of a tall palm-tree. At its foot, though the season was December, there were bright flower-beds and green lawns; and beyond there was a park-like stretch of grass, dotted with magnificent trees all in leaf, sloping down to the soft blue waters of the lake under the bright sun. Suddenly a song came from just outside the window—the song of a willow wren, a willow wren on migration three or four thousand miles from the place where it was hatched; and automatically, as I heard the fresh and delicate dying fall of the notes, they brought back to me all the other attributes and associations which give the willow wren its particular character—the slender, modest green-brown body of the singer, the cool of an English spring, a piece of rough furzeland, with the leaves barely unfolded on the birch-trees, the bird prying about for the few early insects. . . .

JULIAN HUXLEY from *Bird Watching and Bird Behaviour*

April Twenty-fourth. The little winter birds are now definitely taking their departures. Gray and brown creatures, they leave us without our thanks for the pleasure of their esteemed company, so intent are we upon the gorgeous tropical fellows that are arriving as fast as thistledown in September. Only the patient thoroughness of a professional ornithologist, perhaps, would suffice to keep accurate count of the flitting away of the winter wren, the brown creeper, the sapsucker, the golden-crowned kinglet. Yet they too are feeling the great impulse to migration. The juncos and Lapland long-spurs and larks take wing, and the white-throat sparrow is already singing, in reverie of the rapture to come.

There is something especially brave and adventurous about these little fellows, who will seek out the frozen tundras of the north for their courting, and will build their nests in the wild fastness, amidst the swiftly-sprung, wide-eyed arctic wildflowers. When they return to us next winter, driven south by shortening days and snow and blast, they will treat our region as a land of exile enforced, a shelter to be endured till they can return to the chill, lost wildness of Ungava.

DONALD CULROSS PEATTIE from *An Almanac for Moderns*

The autumnal migration, which was always a more impressive spectacle than that of the spring, began in February when the weather was still hot, and continued for three long months; for after the departure of all our own birds, the south Patagonian species that wintered with us or passed on their way to districts further north would begin to come in. During all these three long months the sight and sound of passage birds was a thing of every day, of every hour, so long as the light lasted, and after dark from time to time the cries of the night-travellers came to us from the sky—the weird laughter-like cry of rails, the shrill confused whistling of a great flock of whistling or tree duck; and, most frequent of all, the beautiful wild trisyllabic alarm cry of the upland plover.   w. h. hudson from *A Hind in Richmond Park*

At 4.30, when the ship was 50 miles from the west end of Crete and 40 miles south of Cape Matapan, making about eleven knots to the westward, there commenced a regular rush of migrants. Some Yellow-bellied Wagtails, a Redstart, a Turtle-Dove, and a Whinchat appeared, the latter settled aft, the Wagtails were shyer and only followed in the wake of the ship, uttering vibrating chirps, the others flew around the ship. . . . At five o'clock two more Wood-Wrens came on board, and a party of seven Yellow-bellied Wagtails, which paddled nimbly about the quarter-deck searching for flies, which, unfortunately, did not exist. The next few minutes brought some Turtle-Doves, Whinchats, a Wheatear, and more Wagtails. The Turtle-Dove, I think, settled in the rigging, the Whinchats were quite tired out, and could only sit miserably hunched up, and next day two of them were found dead in the boats. About 5.30 Swallows started to arrive, and their numbers rapidly increased until Swallows were perched all over the ship in the most confiding way. They would crowd up together on the rim of a ventilator or a hatchway rail, heads and tails, as if to keep one another warm, and they did not mind us in the least when we walked up within a foot of them. They subsequently roosted all over the ship, several inside the chart-house, in the captain's cabin

Turtle-Doves

(half-deck); there must have been more than one hundred Swallows roosting altogether. Many were captured by the ship's company and liberated again. Although obviously very tired those Swallows that came under our particular notice did not seem to be wet, at any rate not drenched.

After dinner some of the officers were walking up and down the quarter-deck, lighted by a single electric light underneath the awning; a Swallow hovered over them and actually settled on the head of one, who was wearing a cap with a white cover on it, put its head under its scapulars, and went to sleep. The officer took his cap off and put it down on a grating. The Swallow just raised its head for a moment, then tucked it away again and was at once asleep.

H. LYNES from *British Birds*

See the young, the rosy Spring,
Gives to the breeze her spangled wing;
While virgin Graces, warm with May,
Fling roses o'er her dewy way!
The murmuring billows of the deep
Have languish'd into silent sleep;
And mark! the flitting sea-birds lave
Their plumes in the reflecting wave;
While cranes from hoary winter fly
To flutter in a kinder sky.

From *Odes of Anacreon*
Trans. by Thomas Moore

Once in each revolving year,
Gentle bird! we find thee here.
When Nature wears her summer-vest,
Thou com'st to weave thy simple nest;

But when the chilling winter lowers,
Again thou seek'st the genial bowers
Of Memphis, or the shores of Nile,
Where sunny hours of verdure smile.

From *Odes of Anacreon*
Trans. by Thomas Moore

Flying Swans

Not less their number than the embodied cranes,
Or milk-white swans in Asius' watery plains.
That, o'er the windings of Caÿster's springs,*
Stretch their long necks, and clap their rustling
    wings,
Now tower aloft, and course in airy rounds,
Now light with noise; with noise the field resounds.

From *The Iliad of Homer*
Trans. by Alexander Pope

The greatest manifestation of migration which the present writer has witnessed, was in the neighbourhood of the German Ornithological Society's Observatory at Rossitten, lying at the south-eastern angle of the Baltic, almost midway along a narrow strip of land which separates a great lagoon from the sea. Here the conditions of observation were practically those of an island, and a great part of the movements took place by day. It was on the 2nd October, 1910, that we first saw a great movement of Hooded Crows (*Corvus cornix*), although on previous days these birds had been passing in smaller numbers. We betook ourselves to the seaward strip of sand stretching uninterruptedly as far as we could see, north-eastward toward Russia and south-westward toward the Gulf of Danzig. On one side lay the quiet waters of the almost tideless sea; on the other rose a line of low dunes over which the tops of the trees behind peeped

* Fresh-water fowl, especially swans, were found in great numbers about the Asian Marsh, a fenny tract of country in Lydia, formed by the river Caÿster, near its mouth. See Virg. Georg. vol I. 383, sq.

here and there. The silence was complete but for the rhythmic murmur of gentle waves; a slight breeze blew from the south-east, and the sky was lightly clouded at a great height, leaving the lower air extremely clear. The sun shone brightly, but the keen nip of October was in

Hooded Crows

the air, showing that despite the glorious weather the autumn had entered on its final phase and winter was at hand. The steady progress of the Crow battalions told the same tale. Every minute or two a flock passed, flying steadily and quietly south-westward along the line of the shore at a height of from 100 to 300 feet. Hooded Crows

OB

were in the majority, Rooks numerous, and Jackdaws present in smaller numbers; Rooks and Crows were generally in separate flocks, the Jackdaws accompanying the former. If we watched one flock pass overhead and recede in the distance, another was already passing before it had disappeared, and a third would be coming into view in the wake of the second. The line of the shore seemed to be followed with some exactness, for a bend a quarter of a mile from us caused the flocks to fly out over the sea for a few hundred yards before they wheeled to take the slightly altered direction. In size the flocks varied from thirty or forty to two or three hundred birds; and we calculated that over two thousand birds passed every hour in an unbroken stream from early morning till after midday.

Next day was as beautiful as its predecessors, and the number of migrants greater than ever. Crows were there, as on the day before; but the flocks were larger and more frequent, and continued to pass till well on in the afternoon. Some twenty or thirty thousand must have passed in the course of the day. It was not merely the vastness of the numbers that made the scene so impressive, but the fact that all these thousands were moving together with one accord, without great speed or appearance of haste, yet without halt or deviation, and still more noticeably without noise. The great army was advancing in column—a column of great length but of no appreciable frontage, and apparently without any parallel columns in its near neighbourhood. Not only was there a continual succession of these silent flocks of Hooded Crows, Rooks, and Jackdaws, but small song-birds were also on the move. Every few seconds a small company of Larks or a little band of Finches passed us flying low down over the ground. Overhead, at a considerable altitude, were less frequent flocks of Wood Pigeons, making more speed than most of the others. Here and there were a few birds of prey; Kestrels were frequent, usually alone, sometimes three or four together; and often, at our approach, some larger predatory bird would rise on broad wings from a meal provided by some weakling which had paid too high a price for the journey.

A narrow strip of barren sand bounded by expanses of desolate water made up the landscape that shimmered in the bright sunlight of that crisp autumn day. Nothing else was in sight but the vast flocks of birds, and every bird was moving onwards with the stream. It seemed to us that we were watching the ebb of the life of half a continent, an ebb which would leave the northern forests deserted and voiceless in the deathlike grip of the sub-arctic winter; but we remembered that this same channel would in a few more months convey a contrary tide which would again fill these lands with the active bustle and cheerful sounds of feathered life.

A. LANDSBOROUGH THOMSON from *Problems of Bird Migration*

The habitat of birds is not circumscribed within such narrow limits as that of quadrupeds, because, by means of their wings, they can traverse more space, and even cross the seas. The aquatic birds, by alternate flying and swimming, can proceed to the most remote countries. Nevertheless, each species adopts a country, chooses a climate suitable to its nature, and, when the change of season obliges it to seek, under new skies, a country analogous to its former one, it is but for a season. These birds always return to their favourite country at the season of reproduction. The stork, indeed, has two separate broods, one brought forth in Europe, and the other in Egypt.

Birds, generally speaking, appear to belong more to the air than to the earth. They constitute moving republics, which traverse the atmosphere at stated periods, in large bodies. These bodies perform their aerial evolutions like an army, crowd into close column, form into triangle, extend in line of battle, or disperse in light squadrons. The earth and its climates have less influence on them than on quadrupeds, because they almost always live in similar degrees of temperature, passing the winter in hot climates, and the summer in cold. The continual interchange of birds establishes a sort of communication between all countries, and keeps up a sort of equilibrium of life. The bird, passing in summer from the equinoctial climates to the cold regions of the north, and again in winter from the poles towards the equator, knows, by an admirable instinct, the winds and the weather which are favourable to his voyage. He can long foresee the approaches of frost, or the return of spring, and learns the science of meteorology from the element in which he almost continually lives. He needs no compass to direct his course through the empire of the cloud, the thunder, and the tempest; and while man and beast are creeping on the earth, he breathes the pure air of heaven, and soars upwards nearer to the spring of day. He arrives at the term of his voyage, and touches the hospitable land of his destination. He finds there his subsistence prepared by the hand of Providence, and a safe asylum in the grove, the forest, or the mountain, where he revisits the habitation he had tenanted before, the scene of his former delights, the cradle of his infancy. The stork resumes his ancient tower, the nightingale the solitary thicket, the swallow his old window, and the redbreast the mossy trunk of the same oak in which he formerly nestled.[1]

All the volatile species which disappear in the winter do not, therefore, change their climate. Some retire into remote places, to some desert cave, some savage rock, or ancient forest. Such are many of the starling kind, the loriots, the cuckow, etc. etc. They sally from their retreats at the close of winter, and spread themselves through the country.

Other families of birds do not, properly speaking, emigrate. They content themselves with approaching the southern climates, in proportion as they are pursued by the cold. The species called erratic, such as the greenfinches of the Ardennes, larks, ortolans, other frugivorous races, and especially parrots, go in troops, begging, as it were, their subsistence on their passage. Others follow the track of cultivation, and spread themselves in proportion with the habitations of men.

Of the birds which emigrate every year, some depart in autumn and return in spring, while others depart in spring and return in autumn. Our insectivorous races, and many granivorous, finding nothing at the beginning of winter but a soil deprived of its productions, presenting

[1] Linnaeus tells us, that a starling came regularly to lay during eight years, in the same trunk of an alder, although it emigrated every winter. Spallanzani having attached a red thread to the legs of the swallows which nestled under his windows, beheld them return for many years in succession.

everywhere the image of desolation and death, are necessitated to betake themselves to more favoured climes. At the commencement of this season of gloom, when the fields are denuded of herbage, and all terrestrial animals have retired each to his peculiar shelter, and many species have fallen into a state of torpor, the birds prepare to set out on their voyages. They assemble in troops at the appointed period, and take advantage of the favourable wind which is to aid them in their course. Their proceedings are fancifully and beautifully depicted by a French poet:—

"Dans un sage conseil par le chef assemblé
   Du départ général le grand jour est réglé.
   Il arrive. Tout part: le plus jeune peut-être
   Demande, en regardant les lieux qui l'ont vu
        naître,
   Quand viendra ce printemps par qui tant d'exilés
   Dans les champs paternels se verront rappellés."
                                    L. Racine, fils.

Those which, through negligence or weakness, remain behind are placed in no very comfortable predicament.
                    BARON CUVIER from *The Class Aves*

Oct. 6, 1768. This week twelve months a gentleman from London, being with us, was amusing himself with a gun, and found, he told us, on an old yew hedge where there were berries, some birds like blackbirds, with rings of white round their necks; a neighbouring farmer also at the same time observed the same; but, as no specimens were procured little notice was taken. I mentioned this circumstance to you in my letter of November the 4th, 1767: (you, however, paid but small regard to what I said, as I had not seen these birds myself :) but last week, the aforesaid farmer, seeing a large flock, twenty or thirty of these birds, shot two cocks and two hens: and says, on recollection, that he remembers to have observed these birds again last spring, about Lady-day, as it were, on their return to the north. Now perhaps these ousels are not the ousels of the north of England, but belong to the more northern parts of Europe; and may retire before the excessive rigour of the frosts in those parts; and return to breed in the spring, when the cold abates. If this be the case, here is discovered a new bird of winter passage, concerning whose migrations the writers are silent: but if these birds should prove the ousels of the north of England, then here is a migration disclosed within our own kingdom never before remarked.

GILBERT WHITE from *Selborne*

May 29, 1769. On the thirteenth of April I went to the sheep-down, where the ring-ousels have been observed to make their appearance at spring and fall, on their way perhaps to the north or south; and was much pleased to see three birds about the usual spot. We shot a cock and a hen; they were plump and in high condition. The hen had but very small rudiments of eggs within her, which proves they are late breeders; whereas those species of the thrush kind that remain with us the whole year have fledged young before that time. In their crops was nothing very distinguishable, but somewhat that seemed like blades of vegetables nearly digested. In autumn they feed on haws and yew-berries, and in the spring on ivy-berries. I dressed one of these birds, and found it juicy and well-flavoured.

GILBERT WHITE from *Selborne*

Ring-Ousel

Dec. 8, 1769. The ring-ousel, you find, stays in Scotland the whole year round; so that we have reason to conclude that those migrators that visit us for a short space every autumn do not come from thence.

And here, I think, will be the proper place to mention that those birds were most punctual again in their migration this autumn, appearing, as before, about the 30th of September: but their flocks were larger than common, and their stay protracted somewhat beyond the usual time. If they came to spend the whole winter with us, as some of their congeners do, and then left us, as they do, in spring, I should not be so much struck with the occurrence, since it would be similar to that of the other winter birds of passage; but when I see them for a fortnight at Michaelmas, and again for about a week in the middle of April, I am seized with wonder, and long to be informed whence these travellers come, and whither they go, since they seem to use our hills merely as an inn or baiting place. GILBERT WHITE from *Selborne*

This is the case of a jackdaw which was found last year, unable to fly, and taken home by a boy in the village of Tilshead in the South Wiltshire downs. In a very few days the bird recovered from his weakness and was perfectly well and able to fly again, but he did not go away; and the reason of his remaining appeared to be not that he had been well treated, but because he had formed an extraordinary attachment, not, as one would naturally suppose, to the boy who had rescued and fed him, but to another, smaller boy, who lived in the next cottage! It was quite unmistakable; the bird, free to go away if he liked, began to spend his time hanging about the cottage of his chosen little friend. He wanted to be always with him, and when the children went to school in the morning the daw would accompany them, and flying into the schoolroom after them settle himself on a perch where he would sit until the release came. But the proceedings were always too long for his patience, and from time to time he would emit a loud caw of remonstrance, which would set the children tittering, and eventually he was turned out and the door shut against him. He then took to sitting on the roof until school was over, whereupon he would fly down to the shoulder of his little friend and go home with him. In the same way he would follow his friend to church on Sunday morning, but even there he could not repress his loud startling caw, which made the congregation smile and cast up its eyes at the roof. My friend the vicar, who by-the-by is a lover of birds, could not tolerate this, and the result was that the daw had to be caught and confined every day during school and church hours. W. H. HUDSON from *Adventures Among Birds*

The first time our cock-chaffinch came in was when we were at dinner, with the door open as usual. When we saw him hop over the step we suspended our breath with out knives and forks, and pressed against the edge of the table in acute suspense.

He hopped again, nearer.

My father, careful to make no brusque movement, crumbled some bread to the floor. The chaffinch eyed it, eyed us. Nobody moved. He hopped again. He seized a crumb and flew off in such a hurry that he almost missed his way out. We burst into a buzz of delight, but almost at once we stilled it. He had re-appeared on the step. He was coming back for more. He had accepted us.

He became so friendly that almost every time we sat down to table he arrived. No matter what the weather was, we would not have the door shut against him. It turned out by and by that he had a wife and family. But his wife was one to keep herself to herself, and she never came in. His children would not exert themselves so far;

Chaffinch

they stood in the grass and shrieked to have their food brought to them. They stretched their beaks to the widest and showed both impatience and temper at being kept waiting a second.

"Well, I never," said Kate, pausing in her work to look at them. "You need a good smacking, and if I was your mother, you'd get it. The poor thing's pulled out with you."

The hen-chaffinch was a meek, harassed creature that would work herself to the bone for her insatiable offspring, but the cock-chaffinch, our bold bright bird, kept very cheerful and came to ask our help.

"Cheep, cheep," he said, and we fell over each other in our anxiety to provide crumbs at once.

But it was not all cupboard love that he felt for us. When my father went down the lane to the station in the morning, the chaffinch flew along from bush to bush beside him, accompanying him as far as the first bridge, but no farther, calling out "Cheep, cheep" in farewell, and my father called back to him.

And in the evening my father often came in smiling and said, with a pleased wag of the head, as he went for crumbs:

"He met me."

Whether our first chaffinch trained a son and that son in turn trained his, I do not know, but the fact remains that we always had a chaffinch, in all the years we were at the cottage, to come in when we were at table, to take my father down to the bridge in the mornings, and to greet us when we came back after the winter in the town. Within the first half-hour of our arrival he would greet us.

"Cheep, cheep," he would say, appearing on the wall, and we rushed to welcome him with crumbs and warm affection.　　　　DOROTHY WHIPPLE from *The Other Day*

A Viennese animal dealer reminded me in May, 1929, that I had ordered young ravens three years before, and now, he said, they had arrived. I went to his shop at once, but disappointment awaited me. I had ordered five or six small nestlings, as older birds were likely to be useless for the experiment I had in mind. Of the seven ravens there, four were fully-fledged and already feeding. Only three could be called nestlings.

While the dealer was packing them I turned to have another look at the four older birds. When I approached their cage three retreated to the back. The fourth, feathers fluffed, came to meet me with that gigantic gape that looks like a red tulip springing into sudden bloom, and with that un-birdlike, deep call of his species, sounding like nothing else, which one of the best bird books feebly renders as " Roah, Roah." I pitied that black infant. It was not his fault that he was four weeks older than I wished him to be. But there was nothing to be done, so I picked up a piece of smelly meat in the cage. He could have had it all the time, but he preferred to have it stuffed down his throat until just below the larynx. This is the way to release the swallowing reflex and give the bird the most enjoyment in eating. Withdrawing my hand from his surprisingly hot inside, I scratched the back of his head.

At this point we were interrupted by the dealer calling that my three nestlings were ready. I turned abruptly from the cage and walked away.

Now, for some kinds of birds, moving away has a particular meaning. It impels the bird to follow, just as he follows a bird of his own species which, taking wing, moves suddenly and rapidly away from him. By standing near and then suddenly running away from a tame jackdaw, crane or greylag goose it can be induced to take wing with a machine-like certainty. This young raven that I had been scratching acted so. He gave the sharp short flying call of his species and started in pursuit of me, hitting the front wires of his cage a resounding smack.

At once I was interested. A caged raven does not as a rule forget, as more stupid birds, such as the eagle, falcon, bustard and quail, so easily forget, that there is wire netting all around him, and start flying into space. To make a raven do this there must be some powerful emotion, such as a great fear. It surprised me that the impulse to follow could have supplied so compelling a motive as to make this raven rush blindly against the bars of his cage. By feeding the youngster in the natural way, and then ruffling his head feathers as his mother used to do when she preened him, I had developed the follow-mother reaction.

On getting home with my basketful of young ravens I put Roah, as I had named him, in a small flying-cage; for the nestlings I built a large artificial raven's nest. After lunch I decided to try whether Roah would give the "following" reaction in his new environment. I stepped close to the cage, and he came to meet me from the inside. After some feeding and head scratching I rushed away, uttering my version of that sharp staccato crackle which represents the starting signal of the old raven. Roah responded instantly, and with so much more intensity than he had done at the dealer's shop that I dared to set him free. Remember that I had bought this bird only four hours before. In eliciting the "following" response to bring him through the open door into freedom I succeeded perfectly. The crucial moment came a moment later. The raven flying in pursuit was not more than a few seconds in overtaking me. Would he turn or would he carry on and disappear I thought it quite possible that he would do the latter. It was an anxious moment when my beautiful and expensive bird sailed onward after overtaking me. All I could do was to call loudly, and to start running at right angles to the direction in which the raven was flying, so that he should see my

Young Raven

moving. (All birds respond better to a moving object than to a still one.) I saw his great curved beak turning as he looked back at me over his shoulder, and then he wheeled and came gliding back to me. Again I started running, this time away from him and up the rather steep incline of the meadow in our garden where all this took place. This I did because I knew the raven would try to land on my body, and that it was difficult for him to come down on a steep gradient, the more so as he had never flown before. Frantically I scrambled up a slippery grass bank and arrived at its upper edge just in time to right myself and offer an outstretched arm to the raven, who made an inelegant landing there, falling off again on the other side. Like myself, the raven was quite exhausted and panting. As it takes much more effort for a bird to circle or to come down at a steep slant than to keep straight on, I do not doubt that he would have flown for a considerable time and got lost if he had not been able to land in his first attempt. I have lost a number of birds, especially water birds, whose minimum planing speed is high, through flying straight on to recover after an unsuccessful attempt at landing.

I have given all this in detail because I want to show how much knowledge of a bird's reactions to a situation is necessary for anyone to carry through " free flying " experiments successfully, and also how surely one may count on a bird to react in a certain manner. Most of the falconer's art is nothing but this knowledge of certain instinctive reactions of the bird.

Here I should interject that the three nestlings in their artificial nest were always carried indoors at night. Roah seemed much more attached to me than to them, but at night he sought their company and sat in the nest with them. When, later on, they roosted, he roosted with them.

It was while the young ravens were in the nest that Roah formed his lifelong attachment to me. I doubt whether he would have become so affectionate if he had had a raven companion during that period. He tried to be with me as much as he possibly could, accompanying me on all my walks, either flying from tree to tree, or, with a favouring breeze, sailing high above my head and following me in the same way as, with other motives, vultures follow a caravan. During the time I was from home he searched for me everywhere, specially and very intelligently in those places where we had been together. This searching took him so far a-wing that he ran considerable danger of being lost. I had to shut him in whenever I had to be from home for a few days. (Some years later a Great Yellow-Crested Cockatoo behaved in exactly the same way as Roah.)

Once when I was going up the Danube in my motor boat I met Roah six miles from home or, more accurately, he met me, because he was looking for me. I doubt whether he would have come home again that day if he had not by chance found me. He knew perfectly well, however, when I was inside the house; then he never went in search of me. He learned to know the creaking of the front door, and whenever I went out into the garden he was waiting and hoping I would go for a walk with him. He was dog-like in this.

As accompanying a walking man means much troublesome wheeling and flying for a raven, I wanted to accelerate my movements by the use of a bicycle. It was difficult at first to convince Roah that the bicycle was harmless, so I shut him in his cage with the bicycle, putting all the food on the saddle. He loved the bicycle for ever afterwards, the more so when he understood that it was much easier and more fun to follow me when I was cycling. I had only to wheel the machine out of the house to make him utter a joyous series of starting calls and send him flying along our usual route. He never understood why I could not fly, and to the end of his days tried to induce me to take wing.

PB

I may mention that he used to visit me regularly in my bedroom at dawn. Then one evening he came walking in resolutely by the open window, flew on to the curtain rod, ruffled his feathers and sat down to roost. The curtain was removed, paper spread on the floor, and every evening the bird roosted on the rod. Two years later when I changed to another room he hardly dared to enter; every change is abhorrent and fearsome to a grown raven. But Roah did change, sleeping under the window-sill of my new bedroom.

I never became on such intimate terms with the other three ravens because their yearning for society was satisfied by each other's company. The older bird had no companion except myself during the first weeks after his fledging period, which appears to be the age at which the social impulses of many birds cause them to attach themselves irrevocably to their chosen object. The other ravens alighted freely on my head and shoulders, ate out of my hand and even learned to roost in my bedroom as Roah did; but when they accompanied me on my excursions they did it chiefly for the company of the older raven. When they were about a year old they were apt to attack me from behind, particularly when I was standing still, creeping up to me and giving a vigorous peck at the calves of my legs. Perhaps this lack of filial piety was caused by my allowing the young ravens to become independent too soon. For a long time I used to feed Roah by hand, thus preserving his begging-for-food reaction; I used to throw their ration of meat to the other three ravens and allow them to tear it up by themselves.

In keeping birds tame it is essential to maintain the child-parent relation as long as possible. It is well even to prevent young birds from eating independently. To prevent the young ravens I am now rearing from pecking at the meat I am feeding to them, and to induce them to beg with beak wide open, I hold the meat in such a way that the bird cannot see it, and I let it slide into its wide-opened beak so that the bird does not feel the meat until it is well inside its throat. All this imitates exactly the way in which the ravens feed their young. A bird's emotions are mechanically coupled with its instinctive actions. If the young raven acts as if receiving from its parents, its emotions correspond. The same is true if it is tearing away a piece of meat from my hand, as it would tear it away from weaker ravens which it dared to bully and deprive of their prey. The fundamental fact that it receives the food from me finds no way into its brain, and therefore does not wake any corresponding gratitude. So curiously enough, the success in retaining a young raven's affection really depends upon the way the food changes from hand to beak. By consistently observing and acting on these facts it is possible to keep the attachment of a young raven even longer than his real parents would be able to do. This is necessary if one wants to preserve that dog-like devotion which is so charming.

Towards the end of August the ravens began to extend their excursions farther and farther, staying away longer at a time. Once they were absent for a week, and when one of them, the weakest, failed to come home, I decided to lock them up in a large flying cage I had built on a flat part of the roof of our house. Roah alone I dared to let out from time to time, as I could be sure that he would not fly away so long as I was there to call him back, and it was easy to lure him back into the cage with an egg or a piece of meat. The tendency to fly away during late summer and early autumn corresponds with the age at which young ravens living in the wild state leave the territory of their parents for good. This shows that they probably do so urged by an instinct of their own, and are not driven away by the parent birds, as is so often dogmatically asserted in bird books. The migrating tendency gradually dies out towards October, so that in November I could leave the ravens at large again.

Ever afterwards the ravens remained faithful to their home, so here the story of rearing the birds really ends, but not the story of the ravens themselves. This proved to be complicated by much love interest and some bloodshed, with Roah as the victorious duellist. To anticipate its sad end, all my ravens were shot, although the raven is " protected " throughout the whole year in Austria. It would be impossible to control all the guns within the wide radius of a raven's daily excursions.

DR. LORENZ from *The Countryman*

I kept a tamed cock sparrow three years. It was so tame that it would come when called, and flew where it pleased. When I first had the sparrow, I was fearful of the cat's killing it, so I used to hold the bird in my hand towards her, and when she attempted to smell of it I beat her. She at last would take no notice of it, and I ventured to let it loose in the house. They were both very shy of each other at first and when the sparrow ventured to chirp the cat would brighten up as if she intended to seize it; but she went no further than a look or smell. At length

she had kittens, and when they were taken away she grew
so fond of the sparrow as to attempt to caress it. The
sparrow was startled at first, but came to by degrees and
ventured so far at last [as] to perch upon her back. Puss
would call for it when out of her sight like a kitten, and
would lay mice before it the same as she would for her

House Sparrow and Cat

own young; and they always lived in harmony; so much
so [that] the sparrow would often take away bits of bread
from under the cat's nose and even put itself in a posture
of resistance, when offended, as if it reckoned her nothing
more than one of its kind. In winter, when we could not
bear the doors open to let the sparrow come out and in,
I was allowed to take a pane out of the window; but in
the spring of the third year my poor Tom Sparrow—for

that was the name he was called by—went out and never returned. I went day after day, calling out for Tom, and eagerly eyeing every sparrow on the house; but none answered the name; for he would come down in a moment to the call, and perch upon my hand to be fed. I gave it out that some cat which it mistook for its old favourite betrayed its confidence and destroyed it.

JOHN CLARE from his *Diary*

The next case is from Penzance and was told to me when I was staying there. A lady of that town, a member of one of its oldest and most distinguished families, is a great bird-lover and feeds the birds during the winter on her lawn. She noticed that a blackbird and thrush always came together to the food, and then that the blackbird fed the other, picking up the morsels and placing them in its open mouth. On looking more closely it was discovered that the thrush had lost its beak; this had been cut off close to the head, probably by a steel or a sudden-death spring-trap, such as the children in Cornwall commonly use to catch or kill small birds. The bird was incapable of feeding itself.

W. H. HUDSON from *Adventures Among Birds*

His hawks grew very tame and would come at a call or whistle. When they were hungry they made a strange noise that pierced the ear with its shrillness. They were very fond of washing themselves, often doing it twice a day in winter. After being fed they would play in the garden, running after each other and seizing bits of clods or fallen apples in their claws, or catching at flies. One was much larger than the other and the large one was the tamer. When I went a-walking in the fields it would attempt to fly after me and as I was fearful of losing it I used to drive it back; but one day it took advantage of watching and following me, and when I got into the fields I was astonished and startled to see a hawk settle on my shoulder. It was mine, who had watched me out of the town and taken a short cut to fly after me. I thought it would fly away for good, so I attempted to catch it; but it would not be made a prisoner, and flew to the trees by the roadside. I gave it up for lost, but as soon as I got out of sight it set up a noise and flew after me again. When I got up on the Heath where there are no trees it would settle upon the ground before me, and if I attempted to catch it, it would run and hide in the rabbit-burrows. When I left it it took wing and flew after me, and so it kept on till the end of the journey, when it found home as soon as I did.

After this I took no more heed of losing them, though they would be missing for days together. A boy caught one by surprise and hurt it so that it died; and the tamer died while I was absent from home four days. It refused food, hunted for me every morning and came to sit in my empty chair as it would do till I got up.

They thought it fretted itself to death in my absence, but I think the meat I gave it was too strong for it, and I believed it was not well a good while before I left it. I felt heartily sorry for my poor, faithful, affectionate hawk.

JOHN CLARE from his *Diary*

A friend of mine, an Anglo-Argentine residing at Buenos Ayres, one day when out duck-shooting winged a teal, one of a common species—*Querquedula flavirostris*. The sight and feel of the bird when he had it in his hand, its graceful shape and beautiful plumage and the bright frightened eyes and beating heart, softened him so that

American Green-Winged Teal

he could not kill it, and putting it in his bag he took it home; and after bandaging the broken wing the best way he could, he placed the bird in the large courtyard and supplied it with food and water. In a short time its wound healed, but it did not recover its power of flight and made no attempt to escape. It became perfectly tame and would come at call to be fed or caressed. The strange thing was that although all the people of the house were interested in the teal and made it a pet, its whole affection was given to the man who had shot it. To the others it was indifferent, although they were always in the house taking notice of and petting it, while this chosen friend was absent on business in the city every day from morning to the late afternoon. The teal would keep near him when he had breakfast, then accompany him to the door opening out of the courtyard to the street, and having seen him off she would return to her place and pass her day in a quiet contented manner as if she had forgotten all about the absent one. But invariably at about four o'clock in the afternoon she would go to the open street door to wait for his return, and if he was an hour or so late she would sit there the whole time on the threshold, her beak turned city-wards, to the astonishment of the passers-by. On his appearance she was all joy and would run to his feet, nodding her head and flirting her wings and emitting all the quacking and other curious little sounds the bird uses to express its happy emotions. Like most teals it is a loquacious bird, and very excitable. After that the great happiness of the teal was to have permission to sit at his feet when he settled himself in his chair to rest and read. She would actually sit *on* his foot.

W. H. HUDSON from *Adventures Among Birds*

And these are they which ye shall have in abomination among the fowls; they shall not be eaten, they are an abomination: the eagle, and the ossifrage, and the ospray, And the vulture, and the kite after his kind;
Every raven after his kind;

And the owl, and the night hawk, and the cuckoo, and the hawk after his kind,

And the little owl, and the cormorant, and the great owl,

And the swan, and the pelican, and the gier eagle,

And the stork, the heron after her kind, and the lapwing, and the bat.

All fowls that creep, going upon all four, shall be an abomination unto you.　　　　　*Leviticus xi.* 13–20

It shall not be quenched night nor day; the smoke thereof shall go up for ever: from generation to generation it shall lie waste; none shall pass through it for ever and ever.

But the cormorant and the bittern shall possess it; the owl also and the raven shall dwell in it: and he shall stretch out upon it the line of confusion, and the stones of emptiness.

And thorns shall come up in her palaces, nettles and brambles in the fortresses thereof: and it shall be an habitation of dragons, and a court for owls.

The wild beasts of the desert shall also meet with the wild beasts of the island, and the satyr shall cry to his fellow; the screech owl also shall rest there, and find for herself a place of rest.

There shall the great owl make her nest, and lay, and hatch, and gather under her shadow: there shall the vultures also be gathered, every one with her mate.

Isaiah xxxiv. 10–15

And he said, I tell thee, Peter, the cock shall not crow this day, before that thou shall thrice deny that thou knowest me.　　　　　*Luke xxii.* 34

The ousel cock so black of hue,
   With orange-tawny bill,
The throstle with his note so true,
   The wren with little quill,

The finch, the sparrow, and the jay,
   The plain-song cuckoo gray,
Whose note full many a man doth mark
And dares not answer nay.

                            SHAKESPEARE

I soon found I had but a little passed by the place where I had been before, when I travelled on foot to that shore; so taking nothing out of my boat but my gun and umbrella, for it was exceedingly hot, I began my march. The way was comfortable enough after such a voyage as I had been upon, and I reached my old bower in the evening, where I found everything standing as I left it; for I always kept it in good order, being, as I said before, my country house.

I got over the fence, and laid me down in the shade to rest my limbs, for I was very weary, and fell asleep; but judge you, if you can, that read my story, what a surprise I must be in when I was awaked out of my sleep by a voice, calling me by my name several times, "Robin, Robin, Robin Crusoe: poor Robin Crusoe! Where are you, Robin Crusoe? Where are you? Where have you been?"

I was so dead asleep at first, being fatigued with rowing, or paddling as it is called, the first part of the day, and with walking the latter part, that I did not wake thoroughly, but dozing between sleeping and waking, thought I dreamed that somebody spoke to me; but as the voice continued to repeat, " Robin Crusoe," at last I began to wake more perfectly, and was at first dreadfully frightened, and started up in the utmost consternation; but no sooner were my eyes open, but I saw my Poll sitting on the top of the

Crusoe and his Parrot

hedge; and immediately knew that it was he that spoke to me; for just in such bemoaning language I had used to talk to him, and teach him; and he had learned it so perfectly that he would sit upon my finger, and lay his bill close to my face, and cry, " Poor Robin Crusoe!

Where are you? Where have you been? How came you here?" and such things as I had taught him.

However, even though I knew it was the parrot, and that indeed it could be nobody else, it was a good while before I could compose myself. First, I was amazed how the creature got thither; and then, how he should just keep about the place, and nowhere else; but as I was well satisfied it could be nobody but honest Poll, I got over it; and holding out my hand, and calling him by his name, " Poll," the sociable creature came to me, and sat upon my thumb, as he used to do, and continued talking to me, " Poor Robin Crusoe! and how did I come here? and where had I been?" just as if he had been overjoyed to see me again; and so I carried him home along with me.   DANIEL DEFOE from *Robinson Crusoe*

And now there came both mist and snow
And it grew wondrous cold:
And ice, mast-high, came floating by,
As green as emerald

.   .   .   .   .

At length did cross an Albatross:
Through the fog it came;
As if it had been a Christian soul,
We hailed it in God's name.

It ate the food it ne'er had eat,
And round and round it flew.
The ice did split with a thunder-fit;
The helmsman steered us through!

And a good south wind sprung up behind;
The Albatross did follow.
And every day, for food or play,
Came to the mariner's hollo!

In mist or cloud, on mast or shroud,
It perched for vespers nine;
Whiles all the night, through fog-smoke white,
Glimmered the white moonshine.

God save thee, ancient Mariner!
From the fiends, that plague thee thus!—

Albatross

Why look'st thou so?—With my cross-bow
I shot the Albatross.

    .   .   .   .   .

And the good south wind did blow behind,
But no sweet bird did follow,
Nor any day for food or play
Came to the mariner's hollo!

And I had done an hellish thing,
And it would work 'em woe:
For all averred, I had killed the bird
That made the breeze to blow.
Ah wretch! said they, the bird to slay,
That made the breeze to blow!

Nor dim nor red, like God's own head,
The glorious Sun uprist:
Then all averred, I had killed the bird
That brought the fog and mist.
'Twas right, said they, such birds to slay,
That bring the fog and mist.

    .   .   .   .   .

Ah! well-a-day! what evil looks
Had I from old and young!
Instead of the cross, the Albatross
About my neck was hung.

    .   .   .   .   .

The self-same moment I could pray;
And from my neck so free
The Albatross fell off, and sank
Like lead into the sea.

                       S. T. COLERIDGE from *The Ancient Mariner*

With a lighter heart and step, and eyes the brighter for the happy tear that dimmed them for a moment, Barnaby resumed his walk; and singing gaily to himself, kept guard upon his quiet post.

His comrade Grip, the partner of his watch, though fond of basking in the sunshine, preferred to-day to walk about the stable; having a great deal to do in the way of scattering the straw, hiding under it such small articles as had been casually left about, and haunting Hugh's bed, to which he seemed to have taken a particular attachment. Sometimes Barnaby looked in and called him, and then he came hopping out; but he merely did this as a concession to his master's weakness, and soon returned again to his own grave pursuits: peering into the straw with his bill, and rapidly covering up the place, as if, Midas-like, he were whispering secrets to the earth and burying them; constantly busying himself upon the sly; and affecting, whenever Barnaby came past, to look up in the clouds and have nothing whatever on his mind: in short, conducting himself, in many respects, in a more than usually thoughtful, deep, and mysterious manner.

As the day crept on, Barnaby, who had no directions forbidding him to eat and drink upon his post, but had been, on the contrary, supplied with a bottle of beer and a basket of provisions, determined to break his fast, which he had not done since morning. To this end, he sat down on the ground before the door, and putting his staff across his knees in case of alarm or surprise, summoned Grip to dinner.

This call, the bird obeyed with great alacrity; crying, as he sidled up to his master, " I'm a devil, I'm a Polly,

I'm a kettle, I'm a Protestant, No Popery! " Having learnt this latter sentiment from the gentry among whom he had lived of late, he delivered it with uncommon emphasis.

Raven

" Well said, Grip! " cried his master, as he fed him with the daintiest bits. " Well said, old boy! "

" Never say die, bow wow wow, keep up your spirits, Grip, Grip, Grip, Holloa! We'll all have tea,

QB

I'm a Protestant kettle, No Popery!" cried the raven.

"Gordon for ever, Grip!" cried Barnaby.

The raven, placing his head upon the ground, looked at his master sideways, as though he would have said, "Say that again!" Perfectly understanding his desire, Barnaby repeated the phrase a great many times. The bird listened with profound attention; sometimes repeat-

Raven

ing the popular cry in a low voice, as if to compare the two, and try if it would at all help him to this new accomplishment; sometimes flapping his wings, or barking; and sometimes in a kind of desperation drawing a multitude of corks, with extraordinary viciousness.

CHARLES DICKENS from *Barnaby Rudge*

" You have brought your bird with you, I suppose? " said Mr. Jarndyce.

" By heaven, he is the most astonishing bird in Europe! " replied the other. " He *is* the most wonderful creature! I wouldn't take ten thousand guineas for that bird. I have left an annuity for his sole support, in case he should outlive me. He is, in sense and attachment, a phenomenon. And his father before him was one of the most astonishing birds that ever lived! "

The subject of this laudation was a very little canary, who was so tame that he was brought down by Mr. Boythorn's man, on his forefinger, and, after taking a gentle flight round the room, alighted on his master's head. To hear Mr. Boythorn presently expressing the most implacable and passionate sentiments, with this fragile mite of a creature quietly perched on his forehead, was to have a good illustration of his character, I thought.

" By my soul, Jarndyce," he said, very gently holding up a bit of bread to the canary to peck at, " if I were in your place, I would seize every Master in Chancery by the throat tomorrow morning, and shake him until his money rolled out of his pockets, and his bones rattled in his skin. I would have a settlement out of somebody, by fair means or by foul. If you would empower me to do it, I would do it for you with the greatest satisfaction! " (All this time the very small canary was eating out of his hand.) . . .

It was impossible not to laugh at this strong measure of reform. When he laughed, he threw up his head, and shook his broad chest, and again the whole country seemed to echo to his Ha, ha, ha! It had not the least effect in disturbing the bird, whose sense of security was complete;

and who hopped about the table with its quick head now on this side and now on that, turning its bright sudden eye on its master, as if he were no more than another bird.

CHARLES DICKENS from *Bleak House*

When Mack first boarded the ship, a group of us, gloved, smothered him with a heavy blanket and fastened a chain to his leg. He knew he was overpowered, and did not struggle, but inside the blanket we heard some horrible chuckles. We took off the blanket and stood back expectantly from that dishevelled and puzzled giant of a parrot. He shook his feathers flat again, quite self-contained, looked at us sardonically and murmured " Gur-r-r " very distinctly; then glanced at his foot. There was a little surprise in his eye when he saw the chain there. He lifted up the chain to examine it, tried it and then quietly and easily bit it through. " Gur-r-r! " he said again. He straightened his vest, and still regarded us solemnly. Then he moved off to a davit, and climbed the mizzen shrouds to the topmast.

When he saw us at food he came down with nonchalance, and overlooked our table from the cross beam of an awning. Apparently satisfied, he came directly to the mess table, sat beside me, took his share with all the assurance of a member, and even allowed me to idle with his beautiful wings and his tail. He was a beauty. He took my finger in his awful bill and rolled it round like a cigarette. I wondered what he would do to it before he let it go; but he merely let it go. He was a great character, magnanimously minded. I never knew a tamer creature than Mack. That evening he rejoined a flock of his wild brothers in the distant tree-tops. But he was back next morning, and put everlasting fear into the terrier, who was at breakfast by suddenly appearing before him with wings outspread on the deck, looking like a disrupted and angry rainbow, and making raucous threats. The dog gave one yell and fell over backwards.

H. M. TOMLINSON from *The Sea and the Jungle*

It is a disagreeable reflection that all these many birds —these being everywhere about one—resent one's presence and wish one away, that every one of all the discordant notes uttered as one walks about under this screaming cloud of witnesses has a distinct and very unflattering reference to oneself, upbraids one, almost calls one a name. To be hated by thousands—and rightly hated too! It is strange, man's callousness in this respect—that he should see his presence affect bird and beast as that of the most odious tyrant affects his fellow-men, yet never sleep or eat a meal the less comfortably for it!

EDMUND SELOUS from *The Bird Watcher in the Shetlands*

This district (Lewes) affords some birds that are hardly ever heard of at Selborne. In the first place considerable flocks of cross-beaks have appeared this summer in the pine-groves belonging to this house; the water-ousel is said to haunt the mouth of the Lewes river, near New-haven; and the Cornish chough builds, I know, all along the chalky cliffs of the Sussex shore.

I was greatly pleased to see little parties of ring-ousels (my newly discovered migrators) scattered, at intervals, all along the Sussex downs from Chichester to Lewes. Let them come from whence they will, it looks very suspicious that they are cantoned along the coast in order to pass the channel when severe weather advances. They visit us again in April, as it should seem, in their return; and are not to be found in the dead of winter. It is remarkable that they are very tame, and seem to have no manner of apprehensions of danger from a person with a gun. There are bustards on the wide downs near Brighthelmstone. No doubt you are acquainted with the Sussex-downs; the prospects and rides round Lewes are most lovely!   GILBERT WHITE from *Selborne*

Cornish choughs abound, and breed on Beachy-head and on all the cliffs of the Sussex coast.

GILBERT WHITE from *Selborne*

A melancholy interest surrounds the Chough, whose glossy black dress, long curved red bill and red legs distinguish it from all other birds; it is a species that is going under. Egg-collecting has helped to weaken it, but competition with, rather than the antagonism of, the increasing pushful Jackdaw, its frequent companion, has much to do with its decrease; it is a gentle, sedentary, conservative bird, rarely met with far from its breeding haunts. Many old stations are now deserted, though the nests were not accessible to even daring cragsmen; its position in the south-west of England, where it was called the Cornish Chough, is insecure.

The Chough has wonderfully buoyant and easy flight. It floats above the beetling cliffs with wide-spread primaries; the tips of these bend upwards as it curves and turns sweeping round gracefully. With wings almost closed it shoots towards the boiling surf at the foot of the crags, then checking itself, sweeps into some wave-washed cave.

T. A. COWARD from *Birds of the British Isles*

Choughs

Sept. 9, 1767. The most unusual birds I ever observed in these parts were a pair of hoopoes (*upupa*) which came several years ago in the summer, and frequented an ornamental piece of ground, which joins to my garden, for some weeks. They used to march about in a stately manner, feeding in the walks, many times in the day; and seemed disposed to breed in my outlet; but were frightened and persecuted by idle boys, who would never let them be at rest.   GILBERT WHITE from *Selborne*

The history of the Hoopoe as a British bird is a long, disgraceful obituary. Not only is it a passage migrant in spring and autumn, but it would be a regular summer visitor to England if stupid and greedy collectors and gunners would leave it alone. It has frequently nested in southern counties, and without doubt would do so again if permitted. To our knowledge it has been striving to establish itself for two and a half centuries, and still in spite of opposition continues its efforts. As a would-be settler, wanderer or passage bird it has occurred in all parts of the British Isles, and though most frequent in the south and east, is by no means unusual in the west; indeed the list of " specimens " in any western county is shockingly lengthy.

The large, black-tipped erectile crest, when elevated like the head-gear of an American Indian, and the conspicuous barring of the back and wings, together with its almost stupid tameness, render the Hoopoe not only too easy to see, but far too easy to shoot.

T. A. COWARD from *Birds of the British Isles*

The story of the Kite as a British resident is, though lamentable, a triumph for the present generation of ornithologists—or for a few of them. In the eighteenth century the bird was common in all parts, a woodland species constantly visiting the towns and villages, though apparently never resident in Ireland, where the few instances of its occurrence rest on slender evidence. In the nineteenth century farmers and game-preservers waged war against the Kite, with the result that by the middle of the century it had vanished from most of its ancient haunts, though a few nested in England and Scotland in the Seventies. Twenty years later some twenty pairs lingered in central Wales, and then the egg-collector, fearing that his collection might not contain "British-taken" eggs, raided its sanctuary. In 1903 a few real bird-lovers awoke and efforts were made to protect the survivors, but in 1905 it is believed only five birds remained, and it is doubtful if any got off broods in safety. Carrion-Crows by robbing the nests complicated the difficulties, but careful watching saved the remnant, and though it is early to boast there does seem a chance that the bird will increase once more. On the authority of two good ornithologists we know that a pair nested in Devonshire in 1913, though unfortunately the eggs were taken. T. A. COWARD from *The Birds of the British Isles*

Throughout a long mid-June day I heard the sound of firing in the woods, beginning at about eight o'clock in the morning, and lasting until dark. The shooters ranged over the whole woods; I had never, even in October, heard so much firing on an estate in one day. I inquired of several persons, some employed on the estate, as to the meaning of all this firing, and was told that the keeper was ridding the woods of some of the vermin. More than that they refused to say; but by-and-by I found a person to tell me just what had happened. The head-keeper had got twenty or thirty persons, the men with guns and a number of lads with long poles with hooks to pull nests down, and had set himself to rid the woods of birds that were not wanted. All the nests found, of whatever species, were pulled down, and all doves, woodpeckers, nuthatches, blackbirds, missel- and song-thrushes, shot; also chaffinches, and many other small birds. The keeper said he was not going to have the place swarming with birds that were no good for anything, and were always eating the pheasants' food.

W. H. HUDSON from *Adventures Among Birds*

The points by which the various species and sub-species of *Pandion* are separated are so slight that some authorities maintain that there is but one, almost cosmopolitan species, for in winter it visits many parts of the world in which it does not nest. Whether it may still be classed as a resident in Britain is an annual question, for one after another its historical eyries have been deserted. Careful efforts to preserve the few remaining sites in the Scottish Highlands have usually ended in failure. In spring and autumn passage birds, mostly immature, visit us with a degree of regularity, and are met with both on the coast and on inland waters.

Blind game-preservation and an objection to rivals on trout and salmon streams were, doubtless, responsible for the rapid diminution of our resident birds, but the greed of collectors and the insane habit of shooting any unfamiliar bird put the finishing touch; the eyrie on Loch Arkaig was deserted in 1911, that on Loch-an-Eilein a few years earlier. In Britain, at any rate, the Osprey is purely a fish-eater, though not particular whether from fresh or salt water; it will capture surface fish at sea, flounders from a muddy estuary, lazy bream in the meres, or trout in the clear streams.

T. A. COWARD from *The Birds of the British Isles*

Osprey

Pennsylvania, Philadelphia, Nov. 9, 1748. All the old Swedes and Englishmen, born in America, whom I ever questioned, asserted that there were not near so many birds fit for eating as present, as there used to be when they were children, and that their decrease was visible. They even said, that they had heard their fathers complain of this, in whose childhood the bays, rivers, and brooks were quite covered with all sorts of water fowl, such as wild geese, ducks, and the like. But at present there is sometimes not a single bird upon them; about sixty or seventy years ago, a single person could kill eighty ducks in a morning; but at present you frequently wait in vain for a single one. A Swede above ninety years old assured me, that he had in his youth killed twenty-three ducks at a shot.

This good luck nobody is likely to have at present, as you are forced to ramble about for a whole day, without getting a sight of more than three or four. Cranes[1] at that time came hither by hundreds in the spring; at present there are but very few. The wild Turkeys, and the birds, which the Swedes in this country call Partridges, and Hazel-hens, were in whole flocks in the woods. But at this time a person is tired with walking before he can start a single bird.

The cause of this diminution is not difficult to find. Before the arrival of the Europeans, the country was uncultivated, and full of great forests. The few Indians that lived here seldom disturbed the birds. They carried on

[1] When Captain Amada, the first Englishman that ever landed in North America, set foot on shore (to use his own words) *such a flock of cranes (the most part white) arose under us with such a cry, redoubled by many echoes, as if an armie of men had shouted together.*

no trade among themselves, iron and gunpowder were unknown to them. One hundredth part of the fowl, which at that time were so plentiful here, would have sufficed to feed the few inhabitants: and considering that they cultivated their small maize fields, caught fish, hunted stags, beavers, bears, wild cattle, and other animals whose flesh was delicious to them, it will soon appear how little they disturbed the birds. But since the arrival of great crowds of Europeans, things are greatly changed: the country is well peopled, and the woods are cut down: the people increasing in this country, they have by hunting and shooting in part extirpated the birds, in part feared them away: in spring the people still take both eggs, mothers, and young indifferently, because no regulations are made to the contrary. And if any had been made, the spirit of freedom which prevails in the country would not suffer them to be obeyed.

PETER KALM from *Travels into North America*

Nov. 2, 1769. Most kinds of birds seem to me to be wild and shy somewhat in proportion to their bulk; I mean in this island, where they are much pursued and annoyed: but in Ascension-island, and many other desolate places, mariners have found fowls so unacquainted with an human figure, that they would stand still to be taken; as is the case with boobies, etc. As an example of what is advanced, I remark that the golden-crested wren (the smallest British bird) will stand unconcerned till you come within three or four yards of it, while the bustard (*otis*), the largest British land fowl, does not care to admit a person within so many furlongs. GILBERT WHITE from *Selborne*

Near Lewes, Dec. 9, 1773. But, notwithstanding all my care, I saw nothing like a summer bird of passage: and, what is more strange, not one wheat-ear, though they abound so in the autumn as to be a considerable perquisite to the shepherds that take them; and though many are to be seen to my knowledge all the winter through in many parts of the south of England. The most intelligent shepherds tell me that some few of these birds appear on the downs in March, and then withdraw to breed probably in warrens and stone-quarries: now and then a nest is plowed up in a fallow on the downs under a furrow, but it is thought a rarity. At the time of wheat-harvest they begin to be taken in great numbers; are sent for sale in vast quantities to Brighthelmstone and Tunbridge; and appear at the tables of all the gentry that entertain with any degree of elegance.

GILBERT WHITE from *Selborne*

Saunders Island is the Arctic bird haven for auks, ducks and fulmars, those strange fowls which cannot walk because their knee-joints are bent almost double. If they are placed on the ground or on the deck of a ship they are unable to take off again, and so they must alight only on the steep cliffs from which they can soar into the air.

The fulmars are the first birds to appear in the spring, long before the ice breaks up. Although the flavour of their flesh is bad, the hunters go after them. After a season of nothing but walrus and bear meat, any change is for the better. The birds soar so high that they are mere specks, but they drop like plummets when blubber is thrown overboard.

Those we got from the cliffs were fat, and the taste not too revolting, but their feathers had a typically nauseating odour. Fortunately the natives in the far north do not use them for pillows, but in South Greenland they do. I remember once at a dance Knud and I saw two lovely native girls whom we could not approach because the family bedding was stuffed with fulmar feathers. It is a drastic but effective protection for any girl.

PETER FREUCHEN from *Arctic Adventure*

I must tell you that we were eating little auks. These birds, hardly bigger than starlings, live in such great numbers in the cliffs near-by that the mountains seem alive. They come in early summer and hatch their eggs. At that time the country is quite different—the flutter of wings, song and babbling are over the earth all day long. When night settles down the birds fly out to sea and return to the cliffs at daybreak. They lay only one egg each among the stones. These birds play an important part in supporting life in the whole district. Their skins are used for clothing, and shirts made of them are soft and warm. Auk meat, too, is delicious. But they serve principally as a lure to the foxes that haunt the same cliffs and collect caches of the birds during the summer to last them through the darkness.

But here we were consuming a special delicacy—auks pickled in oil. This is done by killing a seal and skinning it through its mouth without splitting the skin. Not every hunter can do this, but when it is accomplished satisfactorily it makes a magnificent poke, because most of the seal blubber still clings to the skin.

The person intending to fill the hide takes it along to a spot where the birds are thicker than fish in an aquarium and, with a net attached to a long stick, he catches the auks as they fly past, often bagging enough in one day to fill his sealskin, which is then latched and covered with stones. The sun must not reach it or the oil will turn rancid. During the summer the blubber turns to oil and soaks into the birds, which decompose slowly without interference from the air.

This makes a dish which tastes like nothing else in the world, and one loved by old and young alike. The white feathers turn pink, and may be easily plucked out. The birds are often eaten frozen, as we ate them, but some connoisseurs say they are better warmed up. In fact, frozen meat never tastes as strong as it does when it is thawed out. When frozen the diner must chop the birds out of the poke with an axe, but after they become soft they may be eaten with grace and elegant manners. The gastronomist takes them by the legs and bites the feet. Then with a deft twist of his hand he removes the feathers —or most of them. After that he skins them, from the bill backwards, and having turned the skin inside out, sucks the most delicious fat out of it. Finally he swallows the skin at one gulp, and then begins on the meat.

PETER FREUCHEN from *Arctic Adventure*

From the beginning of October till the sea froze over, we used to go out shooting sea-birds from the *Stella*. This was perhaps the most profitable of our various hunting methods. Throughout the autumn Black Guillemots were very plentiful out in the main fjord and on the open coast, and sometimes we would get the larger Brunnich's Guillemot which rarely ventures into the fjords. The Guillemots were usually in pairs or in small parties of six or seven. We would approach them, one man handling the boat and the other waiting in the bows with a 12 bore shotgun. When we were within a couple of hundred yards we would run the motor dead slow and gradually get within range. As there was usually a heavy swell, shooting was not as easy as might be expected, especially as a long shot rarely had any effect on their dense plumage. They usually dived rather than flew away, and we would sometimes follow one bird for a considerable time before he came up within range, and then it was a case of rapid snap-shooting before he dived again. There were always a few Glaucous and Iceland Gulls about and, once one had been shot, others could often be decoyed within range by whistling and by flapping the dead bird. After mid-October, parties of Eider and Long-tailed Ducks visited the fjords; these were very much sought after, being even more palatable than the Guillemots. On a good day's shooting we would bring back perhaps twenty Black Guillemots, two Brunnich's Guillemots, an Eider, a brace of Long-tails, and an odd Gull.

On October 10th we saw a most unusual sight. There was no wind, but low cloud, mist and falling snow restricted the visibility to about half a mile. Out by Ailsa the sea was suddenly alive with birds. Whereas formerly we had seen only one or two Brunnich's Guillemots a day, here we saw literally hundreds. Flock after flock of Little Auks were going south, either flying or swimming in their jerky way upon the water. We saw more Black

RB

Guillemots in an hour than we had seen during the rest of the autumn. Owing to the poor visibility it was impossible to estimate the numbers of these migrating birds. The day before we had seen only the usual number, and two days later the Brunnich's Guillemots and Little Auks had passed on; only a few Black Guillemots remained. We shot a good many Brunnich's Guillemots that day before we ran out of cartridges. We removed the guts of these birds and without plucking or skinning them hung them up by hundreds in the " little house," where they soon froze solid and supplied us with fresh meat till well into the winter.

F. SPENCER CHAPMAN from *Watkins' Last Expedition*

As soon as there was enough open water for them, the migrant birds started to arrive. There were two Glaucous Gulls by the open water in Kangerdlugsuatsiak on April 11th, but the temperature was - 5°F. and they sat huddled up and disconsolate on the edge of the ice. Next day they had gone.

Small parties of Snow Buntings reached the Base in the middle of April, and by the end of the month most of the males had claimed territories and were singing vigorously all day and most of the night. The Greenland Wheatears did not come till the beginning of May. On May 2nd, at Nigertusok, a Redpoll flew over calling, a pair of Purple Sandpipers followed the tide-crack and several Black Guillemots swam around in a pool of open water. Each day several Glaucous Gulls scavenged round the shark-hole, and sometimes Greater Black-backed

Gulls joined them too, much to the delight of the natives, who were by now hungry for boiled seagull. On May 7th we saw a flock of about 70 geese—probably Pink-footed Geese—flying northwards. A week later the first drake Eider appeared, and the next day a Mallard was flying round above the open water. . . . at the end of May we found that White Wagtails, Ringed Plover, Turnstone and Red-throated Divers had come. . . .

F. SPENCER CHAPMAN from *Watkins' Last Expedition*

Drake Eider

I again started before daylight, and as day began to break I found myself in an open, well-cultivated valley, near a village called Ugerbai; the hills on either side were covered with scrubby jungle, and the country very much resembled the Salt range below Jhelum, and had a very parched appearance; in fact, the climate for thirty miles

Cuckoo

into the low hills differs very slightly from that of the Panjáb plains.

The European Cuckoo was calling in every valley, and reminded me of home, for during eleven years on the plains I had never seen it or heard its call, although another species of cuckoo is common enough in Lahore.

HENDERSON AND HUME from *Lahore to Yārkand*

The first two or three days of our stay here were very wet, and I obtained but few insects or birds, but at length, when I was beginning to despair, my boy Baderoon returned one day with a specimen which repaid me for months of delay and expectation. It was a small bird, a little less than a thrush. The greater part of its plumage was of an intense cinnabar red, with a gloss as of spun glass. On the head the feathers became short and velvety, and shaded into rich orange. Beneath, from the breast downwards, was pure white, with the softness and gloss of silk, and across the breast a band of deep metallic green separated this colour from the red of the throat. Above each eye was a round spot of the same metallic green; the bill was yellow, and the feet and legs were of a fine cobalt blue, strikingly contrasting with all the other parts of the body. Merely in arrangement of colours and texture of plumage this little bird was a gem of the first water; yet these comprised only half its strange beauty. Springing from each side of the breast, and ordinarily lying concealed under the wings, were little tufts of greyish feathers about two inches long, and each terminated by a broad band of intense emerald green. These plumes can be raised at the will of the bird, and spread out into a pair of elegant fans when the wings are elevated. But this is not the only ornament. The two middle feathers of the tail are in the form of slender wires about five inches long, and which diverge in a beautiful double curve. About half an inch of the end of this wire is webbed on the outer side only, and coloured of a fine metallic green, and being curled spirally inwards form a pair of elegant glittering buttons, hanging five inches below the body, and the same distance apart. These two ornaments,

the breast fans and the spiral tipped tail wires, are altogether unique, not occurring on any other species of the
eight thousand different birds that are known to exist
upon the earth; and, combined with the most exquisite
beauty of plumage, render this one of the most perfectly
lovely of the many lovely productions of nature. My
transports of admiration and delight quite amused my
Aru hosts, who saw nothing more in the " Burong raja "
than we do in the robin or the goldfinch.

Thus one of my objects in coming to the far East was
accomplished. I had obtained a specimen of the King
Bird of Paradise (*Paradisea regia*), which had been described by Linnaeus from skins preserved in a mutilated
state by the natives. I knew how few Europeans had ever
beheld the perfect little organism I now gazed upon, and
how very imperfectly it was still known in Europe. The
emotions excited in the mind of a naturalist, who has
long desired to see the actual thing which he has hitherto
known only by description, drawing, or badly-preserved
external covering—especially when that thing is of surpassing rarity and beauty—require the poetic faculty
fully to express them. The remote island in which I found
myself situated, in an almost unvisited sea, far from the
tracks of merchant fleets and navies; the wild, luxuriant
tropical forest, which stretched far away on every side;
the rude, uncultured savages who gathered round me—
all had their influence in determining the emotions with
which I gazed upon this " thing of beauty." I thought
of the long ages of the past, during which the successive
generations of this little creature had run their course—
year by year being born, and living and dying amid these
dark and gloomy woods, with no intelligent eye to gaze

upon their loveliness; to all appearance such a wanton
waste of beauty. Such ideas excite a feeling of melancholy.
. . . One day I got under a tree where a number of the
Great Paradise birds were assembled, but they were high
up in the thickest of the foliage, and flying and jumping
about so continually that I could get no good view of
them. At length I shot one, but it was a young specimen,
and was entirely of a rich chocolate-brown colour, without either the metallic green throat or yellow plumes of
the full-grown bird. All that I had yet seen resembled
this, and the natives told me that it would be about two
months before any would be found in full plumage. I
still hoped, therefore, to get some. Their voice is most
extraordinary. At early morn, before the sun has risen,
we hear a loud cry of " Wawk—wawk—wawk, wŏk—
wŏk—wŏk," which resounds through the forest, changing
its direction continually. This is the Great Bird of Paradise going to seek his breakfast. Others soon follow his
example; lories and parroquets cry shrilly; cockatoos
scream; king-hunters croak and bark; and the various
smaller birds chirp and whistle their morning song. As
I lie listening to these interesting sounds, I realize my
position as the first European who has ever lived for
months together in the Aru Islands, a place which I had
hoped rather than expected ever to visit. I think how
many besides myself have longed to reach these almost
fairy realms, and to see with their own eyes the many
wonderful and beautiful things which I am daily en-
countering. But now Ali and Baderoon are up and getting
ready their guns and ammunition, and little Baso has his
fire lighted and is boiling my coffee, and I remember that
I had a black cockatoo brought in late last night, which I

must skin immediately, and so I jump up and begin my day's work very happily.

This cockatoo is the first I have ever seen, and is a great prize. It has a rather small and weak body, long weak legs, large wings, and an enormously developed head, ornamented with a magnificent crest, and armed with a sharp-pointed hooked bill of immense size and length. The plumage is entirely black, but has all over it the curious powdery white secretion characteristic of cockatoos. The cheeks are bare, and of an intense blood-red colour. Instead of the harsh scream of the white cockatoos, its voice is a somewhat plaintive whistle. The tongue is a curious organ, being a slender fleshy cylinder of a deep red colour, terminated by a horny black plate, furrowed across and somewhat prehensile. The whole tongue has a considerable extensile power. I will here relate something of the habits of this bird, with which I have since become acquainted. It frequents the lower parts of the forest, and is seen singly, or at most two or three together. It flies slowly and noiselessly, and may be killed by a comparatively slight wound. It eats various fruits and seeds, but seems more particularly attached to the kernel of the kanary-nut, which grows on a lofty forest tree (*Canarium commune*), abundant in the islands where this bird is found; and the manner in which it gets at these seeds shows a correlation of structure and habits, which would point out the "kanary" as its special food. The shell of this nut is so excessively hard that only a heavy hammer will crack it; it is somewhat triangular, and the outside is quite smooth. The manner in which the bird opens these nuts is very curious. Taking one endways in its bill and keeping it firm by a pressure of the tongue, it cuts a transverse notch by a lateral sawing motion of the sharp-edged lower mandible. This done, it takes hold of the nut with its foot, and biting off a piece of leaf retains it in the deep notch of the upper mandible, and again seizing the nut, which is prevented from slipping by the elastic tissue of the leaf, fixes the edge of the lower mandible in the notch, and by a powerful nip breaks off a piece of the shell. Again taking the nut in its claws, it inserts the very long and sharp point of the bill and picks out the kernel, which is seized hold of, morsel by morsel, by the extensible tongue. Thus every detail of form and structure in the extraordinary bill of this bird seems to have its own use, and we may easily conceive that the black cockatoos have maintained themselves in competition with their more active and more numerous white allies, by their power of existing on a kind of food which no other bird is able to extract from its stony shell. The species is the *Microglossum aterrimum* of naturalists.

ALFRED RUSSEL WALLACE from *The Malay Archipelago*

The great contrast between the two divisions of the Archipelago is nowhere so abruptly exhibited as on passing from the island of Bali to that of Lombock, where the two regions are in closest proximity. In Bali we have barbets, fruit-thrushes, and woodpeckers; on passing over to Lombock these are seen no more, but we have abundance of cockatoos, honeysuckers, and brush-turkeys, which are equally unknown in Bali*, or any island further west.

* I was informed, however, that there were a few cockatoos at one spot on the west of the Bali, showing that the intermingling of the productions of these islands is now going on.

The strait is here fifteen miles wide, so that we may pass in two hours from one great division of the earth to another, differing as essentially in their animal life as Europe does from America. If we travel from Java or Borneo to Celebes or the Moluccas, the difference is still more striking. In

Neck-Lace Trogon

the first, the forests abound in monkeys of many kinds, wild cats, deer, civets, and otters, and numerous varieties of squirrels are constantly met with. In the latter none of these occur; but the prehensile-tailed cuscus is almost the only terrestrial mammal seen, except wild pigs, which are found in all the islands, and deer (which have probably

been recently introduced) in Celebes and the Moluccas.
The birds which are most abundant in the Western
Islands are woodpeckers, barbets, trogons, fruit-thrushes,
and leaf-thrushes; they are seen daily, and form the great
ornithological features of the country. In the Eastern
Islands these are absolutely unknown, honeysuckers and
small lories being the most common birds; so that the
naturalist feels himself in a new world, and can hardly
realize that he has passed from the one region to the
other in a few days, and without ever being out of sight
of land.

ALFRED RUSSEL WALLACE from *The Malay Archipelago*

The very first time I fired my gun I brought down one
of the most curious and beautiful of the Malacca birds,
the blue-billed gaper (*Cymbirhynchus macrorhynchus*),
called by the Malays the " Rain-bird." It is about the
size of a starling, black and rich claret colour with white
shoulder stripes, and a very large and broad bill of the
most pure cobalt blue above and orange below, while the
iris is emerald green. As the skins dry the bill turns dull
black, but even then the bird is handsome. When fresh
killed, the contrast of the vivid blue with the rich colours
of the plumage is remarkably striking and beautiful. The
lovely Eastern trogons, with their rich brown backs,
beautifully pencilled wings, and crimson breasts, were
also soon obtained, as well as the large green barbets
(*Megalaema versicolor*)—fruit-eating birds, something like
the small toucans, with a short, straight bristly bill, and
whose head and neck are variegated with patches of the

most vivid blue and crimson. A day or two after, my hunter brought me a specimen of the green gaper (*Calyptomena viridis*), which is like a small cock-of-the-rock, but entirely of the most vivid green, delicately marked on the wings with black bars. Handsome woodpeckers and gay kingfishers, green and brown cuckoos with velvety red faces and green beaks, red-breasted doves and metallic honeysuckers, were brought in day after day, and kept me in a continual state of pleasurable excitement.

ALFRED RUSSEL WALLACE from *The Malay Archipelago*

The Moluccas are especially rich in the parrot tribe, no less than twenty-two species, belonging to ten genera, inhabiting them. Among these is the large red-crested cockatoo, so commonly seen alive in Europe, two handsome red parrots of the genus Eclectus, and five of the beautiful crimson lories, which are almost exclusively confined to these islands and the New Guinea group. The pigeons are hardly less abundant or beautiful, twenty-one species being known, including twelve of the beautiful green fruit-pigeons, the smaller kinds of which are ornamented with the most brilliant patches of colour on the head and the under-surface. Next to these come the kingfishers, including sixteen species, almost all of which are beautiful, and many are among the most brilliantly-coloured birds that exist.

One of the most curious groups of birds, the Megapodii, or mound-makers, is very abundant in the Moluccas. They are gallinaceous birds, about the size of a small fowl, and generally of a dark ashy or sooty colour, and they have remarkably large and strong feet and long claws. They are allied to the " Maleo " of Celebes, of which an account has already been given, but they differ in habits, most of these birds frequenting the scrubby jungles along the sea-shore, where the soil is sandy, and there is a considerable quantity of *débris*, consisting of sticks, shells, seaweed, leaves, etc. Of this rubbish the Megapodii form immense mounds, often six or eight feet high and twenty or thirty feet in diameter, which they are enabled to do with comparative ease by means of their large feet, with which they can grasp and throw backwards a quantity of material. In the centre of this mound, at a depth of two or three feet, the eggs are deposited, and are hatched by the gentle heat produced by the fermentation of the vegetable matter of the mound. When I first saw these mounds in the island of Lombock, I could hardly believe that they were made by such small birds, but I afterwards met with them frequently, and have once or twice come upon the birds engaged in making them. They run a few steps backwards, grasping a quantity of loose material in one foot, and throw it a long way behind them. When once properly buried the eggs seem to be no more cared for, the young birds working their way up through the heap of rubbish, and running off at once into the forest. They come out of the egg covered with thick downy feathers, and have no tail, although the wings are fully developed.

I was so fortunate as to discover a new species (*Megapodius wallacei*), which inhabits Gilolo, Ternate, and Bouru. It is the handsomest bird of the genus, being richly banded with reddish brown on the back of the wings; and it differs from the other species in its habits. It frequents the forests of the interior and comes down to the sea-beach to deposit its eggs, but instead of making a mound, or scratching a hole to receive them, it burrows into the sand to the depth of about three feet obliquely downwards, and deposits its eggs at the bottom. It then loosely covers up the mouth of the hole, and is said by the natives to obliterate and disguise its own footmarks leading to and from the hole, by making many other tracks and scratches in the neighbourhood. It lays its eggs only at night, and at Bouru a bird was caught early one morning as it was coming out of its hole, in which several eggs were found. All these birds seem to be semi-nocturnal, for their loud wailing cries may be constantly heard late into the night and long before daybreak in the morning. The eggs are all of a rusty red colour, and very large for the size of the bird, being generally three or three and a quarter inches long, by two or two and a quarter wide. They are very good eating, and are much sought after by the natives.

Another large and extraordinary bird is the Cassowary, which inhabits the island of Ceram only. It is a stout and strong bird, standing five or six feet high, and covered with long coarse black hair-like feathers. The head is ornamented with a large horny casque or helmet, and the bare skin of the neck is conspicuous with bright blue and red colours. The wings are quite absent, and are replaced by a group of horny black spines like blunt porcupine quills. These birds wander about the vast mountainous forests that cover the island of Ceram, feeding chiefly on fallen fruits, and on insects or crustacea. The female lays from three to five large and beautifully shagreened green eggs upon a bed of leaves, the male and female sitting upon them alternately for about a month. This bird is the helmeted cassowary (*Casuarius galeatus*) of naturalists, and was for a long time the only species known. Others have since been discovered in New Guinea, New Britain, and North Australia.

ALFRED RUSSEL WALLACE from *The Malay Archipelago*

Sept., 1851. The only live animals I had with me were a couple of parrots, which were a never-failing source of amusement. One was a little "Marianna," or Macai of the Indians, a small black-headed, white-breasted, orange-neck and thighed parrot; the other, an Anaca, a most beautiful bird, banded on the breast and belly with blue and red, and the back of the neck and head covered with long bright red feathers margined with blue, which it would elevate when angry, forming a handsome crest somewhat similar to that of the harpy eagle; its ornithological name is *Derotypus accipitrinus*, the hawk-headed parrot. There was a remarkable difference in the characters of these birds. The Anaca was of a rather solemn, morose, and irritable disposition; while the Marianna was a lively little creature, inquisitive as a monkey, and playful as a kitten. It was never quiet, running over the whole canoe, climbing into every crack and cranny, diving into all the baskets, pans, and pots it could discover, and tasting everything they contained. It was a most omnivorous feeder, eating rice, farinha, every kind of fruit, fish, meat, and vegetable, and drinking coffee too as well as myself; and as soon as it saw me with basin in hand, would climb up to the edge, and not be quiet without having a share, which it would lick up with the greatest satisfaction, stopping now and then, and looking knowingly round, as much as to say, "This coffee is very good," and then sipping again with increased gusto. The bird evidently liked the true flavour of the coffee, and not that of the sugar, for it would climb up to the edge of the coffee-pot, and hanging on the rim plunge boldly down till only its little tail appeared above, and then drink the coffee-grounds for five minutes together. The Indians in the canoe delighted to imitate its pretty clear whistle, making it reply and stare about, in a vain search after its companions. Whenever we landed to cook, the Marianna was one of the first on shore—not with any view to an escape, but merely to climb up some bush or tree and whistle enjoyment of its elevated position, for as soon as eating commenced, it came down for a share of fish or coffee. The more sober Anaca would generally remain quietly in the canoe, till, lured by the cries and whistles of its lively little companion, it would venture out to join it; for, notwithstanding their difference of disposition, they were great friends, and would sit for hours side by side, scratching each other's heads, or playing together just like a cat and a kitten; the Marianna sometimes so exasperating the Anaca by scratches and peckings, and by jumping down upon it, that a regular fight would ensue, which, however, soon terminated, when they would return to their former state of brotherhood. I intended them as presents to two friends in Barra, but was almost sorry to part them.

ALFRED RUSSEL WALLACE from

A Narrative of Travels on the Amazon and Rio Negro

Ever since leaving Dobbo I had suffered terribly from insects, who seemed here bent upon revenging my long-continued persecution of their race. . . . On arriving here we were delighted to find the house free from sand-flies or mosquitoes, but in the plantations where my daily walks led me, the day-biting mosquitoes swarmed, and seemed especially to delight in attacking my poor feet. After a month's incessant punishment, those useful members rebelled against such treatment and broke into open insurrection, throwing out numerous inflamed ulcers, which were very painful, and stopped me from walking.

King Bird of Paradise

. . . The stings and bites and ceaseless irritation caused by these pests of the tropical forests would be borne uncomplainingly; but to be kept prisoner by them in so rich and unexplored a country, where rare and beautiful creatures are to be met with in every forest ramble—a country reached by such a long and tedious voyage, and which might not in the present century be again visited for the same purpose—is a punishment too severe for a naturalist to pass over in silence.

I had, however, some consolation in the birds my boys brought home daily, more especially the Paradiseas, which they at length obtained in full plumage. It was quite a relief to my mind to get these, for I could hardly have torn myself away from Aru had I not obtained specimens. But what I valued almost as much as the birds themselves, was the knowledge of their habits, which I was daily obtaining both from the accounts of my hunters, and from the conversation of the natives. The birds had now commenced what the people here call their " sacaleli," or dancing parties, in certain trees in the forest, which are not fruit trees as I at first imagined, but which have an immense head of spreading branches and large but scattered leaves, giving a clear space for the birds to play and exhibit their plumes. On one of these trees a dozen or twenty full-plumaged male birds assemble together, raise up their wings, stretch out their necks, and elevate their exquisite plumes, keeping them in a continual vibration. Between whiles they fly across from branch to branch in great excitement, so that the whole tree is filled with waving plumes in every variety of attitude and motion. The bird itself is nearly as large as a crow, and is of a rich coffee brown colour. The head and neck is of a pure straw yellow above, and rich metallic green beneath. The long plumy tufts of golden orange feathers spring from the sides beneath each wing, and when the bird is in repose are partly concealed by them. At the time of its excitement, however, the wings are raised vertically over the back, the head is bent down and stretched out, and the long plumes are raised up and expanded till they form two magnificent golden fans striped with deep red at the base, and fading off into

Great Bird of Paradise

the pale brown tint of the finely divided and softly waving points. The whole bird is then overshadowed by them, the crouching body, yellow head, and emerald green throat forming but the foundation and setting to the golden glory which waves above. When seen in this attitude, the Bird of Paradise really deserves its name, and must be ranked as one of the most beautiful and most wonderful of living things. I continued also to get specimens of the lovely little king-bird occasionally, as well as numbers of brilliant pigeons, sweet little parroquets, and many curious small birds, most nearly resembling those of Australia and New Guinea.

ALFRED RUSSEL WALLACE from *The Malay Archipelago*

Oct. 24, 1748. Of all the rare birds of North America, the Humming Bird is the most admirable, or at least most worthy of peculiar attention. Several reasons induce me to believe, few parts of the world can produce its equal. Dr. Linnaeus calls it *Trochilus Colubris*. The Swedes, and some Englishmen, call it the King's bird; but the name of Humming Bird is more common. Catesby, in his *Natural History of Carolina*, Vol. 1, p. 65, tab. 65, has drawn it, in its natural size, with its proper colours, and added a description of it. In size it is not much bigger than a large humble bee, and is therefore the least in the world. Its plumage is most beautifully coloured, of all birds,[1] or it is much if there is a lesser species

[1] There is a much lesser species of humming bird, by Linnaeus called *Trochilus minimus*, being the least bird known; Sir Hans Sloane's living one weighed only twenty grains, and Mr. Edwards's dry one forty-five.

most of its feathers being green, some grey, and others forming a shining red ring round its neck; the tail glows with fine feathers, changing from green into a brass colour. These birds come here in spring, about the time when it begins to grow very warm, and make their nests in summer; but, towards autumn, they retreat again into the more southern countries of America. They subsist barely upon the nectar, or sweet juice of flowers, contained in that part which botanists call the *nectarium*, and which they suck up with their long bills. Of all the flowers, they like those most, which have a long tube; and I have observed that they have fluttered chiefly about the *Impatiens Noli tangere*, and the *Monarda* with crimson flowers. An inhabitant of the country is sure to have a number of these beautiful and agreeable little birds before his windows all the summer long, if he takes care to plant a bed with all sorts of fine flowers under them. It is indeed a diverting spectacle to see these little active creatures flying about the flowers like bees, and sucking their juices with their long narrow bills. The flowers of the above-mentioned *Monarda* grow *verticillated*, that is, at different distances they surround the stalk as the flowers of our mint (*Mentha*) bastard hemp (*Galeopsis*) mother-wort (*Leonurus*) and dead nettle (*Lamium*). It is therefore diverting to see them putting their bills into every flower in the circle. As soon as they have sucked the juice of one flower, they flutter to the next. One that has not seen them would hardly believe in how short a space of time they have had their tongues in all the flowers of a plant, which when large, and with a long tube, the little bird, by putting its head into them, looks as if it has crept with half its body into them.

During their sucking the juice out of the flowers, they never settle, but flutter continually like bees, bend their feet backwards, and move their wings so quick, that they are hardly visible. During this fluttering, they make a humming like bees, or like that which is occasioned by the turning of a little wheel. After they have thus, without resting, fluttered for a while, they fly to a neighbouring tree or post, and resume their vigour again. They then return to their humming and sucking. They are not very shy; and I, in company with several other people, have not been full two yards from the place where they fluttered about and sucked the flowers; and though we spoke and moved, yet they were no ways disturbed; but, on going towards them, they would fly off with the swiftness of an arrow. When several of them were on the same bed, there was always a violent combat between them, in meeting each other at the same flower (for envy was likewise predominant amongst these little creatures) and they attacked with such impetuosity, that it would seem as if the strongest would pierce its antagonist through and through with its long bill. During the fight, they seem to stand in the air, keeping themselves up by the incredibly swift motion of their wings. When the windows towards the garden are open, they pursue each other into the rooms, fight a little, and flutter away again. Sometimes they come to a flower which is withering, and has no more juice in it; they then, in a fit of anger, pluck it off, and throw it on the ground, that it may not mislead them for the future. If a garden contains a great number of these little birds, they are seen to cut off the flowers in such quantities, that the ground is quite covered with them. . . .

Commonly you hear no other sound than their humming; but when they fly against each other in the air, they make a chirping noise like a sparrow or chicken. I have sometimes walked with several other people in small gardens, and these birds have on all sides fluttered about us, without appearing very shy. They are so small that

Trochilus Colubris

one would easily mistake them for great humming bees or butterflies, and their flight resembles that of the former, and is incredibly swift. They have never been observed to feed on insects or fruit; the nectar of flowers seems therefore to be their only food. Several people have caught some humming birds, on account of their singular beauty, and have put them into cages, where they died for want of proper food. However, Mr. Bartram has kept a couple of them for several weeks together, by feeding them with water in which sugar had been dissolved; and I am of opinion, that it would not be difficult to keep them all winter in a hot house.

The humming bird always builds its nest in the middle of a branch of a tree, and it is so small, that it cannot be seen from the ground, but he who intends to see it must get up to the branch. For this reason it is looked upon as a great rarity if a nest is accidentally found, especially as the trees in summer have so thick a foliage. The nest is likewise the least of all; that which is in my possession is quite round, and consists in the inside of a brownish and quite soft down, which seems to have been collected from the leaves of the great mullein or *Verbascum Thapsus*, which are often found covered with a soft wool of this colour, and the plant is plentiful here. The outside of the nest has a coating of green moss, such as is common on old pales, or enclosures, and on trees; the inner diameter of the nest is hardly a geometrical inch at the top, and its depth half an inch. It is however known, that the humming birds make their nests likewise of flax, hemp, moss, hair, and other such soft materials; they are said to lay two eggs, each of the size of a pea.

PETER KALM from *Travels into North America*

In the grounds of the Empress Hotel I found a lovely rose-garden, and again I wasted more hours than I like to think of looking at roses. But the only bird that appeared was the Canadian robin, which does its best to sing the first notes of a thrush, to scuttle like a blackbird and to be as fearless and as red-breasted as a robin.

Luckily, the day before I left Victoria, I met a charming lady who told me that the humming-bird detests roses, and that its favourite flowers are honey-flowers, such as the fuchsia and the honeysuckle. As the honeysuckle was in bloom in the gardens of the hotel, I resolved to be up betimes the next morning and sit in a deck-chair under the honeysuckle and see whether the British Columbia humming-bird was or was not a myth.

A friend who suffers from morning insomnia promised to ring me up when he woke, and at a quarter to six the telephone at my bedside buzzed, and leaping out of bed I hauled on my trousers and coat over my pyjamas. The problem then was how to get out of the hotel. No one who has not tried knows how difficult it is to find one's way from an upper story of a large hotel to the ground floor at an hour at which the lifts are not working. In the end, after losing our way again and again, we had to steal out into the gardens by the fire-escape.

It had rained during the night, and it was impossible to sit down in the deck-chairs under the honeysuckle. Consequently, we were compelled to walk up and down in the exquisitely clear and sunny morning air. After ten minutes of perambulating, one of us said: " I hear a spinning noise like a grasshopper." After fifteen minutes, another of us said: " I saw something flash by." After twenty minutes, she said: " There it is." I could see nothing. " On that delphinium," she said.

By the time we reached the delphinium there was nothing there. " Wait," she said, " it will come back." We stood in the doorway of a hothouse within three feet of the delphinium, and suddenly, as if it had been created and put there by a miracle, a little bird with its throat on fire was stationed in the air, with its long beak in one of the cerulean flowers. It hovered there, its wings beating so fast that they were almost invisible, and then with a sound like a tiny kiss it flew a few inches backwards— it is, I believe, the only bird that can fly backwards—and

Rufous Humming Bird

darted to drink at another of the delphinium's Cambridge-blue flowers.

If you look at a picture of a rufous humming-bird you will see that the patch of red on its throat is comparatively small, and that the bird is mainly green and brown. But if you see it three feet away in the early morning sunshine the bird seems a blazing jewel. I have seen no colour so radiant except in a kingfisher in flight. It is as though the humming-bird's breast were alight, so dazzling, so iridescent it is. Something of the kingfisher and something of the dragonfly and with ten times the dragonfly's speed—that will give you some conception of the beauty of the humming-bird.

I could have stood all the morning watching it suspended at one flower after another, backing an inch or two and darting to another flower, and giving a little parting kiss to each flower that had yielded up its honey. But suddenly, as if at the waving of a wand, the bird vanished, its flight so thunderbolt-fast that the eye could not follow it. Then gardeners appeared and then an early guest or two, and we moved into the hotel, satisfied that it was worth travelling all the way from London to Quebec, and from Quebec to Vancouver Island if only to have seen so much of the loveliness of the world concentrated in one tiny creature measuring three and a quarter inches from tip of beak to tip of tail.

I was talking to a Canadian country boy afterwards, and he said: " I'm scared of humming-birds. They fly so fast, and, if one of them flew against your forehead, its beak would go right into your brain and kill you. Oh," he said, " I don't like humming-birds."

ROBERT LYND from the *News-Chronicle*

Close to the very entrance of the Convict Trail behind
Kalacoon stood four sentinel trees. Every day we passed
and repassed them on the way to and from the jungle.
For many days we paid very little attention to them,
except to be grateful for the shade cast by their dense
foliage of glossy leaves. Their trunks were their most
striking feature, the bark almost concealed by a maze of
beautifully coloured lichens, different forms overlapping
one another in many places, forming a palimpsest of gray,
white, pink, mauve and lilac. One day a streaked fly-
catcher chose the top of a branch for her nest, and this
we watched and photographed and robbed for science's
sake, and again we thought no more of the four trees.

Late in April, however, a change came over the trees.
The leaves had been shed sometime in January and the
fallen foliage formed a dry mass on the ground which
crackled under foot. Now each branch and twig began
to send out clusters of small buds, and one day,—a week
after Easter,—these burst into indescribable glory. Every
lichened bough and branch and twig was lined with a
soft mass of bloom, clear, bright cerise, which reflected
its brilliance on the foliage itself. After two days a rain
of stamens began and soon the ground beneath the trees
was solid cerise, a carpet of tens of thousands of fallen
stamens, and within the length of a foot on one small
branch were often a score of blooms. This feast of colour
was wonderful enough, and it made us want to know more
of these trees. But all the information we could glean was
that they were called French cashew. Yet they had not
nearly finished with the surprises they had in store. A
humming-bird or two was not an uncommon sight along
the trail at any time, but now we began to notice an

increase in numbers. Then it was observed that the tiny
birds seemed to focus their flight upon one part of the
clearing, and this proved to be the four cashew trees.

The next few days made the trees ever memorable:
they were the Mecca of all the humming-birds in the
jungle. In early morning the air for many yards resounded
with a dull droning, as of a swarming of giant bees. Standing or sitting under the tree we could detect the units of
this host and then the individuals forced themselves on
our notice. Back and forth the hummers swooped and
swung, now poising in front of a mass of blossom and
probing deeply among the stamens, now dashing off at a
tangent, squeaking or chattering their loudest. The mag-
nitude of the total sound made by these feathered atoms
was astounding; piercing squeaks, shrill insect-like tones,
and now and then a real song, diminutive trills and warbles
as if from a flock of song birds a long distance away.
Combats and encounters were frequent, some mere sparring bouts, while, when two would go at it in earnest,
their humming and squeaks and throb of wings were
audible above the general noise.

WILLIAM BEEBE from *Jungle Peace*

I observed closely for one hour and counted one hundred
and forty-six humming-birds coming to the tree. During
the day at least one thousand must visit it.

They did not have a monopoly of the cashew manna,
for now and then a honey-creeper or flower-pecker flew
into the tree and took toll of the sweets. But they were
scarcely noticeable. We had almost a pure culture of
humming-birds to watch and vainly to attempt to study,

for more elusive creatures do not exist. Convict Trail
revealed no more beautiful a sight than this concentration
of the smallest, most active and the most gorgeous birds
in the world.

Such treats—floral and avian—were all that might be
expected of any tree, but the cashews had still more
treasures in store. The weeks passed and we had almost

Scarlet Tanagers on a Cashew Branch

forgotten the flowers and humming-birds, when a new
odour greeted us, the sweet, intense smell of overripe
fruit. We noticed a scattering of soft yellow cashews
fallen here and there, and simultaneously there arrived
the hosts of fruit-eating birds. From the most delicate
turquoise honey-creepers to great red and black gros-
beaks, they thronged the trees. All day a perfect stream

of tanagers—green, azure and wine-coloured—flew in
and about the manna, callistes and silver beaks, dacnis and
palm tanagers.   WILLIAM BEEBE from *Jungle Peace*

THE HUMMING BIRD (PRINCETON, NEW JERSEY)

Green wing and ruby throat,
  What shining spell, what exquisite sorcery,
Lured you to float
  And fight with bees round this one flowering tree?

Petulant imps of light,
  What whisper or gleam or elfin-wild perfume,
Thrilled through the night
  And drew you to this hive of rosy bloom?

One tree, and one alone,
  Of all that load this magic air with spice
Claims for its own
  Your brave migration out of Paradise;

Claims you, and guides you, too,
  Three thousand miles across the summer's waste
Of blooms ye knew
  Less finely fit for your ethereal taste.

To poets' youthful hearts,
  Even so the quivering April thoughts will fly,—
Those irised darts,
  Those winged and tiny denizens of the sky.

Through beaks as needle fine
  They suck a redder honey than bees know.
Unearthly wine
  Sleeps in this bloom; and, when it falls, they go.
                                        ALFRED NOYES

There is just a short half-hour after sunset when the bats begin to fly and one can see to shoot them against the fast waning light in the west. On one of our last evenings of camp life I was trying to shoot some small bats that were flitting round the tents. The first that dropped I failed to find in the darkness, so I marked the place where it seemed to fall by a small pyramid of mud. By this time the sun's glow had faded, but a brilliant moon had risen, and thinking I should be able to see the bats flying over the water, I moved down to the edge of the river. As I was standing there a hawk-like bird appeared like a ghost from over the river. As it passed me I raised my gun mechanically and fired, but the bird went on and in ten yards or so was out of sight. I thought no more about it as my gun was loaded with dust shot and the bird seemed large and some distance off. Tiring at length of shooting by moonlight I returned to the camp, and calling for a lantern, went to search for the bat at the place I had marked with a heap of mud. As the light flashed on the spot, there lying dead with outspread wings was the glorious golden goatsucker. I picked it up and rushed madly to my companions. The Arabs looked on in wonder at three frantic Englishmen dancing and shouting round a bird. It was one of those rare occasions in a naturalist's camp when champagne would seem a necessity. Having none we drank to the goatsucker in whisky and White Nile water.

H. F. WITHERBY from *Bird Hunting on the White Nile*

I am delighted to hear you say that you have *one* egg of the Flamingo for me, but when shall I see it is another

affair?—You say also that you have young ones under
way to make experiments as regards their progressive
changes of plumage, but would it not be much better to
send me one of these young birds to figure (a thing quite
new to the world of Science) and thereby enable ourselves
to fulfil the whole of our enquiries respecting this very
remarkable Bird?—I have noted what you have gathered
of their habits—but to me the most essential point remains in darkness—to wit—Whether they set on their
nest with legs dangling on the outsides??? a thing which
I cannot believe, until I hear *you* affirm it!

JOHN JAMES AUDUBON in a letter (1837)

Philadelphia, Sun., Oct. 23, 1836. Now Good Friend open
your Eyes! aye open them tight!! Nay place specks on
your probosis if you chuse! Read aloud!! quite aloud!!!
—I have purchased *Ninety Three Bird Skins!* Yes 93
Bird Skins sent from the Rocky Mountains and the
Columbia River by Nuttall & Townsend!—Cheap as
Dirt too—only one hundred and Eighty Four Dollars
for the whole of these, and hang me if you do not echo
my saying so when *you see them! !*—Such beauties! such
rarities! Such Novelties! Ah my Worthy Friend how we
will laugh and talk over them!

JOHN JAMES AUDUBON in a letter (1836)

April 22, 1749. The Swedes give the name of Whipperiwill,
and the English that of Whip-poor-will, to a kind of
nocturnal bird whose voice is heard in North America,
TB

almost throughout the whole night. Catesby and Edwards both have described and figured it. Dr. Linnaeus calls it a variety of the *Caprimulgus Europaeus*, or Goatsucker; its shape, colour, size, and other qualities, make it difficult to distinguish them from each other. But the peculiar note of the American one distinguishes it from the European one, and from all other birds; it is not found here during winter, but returns with the beginning of summer. I heard it to-day, for the first time, and many other people said that they had not heard it before this summer; its English and Swedish name is taken from its note; but, accurately speaking, it does not call Whipperiwill, nor Whip-poor-will, but rather, Whipperiwip, so that the first and last syllables are accented, and the intermediate one but slightly pronounced. The English change the call of this bird into Whip-poor-will, that it may have some kind of signification: it is neither heard nor seen in day-time; but soon after sunset it begins to call, and continues for a good while, as the cuckoo does in Europe. After it has continued calling in a place for some time, it removes to another, and begins again: it usually comes several times in a night, and settles close to houses; I have seen it coming late in the evening, and settling on the steps of the house in order to sing its song; it is very shy and when a person stood still, it would settle close by him, and begin to call. It came to the houses in order to get its food, which consists of insects; and those always abound near the houses at night; when it sat and called its whip-periwhip, and saw an insect passing, it flew up and caught it, and settled again. Sometimes you hear four or five, or more, near each other, calling as it were for a wager, and raising a great noise in the woods. They were seldom heard in towns, being either extirpated there, or frightened away, by frequent shooting. They do not like to sit on trees, but are commonly on the ground, or very low in bushes, or on the lower poles of the enclosures. They always fly near the ground: they continue their calling at night till it grows quite dark; they are silent till the dawn of day comes on, and then they call till the sun rises. The sun seems to stop their mouths, or dazzle their eyes, so as to make them sit still. I have never heard them call in the midst of night, though I harkened very attentively on purpose to hear it; and many others have done the same. I am told they make no nest, but lay two eggs in the open fields. My servant shot at one which sat on a bush near the house, and though he did not hit it, yet it fell down through fear, and lay for some time as if dead; but recovered afterwards. It never attempted to bite when it was held in the hands, only endeavouring to get loose by stirring itself about. Above, and close under the eyes, were several black, long, and stiff bristles, as in other nocturnal birds. The Europeans eat it. Mr. Catesby says the Indians affirm that they never saw these birds, or heard of them, before a certain great battle, in which the Europeans killed a great number of Indians. Therefore, they suppose that these birds, which are restless, and utter their plaintive note at nights, are the souls of their ancestors who died in battle.

PETER KALM from *Travels into North America*

Of all the birds of Lombock, however, I sought most after the beautiful ground thrushes (*Pitta concinna*), and always thought myself lucky if I obtained one. They were found only in the dry plains densely covered with thickets, and carpeted at this season with dead leaves. They were so shy that it was very difficult to get a shot at them, and it was only after a good deal of practice that I discovered how to do it. The habit of these birds is to hop about on the ground, picking up insects, and on the least alarm to run into the densest thicket or take a flight close along the

Jungle Cock

ground. At intervals they utter a peculiar cry of two notes which when once heard is easily recognized, and they can also be heard hopping along among the dry leaves. My practice was, therefore, to walk cautiously along the narrow pathways with which the country abounded, and on detecting any sign of a Pitta's vicinity to stand motionless and give a gentle whistle occasionally, imitating the notes as near as possible. After half an hour's waiting I was often rewarded by seeing the pretty bird hopping along in the thicket. Then I would perhaps lose sight of it again, till, having my gun raised and ready for a shot, a second glimpse would enable me to secure my prize, and admire its soft puffy plumage and lovely colours. The upper part is rich soft green, the head jet black with a stripe of blue and brown over each eye; at the base of the tail and on the shoulders are bands of bright silvery blue, and the under side is delicate buff with a stripe of rich crimson, bordered with black on the belly. Beautiful grass-green doves, little crimson and black flower-peckers, large black cuckoos, metallic king-crows, golden orioles, and the fine jungle-cocks—the origin of all our domestic breeds of poultry—were among the birds that chiefly attracted my attention during our stay at Labuan Tring.

ALFRED RUSSEL WALLACE from *The Malay Archipelago*

The Megapodidae are a small family of birds found only in Australia and the surrounding islands, but extending as far as the Philippines and North-west Borneo. They are allied to the gallinaceous birds, but differ from these and from all others in never sitting upon their eggs, which they bury in sand, earth, or rubbish, and leave to be hatched by the heat of the sun or of fermentation. They are all characterized by very large feet and long curved claws, and most of the species of Megapodius rake and scratch together all kinds of rubbish, dead leaves, sticks, stones, earth, rotten wood, etc., till they form a large mound, often six feet high and twelve feet across, in the middle of which they bury their eggs. The natives can tell by the condition of these mounds whether they contain eggs or not; and they rob them whenever they can, as the brick-red eggs (as large as those of a swan) are considered a great delicacy. A number of birds are said to join in making these mounds and lay their eggs together, so that sometimes forty or fifty may be found. The mounds are to be met with here and there in dense thickets, and are great puzzles to strangers, who cannot understand who can possibly have heaped together cartloads of rubbish in such out-of-the-way places; and when they inquire of the natives they are but little wiser, for it almost always appears to them the wildest romance to be told that it is all done by birds. The species found in Lombock is about the size of a small hen, and entirely of dark olive and brown tints. It is a miscellaneous feeder, devouring fallen fruits, earth-worms, snails, and centipedes, but the flesh is white and well-flavoured when properly cooked.

ALFRED RUSSEL WALLACE from *The Malay Archipelago*

Jan. 1850. In the evening after dark he returned, bringing one fine specimen. This singular bird is about the size of a raven, and is of a similar colour, but its feathers have a more scaly appearance, from being margined with a different shade of glossy blue. It is also allied to the crow in its structure, being very similar to them in its feet and bill. On its head it bears a crest, different from that of any other bird. It is formed of feathers more than two inches long, very thickly set, and with hairy plumes curling over at the end. These can be laid back so as to be hardly visible, or can be erected and spread out on every side, forming a hemispherical, or rather a hemi-ellipsoidal dome, completely covering the head, and even reaching beyond the point of the beak: the individual feathers then stand out something like the down-bearing seeds of the dandelion. Besides this, there is another ornamental appendage on the breast, formed by a fleshy tubercle, as thick as a quill and an inch and a half long, which hangs down from the neck, and is thickly covered with glossy feathers, forming a large pendent plume or tassel. This also the bird can either press to its breast,

Umbrella Bird

so as to be scarcely visible, or can swell out, so as almost to conceal the forepart of its body. In the female the crest and the neck-plume are less developed, and she is altogether a smaller and much less handsome bird. It inhabits the flooded islands of the Rio Negro and the Solimões, never appearing on the mainland. It feeds on fruits, and utters a loud, hoarse cry, like some deep musical instrument; whence its Indian name, *Ueramimbé*, "trumpetbird." The whole of the neck, where the plume of feathers springs from, is covered internally with a thick coat of hard, muscular fat, very difficult to be cleaned away,—which, in preparing the skins, must be done, as it would putrefy, and cause the feathers to drop off. The birds are tolerably abundant, but are shy, and perch on the highest trees, and, being very muscular, will not fall unless severely wounded. My hunter worked very perseveringly to get them, going out before daylight and often not returning till nine or ten at night, yet he never brought me more than two at a time, generally only one, and sometimes none.

ALFRED RUSSEL WALLACE from *A Narrative of Travels on the Amazon and Rio Negro*

Between Makalla and Bir Ali. . . . As we drove back by the sea, along the strip of wet sand at the edge of the waves, gulls rose like a fluttering grey ribbon before us and sank again behind. They live here in countless numbers. They seem black and white as raindrops when they fly against the water. On the white sands they look like white pearls, and like grey pearls on the brown, and they swim strung out like pearls upon the waves. Now,

as their barrage rose and fell, they made a canopy of
shadow with their wings. They rose only just high enough
to clear us, wheeling and almost touching; and one mis-
judged his distance and hit me and fell stunned in my lap.
I picked him up, stiff with fear; only his eyes moved,
surrounded by a delicate black beading like the glass of
a miniature; his beak was red, its upper point curved over
the lower; his feet were webbed and pale; and as I let
his body slip away to freedom, the grey feathers felt cool
and smooth as the sea they live on.

FREYA STARK from *The Southern Gates of Arabia*

I was on my way to the Leakeys' archaeological camp at
Elmenteita.

The camp—a couple of huts and some tents—is set
over against the far scarp of the Kenya rift, in wildish
country. Coming hither you must pass close to the southern
end of Elmenteita Lake. As we came in view of it, I could
not help exclaiming at its strange likeness to the English
lakes—dark grey-blue waters hemmed in by low hills,
regular north-country fells on which grew yellowish grass
and patches of bushes and small dark trees among the
rocky scars. (I later found this same yellowish grass, so
like the moor-grass of our northern hills, combining with
the hill shapes to give to the north end of the neighbouring
Lake Nakuru a delusive, derisory likeness to Capel Curig
or other North Welsh scenery.)

A little bay, charming in the extreme, irregular with
promontories and rocky knolls crowned with scattered
trees, ran in towards us. It might have been transplanted

from Windermere, after having been commemorated by Wordsworth in one of his innumerable sonnets. But the final touch was most un-Wordsworthian. Not daffodils bordered it, but flamingoes. At first sight they too had a flowerlike air, as of enormous lotuses or lilies thrusting themselves out of water to burst into bloom. But then the lotuses raised sinuous necks from their subaqueous browsing; they looked at us with suspicion; they began to walk. Flamingoes, supreme combination of the grotesque and the beautiful: Windermere with its shores bordered by great rosy birds! Then suddenly I saw that the far shore, four or five miles away, was bordered with pink. Surely this could not be birds?—it must be some geological deposit, some incrustation. But the glasses insisted on the fantastic truth—it was all birds, battalions of birds, massed in a pink continuous army. JULIAN HUXLEY from *Africa View*

The bird was a *Vanellus*, a lapwing in its shape, crest, and the colour of its plumage, closely allied to our familiar bird of the moors and pasture-lands but a third bigger, with pink beak, crimson eyes, scarlet spurs on its wings, and bright red legs, and these touches of colour, " angrie and brave," give it a strikingly bold appearance. Our green plover is like a small weak copy of the Argentine bird. The voice of the latter, too, is twice as loud, and its temper more jealous and violent. In its habits it resembles the peewit, but has a greater love of play, which it practises, both when flying and on the ground. This play on the ground, called by the natives the bird's " dance," is performed by a set of three, and is indulged in every day

Flamingoes

at intervals all the year round. So fond of it are they that when the birds are distributed in pairs all over the plains, for some time before and during the breeding season, one bird may frequently be seen to leave his mate at home and fly away to visit another pair in the neighbourhood. These, instead of rising up with angry screams to hunt him furiously away from their sacred ground as they would any other bird, receive his visit with manifest pleasure, and running to him where he stands motionless, they place themselves behind him, standing abreast, their plumage puffed out, and then with loud, rhythmical, drumming notes uttered by the pair, and loud single measured notes by the leader, they begin a rapid march, stepping in time to the music; then, when the march is ended the leader as a rule lifts his wings and holds them erect, still emitting loud notes, while the two behind, still standing abreast with slightly opened wings and puffed-out feathers, lower their heads until the tips of their beaks touch the ground, at the same time sinking their voices until the drumming sound dies to a whisper. The performance is then over, and is repeated, or if the visitor is in a hurry he takes his departure, to rejoin his mate and receive a visitor himself by-and-by.

One dry summer, long after the breeding season was over, while out riding I passed by a lagoon, or lakelet, where the birds from all the plain for some miles round were accustomed to come to drink, and noticed a gathering of about a hundred lapwings standing quietly near the water. It was evident they had all had their drink and bath, and were drying and preening their feathers and resting before going back to their several feeding-grounds. On seeing them my attention was instantly arrested by the singular behaviour of two birds, the only restless noisy ones in that quiet, silent company. It was not a close company; every bird had a good space to himself, his nearest neighbour standing a foot or more away, and right in among them the two restless birds were trotting freely about, uttering loud commanding notes, and apparently greatly excited about something. I had seen nothing like that before, and it puzzled me to account for their action. By-and-by there was a fresh arrival; a lapwing came to drink, and instead of dropping down on the edge of the water, he alighted about thirty feet away, at a distance of two or three yards from the others, and remained there, standing erect and motionless as if waiting. The two busy birds, still crying aloud, now made their way to him, and placing themselves behind him and observing all the attitudes and gestures used in their " dances " or marches and giving the signal, the three set off at a trot to the sound of drums and the thirsty bird was run down to the water. He at once went in to the depth of his knees and drank, then squatting down, bathed his feathers, the whole process lasting about half a minute. He would, no doubt, have taken much longer over his refreshment but for the two birds who had run him down to the water, and who continued standing on the margin emitting their loud authoritative cries. Coming out, he was again received as at first, and trotted briskly away with drumming sounds to a place with the others. No sooner was this done than the two, smoothing their feathers and changing their notes, resumed their marching about among their fellows, until another lapwing arrived, whereupon the whole ceremony was gone through again.

Without a doubt this performance had nothing but

play for a motive, the remarkable thing about it was that it was made to fit so admirably into the serious business which brought them together at that spot. They came, one by one, from all over the plain, at noon on a hot thirsty day, solely for refreshment, yet every bird on arrival instantly fell into the humour of the moment and took his appointed part and place in the game. It struck me at the time as a very strange thing, for well as I knew the bird, I had never witnessed an act precisely like this before. Yet it does not stand alone, except in form; any day and every day we may see acts in other species of social disposition or habits, which are undoubtedly inspired by a similar spirit. Little sham quarrels and flights and chases; we see them squaring up to one another with threatening gestures and language; playing little practical jokes too, as when one approaches another in a friendly way and subtly watches him to snatch a morsel from his beak; or when another pretends to have found something exceptionally good and makes a great fuss about it to deceive a comrade, and when the other carries the joke further by capturing and carrying off the bit of dry stick or whatever it is, and pretending to feast on it with great satisfaction. These and a hundred other little playful acts of the kind are common enough and mingle with and are like a part of the food-getting or other business of the moment.

The strangeness of the plover's performance was due to the singular form which play in them almost invariably takes—the military discipline in all their movements, their drumming sounds and commanding cries, the tremendous formality of it all! The two birds were like little children pretending to be some mighty personages who owned everything and lorded it over the others. They were dispensers of the water of the lake, and were graciously pleased to allow any thirsty bird that came to drink and bathe, but only after the proper ceremonies had been performed; also the drinking and bathing had to be cut rather short on these occasions.

W. H. HUDSON from *Adventures Among Birds*

Wild Turkeys

Striped like a gaudy convict—and for the same reasons, for he was a dangerous murderer—a large coral snake lay coiled near the foot of the tallest obelisk. At our approach, he woke and oozed slowly away, inch after tricoloured inch, into his hole. And while we were standing in front of the most extraordinary of the monuments— the huge mythological animal that lies at one corner of the southern pyramid—there was a sudden noise in the trees overhead. Looking up, we saw a flock of toucans hopping clumsily among the branches; grotesque, like a ribald human invention; and as they moved, their great bills would flash startlingly in the light, like drawn daggers. ALDOUS HUXLEY from *Beyond the Mexique Bay*

The wild turkey, the burrowing owl, the whip-poor-will, the cardinal—in the Old World there is nothing like these. The family of mocking-birds is wholly American, with its catbirds and thrashers. Ours only are the hummingbirds, the vireos, and the gorgeous, black-dashed, whistling *Ictaridae*—orioles and meadow-larks, bobolinks and grackles and redwinged blackbirds. The tanagers are ours, the phoebe and pewee; the two families of warblers keep each to its own side of the Atlantic, and though they are like enough in their habits, they sing to different tunes.

DONALD CULROSS PEATTIE from *Singing in the Wilderness*

So I fell to dreaming on my country, the past and the present indistinguishable. Ox-teams and covered wagons lumbering down a bank between sallows to a ford of the

Platte; men going west for gold that most of them would never find. Farmers getting into their Fords in a green twilight, their children hugging their own ribs with excitement, to go to the movies in the town and see people rich as they are rich only on the screen. . . . The Puritan Fathers, writing home about the fertility of New England, the wonderful climate, God's hand over them. The subdivision: lonely pavements and street signs, " Broadway," and " Rosemount Boulevard "; God's hand over advertising men. Black men and women let up out of the slaver's hold, to look at the palmetto-lined shore they shall inherit. Daniel Boone, blazing death among the antlers and the wigwams of Kentucky. Young men digging to-day, to put the forests back; billions for relief in a country that could not slay the bison fast enough, that feasted on the tongues and left the carcasses to rot.

This is the land to which came other men, but not Jean Jacques Audubon. Nothing ever really happened to him except birds, for he took nothing else seriously. Even his love affair, his marriage and his home were as those of the birds—a mating for life, a nesting here and there, a foraging by God's grace, a wide roaming and a sure return.

The America to which Audubon came is the bittern and the kinglet, the flamingo and the flicker.

DONALD CULROSS PEATTIE from *Singing in the Wilderness*

When the Mormons established their earliest settlement in Utah, their first crops were almost destroyed by myriads of black crickets. In the following season the crickets

UB

again appeared and the settlers were in despair, as the failure of their second crop would have meant starvation. Then Sea-Gulls came in thousands and devoured the insects so that the fields were freed from them. The settlers regarded this as a heaven-sent miracle and the event is commemorated in Salt Lake City by a monument. . . .   W. B. ALEXANDER from *Birds of the Ocean*

Of all the descriptions of prairie creatures, that of a certain bird charmed me most. This bird was the Road-Runner, a bloodthirsty killer whose eyes were " flaming red," and whose speed was the speed of a race horse. He was known by such colloquial names as Chapparal Cock, Ground Cuckoo, and Snake Killer. He was the ancient foe of the rattlesnake, round whom he built walls of cactus and whom he fought to the death. What prowess, what strength, what craftiness must be the Road-Runners's, I thought, as I longed to see this terror of the sandy wilderness. I was not anxious, however, that our first meeting should be intimate.

This meeting was inevitable. Walking across the prairie, I entered a ravine whose nearer bank was covered with bushes and vines. Instantly, hearing a sharp rattle, I halted. Was I in a snake's den? Turning cautiously I saw a bird, about two feet long, with coarsely streaked plumage. For a second he looked at me, then raised his high, steel-black crest, disclosing a red-orange, featherless patch back of his eye. Again I heard the arresting rattle as his mandibles clapped together. He bounded with unbelievable ease over some low bushes, then, spreading his short wings which

were obviously unfit for sustained flight, soared down the
gully, dropped into the maze of gray-green, and was gone.
I had met the Road-Runner! I had been close enough to
ascertain that not his eyes, but the bare patches *back of
his eyes* were red, and that his tail was very long. His
perfectly calculated leaping haunted my memory for days.

During the following care-free years I was to learn
much about this famous bird. I saw him often. I found
his nest. Finally, I took it upon myself to raise two young
from early infancy.

One day in late April, 1914, while pushing my way
through a dense, cobweb-hung thicket, I spied not far
in front of me a crude mass of twigs. Instantly on the alert,
I wiped the caterpillar silk from my eyelashes and looked
at the unshapely structure more closely. A hopelessly
lopsided, poorly anchored nest it was, but above it,
parallel with a supporting branch, was the long, iridescent
tail of a bird. In moving, I disturbed a small vine. At
once there peered over the rim an angular face with lifted
crest and blazing eyes. There was a flash of scarlet; then,
with scarcely a rustle of leaf or tremor of tendril, the
muscular creature slid away. There was a soft thud as
strong feet touched the ground. A thin form faded into
the weeds. Wings unspread, the mother Road-Runner had
bounded clear of the dense tangle.

There was a weird nestful. Crouching beside a soiled
egg were five ugly youngsters whose dark-skinned bodies
were sparsely covered with long, white hairs, and whose
beaks were tipped with the hard egg-tooth of babyhood.
Their flabby feet, two toes pointing forward, two backward,
were dull blue. Their eyes were gray-brown, with steel-
blue pupils and a reptilian stare. Pinfeathers had just

begun to appear on the edge of the wings. Were these four-inch, greasy-looking, uncouth things really baby birds? Though I had had no experience in caring for such charges I decided to take two of them home.

Young Road-Runner

As I stood there I wondered what I was to feed these infant dragons. Accidentally I touched an upturned beak and four great mouths, wabbling uncertainly on scrawny necks, rose in unison. I jerked back my hand—the pink-blotched lining of those mouths had an almost poisonous appearance. From the depths of the small frames came a hoarse, many-toned buzzing which gave the impression that a colony of winged insects had been stirred to anger.

Puzzled by the motionlessness of one of the young I examined him more closely and was startled at finding an inch of the tail of a large lizard protruding from his mouth. He had been fed enough to keep his digestive apparatus busy for some time; for, as the gastric fluids would make assimilable that part of the lizard which had entered his stomach, he had only to swallow a little more to prolong his meal. For a four-inch Road-Runner a lizard nine inches long should furnish an enduring repast.

I had learned at least that my pets were carnivorous. At home my long-suffering family gathered round the unattractive pair, exhibiting all the enthusiasm at their command, and wondering, no doubt, when this gathering of crawling, creeping, buzzing and squeaking creatures was to end. We found an old bucket, lined it with dry grass, and placed the birds in their new nest. It took them but an instant to adjust themselves. Once they had assumed their normal attitude they began buzzing for food. For the following two weeks this clamour was almost incessant. It greeted us early in the morning; the merest human whisper or footfall near the bucket roused it instantly. I was to learn much, sometimes to my annoyance, about the rapidity with which young Road-Runners digest their food.

After three weeks they became sturdy enough to catch part of their own food. With patient coaxing they were taught to pick up grasshoppers tossed to them, and finally to run after and capture crippled insects. Content at first, perforce, with sluggish, wingless nymphs which were abundant, they stole about through the weeds, wings pressed neatly against their slender bodies, snapping up the insects as fast as they could find them. Grasshoppers, often still alive and kicking, they swallowed with a toss of the head and a hollow gulp. Large green or gray cave-crickets which lived in piles of boards, or in damp, shadowy places, were especially prized. When a yellow- or coral-winged grasshopper rose noisily from the path, the birds crouched in momentary fear, but soon began to mark the return to earth of the clackety aeronaut and to steal up behind tufts of grass, intent upon a killing.

Finally they learned to capture the biggest, noisiest, and wariest grasshoppers on the prairie. They would watch a coral-wing in his courtship flight and, running stealthily, wait until the performer dropped to the ground. With a bound over low weeds, a dart across the open, and a final rush with outspread wings and tail they would frighten their prey into the air, leap nimbly after him, nab him unerringly with their bills, and descend gracefully on outspread wings to beat him to insensibility with a whack or two on a stone.

Once they had learned to capture grasshoppers, their food problem was largely solved and, since they showed no inclination to run away, they were at liberty most of the time. They ran about the yard, playing with each other, or catching insects. In the heat of mid-day they sought the shelter of broad, cool leaves, and sprawled in the sand. Daily, often many times daily, I took them for a walk across the prairie. Following me closely or running at my side, they watched the big world with eyes far keener than my own. Grasshoppers which I frightened from the grass they captured in side expeditions. If I paused near a flat stone, they urged me on with grunts, bit gently at my hands, and raced back and forth in an ecstasy of anticipation.

I entertained misgivings concerning these flat stones. What savage creatures might not they conceal! Could young Road-Runners manage swift-tailed scorpions, sharp-toothed mice, or poisonous spiders? Under the first stone there were scorpions. The Road-Runners hesitated an instant, as if permitting an untried instinct to take possession of their brains, then rushed forward, thrust out their heads, and attacked the scorpions precisely at their tails. Perhaps these venomous tails received more than the usual number of benumbing blows, but the scorpions were swallowed with gusto.

I had not supposed that a Road-Runner would capture and devour a tarantula. One day, however, we paused at the tunnel of one of these big, furred spiders. Somewhat in the spirit of experimentation, and following the method known to all Texas boys, I teased the black Arachnid from her lair by twirling a wisp of grass in her face. She popped out viciously and jumped a good ten inches to one side. With a dash one bird was upon the monster before she had opportunity to leap a second time. A toss of the bird's head and one of the eight legs was gone. Free again, the spider leaped upon her captor. The other bird now entered the combat, snatched up the spider, and flicked off another leg. One by one the legs went down, and finally the two birds pulled apart and gulped the sable torso.

Tarantulas were now our prey. Whenever we came upon a burrow the birds ran about wildly, looked longingly at the hole, begged noisily for food, then rushed back and forth flashing their tails. Imagine my delight, my wonder too, one day, at seeing one of the birds pick up a tiny pebble and, after creeping up slyly, drop it into the neat orifice.

Life on the prairie was pleasant and eventful. Each dawn promised new conquests; each expedition along the roads had its excitement and rewards. But these happy days were numbered. In July, when the birds were almost three months old, we moved to northern West Virginia. I was exceedingly fond of my pets, and feared leaving them behind would mean their early death. We made a wire cage, covered it with a cloth, and took them with us on the train. . . .

Arrived at our destination, a hamlet sequestered among cool hills, I thought first of all of the Road-Runners. Chilled by fog, sick from lack of exercise and improper food, and, worst of all, minus their handsome tails, they were forlorn indeed as they walked about sedately on the cement walks and neat lawn of the college campus. . . .

In September the campus hummed with the return of students. Frosty mornings with their lavender-coloured asters and scarlet maple leaves heralded a winter which would be difficult indeed for the aliens. I was so busy that I could not properly care for my pets, which now ran hither and yon through the countryside. For a week or two I saw little of the Road-Runners, though daily I heard reports of strange birds seen here and there along the roads sometimes some distance from town.

Winter in West Virginia is rarely severe; but it is damp, and there is little in the way of food for Road-Runners. I made plans for sending them back to their Texas prairie. I considered feeding and keeping them indoors for winter. But when I tried to locate them, they were not to be found. I spent many hours, day after day, in searching. Through likely meadows, now rank with iron-weed and strewn with silken milkweed balloons, I wandered in the morning, or after school hours, eager to glimpse a familiar slender form, or to hear the sharp rattle of mandibles. But I failed to find the birds.

One afternoon, when I returned from college, my mother told me of a dead bird, wrapped in a newspaper, brought by a man who had heard I was interested in collecting specimens. Two odd creatures had rushed up to him from the roadside, he had said, fluttering their wings as if they were baby birds, begging for food; and he had killed one of them with a stick.

I did not need to unwrap the slender package, for I saw a familiar foot sticking out at the end. I should not have known, anyway, whether it was Titania or Oberon who had been returned to me.

GEORGE MIKSCH SUTTON from *Birds in the Wilderness*

July Seventh. It was to an America still partly wilderness, fresh with adventure, that the weary and driven little Scotsman came. You could expect in our woods then an ivory-billed wood-pecker, the largest of all its tribe, a creature known to me only as a perfectly incredible specimen in museums. It has a glossy black body almost two feet long, a head crested with scarlet, and a great bill, ivory white. A native of Brazil and Mexico, it is now extinct without our borders.

Not so in Wilson's time. He easily captured a specimen in the cypress swamps near Wilmington, North Carolina, and was conveying it, imprisoned under a blanket, in a large basket, to an inn, when it suddenly burst into the most ear-splitting and dismal sounds, like the voice of a baby in agony. Several women on the porch of the inn cast dark looks at the poor little man, as though he had been a kidnapper or an ogre. Marching proudly by them, Wilson conveyed the bird to his room to paint it. But it abruptly left off sitting for its portrait, and violently attacked Wilson about the face with the bill that is made to split oak. Fleeing the room, Wilson after an hour returned to hear the sound as of twenty wood choppers at work. He threw open the door, and discovered that his tropical carpenter had battered his way through the inner wall, and at that moment was engaged in enlarging an opening in the clapboards outside wide enough to admit his scarlet-crested head. Restrained in this, the proud spirited fowl moped and died, leaving Wilson his ivory bill and the inn-keeper's bill for repairs.

DONALD CULROSS PEATTIE from *An Almanac for Moderns*

You will not find the word *Kint* in the dictionaries. You will not hear any of your friends using it. But if you go

to the wooded swamps along the Tinsaw River (this is
spelled *Tensas* River on the maps) in the northeastern
Loosiana (this is spelled *Louisiana*), you will sooner or
later hear about a big black and white woodpecker-bird,

Ivory-Billed Woodpecker

bigger than a crow, and with a white bill, that lives way back among the maples and gums and cypresses along Methiglum Bough and John's Bough (and Bough is spelled *Bayou*). This little-known, little-seen bird is the *Kint*, the famous Ivory-bill, a woodpecker that for decades has been considered one of the rarest of North American birds. . . .

Since my companions had failed to find Ivory-bills in other parts of Florida they had visited earlier in the season, we decided to try Louisiana. Driving westward across Alabama, Mississippi, and Ol' Man River, we found ourselves in a land that was entirely new to me—a land of timber wolves, panthers, razor-back hawgs, and deer—the broad, wet valley of the Tinsaw.

Here, after making inquiries, we found an attorney-at-law named Spencer, who was good enough to tell us what he knew about the country, to show us his big maps, to warn us about the mosquitoes and the dangers of becoming lost, and to put us in touch with friends of his who would help us find the Ivory-bills.

The talk in Mr. Spencer's office kept us on the edge of our chairs. There could be no doubt that we were in a fearful and wonderful country. We were amazed to learn that mammalogists considered wolves more common in this section of Louisiana than in any other part of the United States. Wild Turkeys were abundant. White-tailed deer thronged the swamplands.

I was still in some doubt, however, about the Ivory-bills. Fearing that Mr. Spencer might, in his eagerness to help us, be confusing the Ivory-bill with the Pileated, which is also a large and showy woodpecker, I said, " Mr.

Spencer, you're sure the bird you're telling us about isn't the big Pileated Woodpecker, the bird the Florida Crackers call the ' Lord God Almighty '? "

" Man alive! " answered Mr. Spencer hotly, " these birds I'm tellin' you all about is Kints! Why, the Pileated Woodpecker's just a little bird about as big as that "— he indicated with his fingers an object a few inches long— " and a Kint's as big as that! " He moved his arms generously apart, fisherman fashion, and glared at me. " Why, man, I've known Kints all my life. My pappy showed 'em to me when I was just a kid. I see 'em every fall when I go deer huntin' down aroun' my place on the Tinsaw. They're *big* birds, I tell you, big and black and white; and they fly through the woods like Pintail Ducks! " . . .

Our search began. Led by Kuhn, an energetic, friendly, and well-informed man, we made our way back through the timber, following first a dim, muddy road; then an old trail across turkey country, where the ground was comparatively dry; and finally an opening through a mile or so of wet swamp, to John's Bough. Here Kuhn showed us the very trees where Kints had recently been seen. Here we found chips of dead wood eight or ten inches long that had been chiselled out by big woodpeckers of some sort. But the big woodpeckers that we saw were all Pileateds. Here, again, the Pileateds were common. . . .

On the third day of our search we decided to plunge more deeply into the swamp. So, crossing John's Bough once more, we walked directly eastward through a twilight of gigantic trees, poison ivy, and invisible pools, turned sharply right, and began a reconnaissance of new country. There were four of us—Professor Allen, leader of the expedition, at the extreme right, then Kuhn, then myself, and to my left Jim Tanner. Shouting loudly, so as not to lose any one, but keeping several rods apart so as to cover more territory, we marched abreast. The tangle was so dense we gave up trying to avoid the ivy.

We had gone about a quarter of a mile when, emerging from a tangle of cat's claw, I thought I heard Kuhn shouting something to me. His voice was way off somewhere, ahead and to the right. I could not make out what he said, for the swamp was ringing with echoes. Shouting to Jim to follow, I finally caught up with Kuhn, who was agog. He had heard an Ivory-bill. He had been shouting to us, imploring us to listen. His face was a study, for he was transported with boyish joy.

" Right there, men! " he was saying in a tense voice. " Didn't any of you hear it? I heard it plain, several times. Right in that direction! " He pointed. We listened. Off to the right there was the cackle of a Pileated Woodpecker. But we heard no other sound. Following Kuhn's suggestion, we started again, walking slowly so as to be able to hear any unfamiliar sound.

Kuhn and I were not far apart. We had walked a hundred steps or so when we came upon a big cypress log. In order to move forward more rapidly and to see the woodland more clearly we climbed upon this log and started for its farther end.

All at once Kuhn, who was ahead, stopped, caught his breath, and whispered hoarsely: " There it goes, Doc! Did you see it? " He turned and, noting my bewilderment, gripped me by the shoulder, moved me round, and pointed so hard at the forest that both of us almost toppled in that direction. " It flew from its nest, too, Doc! What do you think of that! A nest! See it! There it is, right up there! " We were both so excited we were not quite coherent. I didn't know whether Kuhn was pointing at the bird or at the nest. I had seen something fly from a dead tree, but the glimpse was not very satisfactory. Now I noted a hole in this same tree, a big hole, about thirty or forty feet from the ground. The nest of an Ivory-billed Woodpecker! . . .

The cries of the Ivory-bill sounded closer at hand. We crouched. The female was returning. Within the following five minutes we watched her fly to the home-tree, go to her nest, look out suspiciously, and fly away again. Much white showed in her wings. Her long black crest curled jauntily upward at the tip. Her eyes were white and fiercely bright. Her flight was swift and direct—somewhat, indeed, like that of a Pintail Duck, though her wings did not beat as rapidly as a duck's.

We hid ourselves among the logs and bushes, making as little noise as possible. Both birds soon returned, the male slightly the larger and with a brilliant flame-red crest.

The whole experience was like a dream. There we sat in the wild swamp, miles and miles from any highway, with two Ivory-billed Woodpeckers so close to us that we could see their eyes, their long toes, even their strongly curved claws with our binoculars. The male bird sighted me, called more rapidly, and then, instead of flying off in alarm, swung to a tree above me, looked at me first with one eye then with the other, and stationed himself not more than thirty feet away. What a splendid creature he was! He called loudly, preened himself, shook out his plumage, rapped defiantly, then hitched down the trunk to look at me more closely. As I beheld his scarlet crest and white shoulder strap I felt that I had never seen a more strikingly handsome bird. His crest was gorgeous. But somehow what struck me most was the rich whiteness of his beak and the staring whiteness of his eye.

GEORGE MIKSCH SUTTON from *Birds in the Wilderness*

A ropeway goes down from the pitch lake to the sea. Its buckets, at the moment, dangle idly; as of everything else, the world has an excess of asphalt. No work is being done at the lake, and the telpher wires, stretched tightly across the sky, serve only as convenient perches for innumerable black pelicans. They sit there like a passage of semi-quavers on a mile-long expanse of ruled paper. We seemed to be landing at the foot of a gigantic page of Liszt.

ALDOUS HUXLEY from *Beyond the Mexique Bay*

In this place (the people being remoued vp into the country, belike for feare of our comming) we found neere vnto the rocks, in houses made for that purpose, as also in diuers other places, great store of Ostriches, at least to the number of 50, with much other foule, some dried and some in drying for their prouision, as it seemed, to carry with them to the place of their dwellings. The Ostriches thighs were in bignes equal to legs of mutton. They cannot flie at all; but they runne so swiftly, and take so long strides, that it is not possible for a man in running by any meanes to take them, neither yet to come so nigh them as to haue any shot at them either with bow or peece; whereof our men had often proofe on other parts of that coast, for all the countrey is full of them. We found there the tools or instruments which the people vse in taking them.

Among other meanes they vse in betraying these Ostriches, they haue a great and large plume of feathers, orderly compact together vpon the end of a staffe, in the forepart bearing the likenesses of the head, necke, and bulke of an Ostrich, and in the hinder part spreading itselfe out very large, sufficient (being holden before him) to hide the most part of the body of a man. With this it seemeth they staulke, driving them into some straite or necke of land close to the sea-side, where spreading long and strong nets, with their dogs which they haue in readinesse at all times, they ouerthrow them, and make a commong quarry. The countrey is very pleasant and seemeth to be a fruitfull soyle.   SIR FRANCIS DRAKE from *The World Encompassed*

The flight of the hoatzin resembles that of an over-fed hen. The hoatzin's voice is no more melodious than the cry of a peacock, and less sonorous than an alligator's roar. The bird's grace is batrachian rather than avian, while the odour of its body resembles that of no bird untouched by dissolution. Still, zoologically considered, the hoatzin is probably the most remarkable and interesting bird living on the earth to-day.

Xʙ

It has successfully defied time and space. For it, the dial of the ages has moved more slowly than for the rest of organic life, and although living and breathing with us to-day, yet its world is an affair of two dimensions— a line of thorny saplings threaded along the muddy banks of a few tropical waters.

A bird in a cage cannot escape, and may be found month after month wherever the cage is placed. A stuffed bird in a case may resist disintegration for a century. But when we go to look for the bluebirds which nest in the orchard, they may have flown a half mile away in their search for food. The plover which scurries before us to-day on the beach may to-night be far away on the first lap of his seven thousand mile flight to the southward.

The hoatzin's status lies rather with the caged bird. In November in New York City an Englishman from British Guiana said to me, " Go to the Berbice River, at the north end of the town of New Amsterdam, in front of Mr. Beckett's house, you will find hoatzins." Six months later as I drove along a tropical river road I saw three hoatzins perched on a low thorn bush at the river's edge in front of a house. And the river was the Berbice, and the house that of Mr. Beckett. . . .

We took a boat opposite Mr. Beckett's house, and paddled slowly with the nearly-flood tide up the Berbice River. It was two o'clock, the hottest time of the day. For three miles we drifted past the chosen haunts of the hoatzins. All were perched in the shade, quiet in the intense heat, squatting prostrate or sleepily preening their plumage. Now and then we saw a bird on her nest, always over the water. If she was sitting on eggs she sat close.

If young birds were in the nest she half-crouched, or perched on the rim, so that her body cast a shadow over the young. . . .

When a mother hoatzin took reluctant flight from her nest, the young bird at once stood upright and looked

Hoatzin (young)

curiously in every direction. No slacker he, crouching flat or awaiting his mother's directing cries. From the moment he was left alone he began to depend upon the warnings and signs which his great beady eyes and skinny ears conveyed to him. Hawks and vultures had swept low over his nest and mother unheeded. Coolies in their boats had paddled underneath with no more than a glance upward. Throughout his week of life, as through his parents' and their parents' parents' lives, no danger had disturbed their peaceful existence. Only for a sudden windstorm such as that which the week before had upset nests and blown out eggs, it might be said that for the little hoatzin chicks life held nothing but siestas and munchings of pimpler leaves.

But one little hoatzin, if he had any thoughts such as these, failed to count on the invariable exceptions to every rule, for this day the totally unexpected happened. Fate, in the shape of enthusiastic scientists, descended upon him. He was not for a second nonplussed. If we had concentrated upon him a thousand strong, by boats and by land, he would have fought the good fight for freedom and life as calmly as he waged it against us. And we found him no mean antagonist, and far from reptilian in his ability to meet new and unforeseen conditions.

His mother, who a moment before had been packing his capacious little crop with predigested pimpler leaves, had now flown off to an adjoining group of mangroves, where she and his father croaked to him hoarse encouragement. His flight feathers hardly reached beyond his finger-tips, and his body was covered with a sparse coating of sooty black down. So there could be no resort to flight. He must defend himself, bound to earth like his assailants.

Hardly had his mother left when his comical head, with thick, blunt beak and large intelligent eyes, appeared over the rim of the nest. His alert expression was increased by the suspicion of a crest on his crown where the down was slightly longer. Higher and higher rose his head, supported on a neck of extraordinary length and thinness. No more than this was needed to mark his absurd resemblance to some strange, extinct reptile. . . .

My man climbed higher and the nest swayed violently. Now the brave little hoatzin reached up to some tiny side twigs and aided by the projecting ends of dead sticks from the nest, he climbed with facility, his thumbs and forefingers apparently being of more aid than his feet. It was fascinating to see him ascend, stopping now and then to crane his head and neck far out, turtle-wise. He met every difficulty with some new contortion of body or limbs, often with so quick or so subtle a shifting as to escape my scrutiny. The branch ended in a tiny crotch and here, perforce, ended his attempt at escape by climbing. He stood on the swaying twig, one wing clutched tight, and braced himself with both feet.

Nearer and nearer crept Sam. Not a quiver on the part of the little hoatzin. We did not know it, but inside that ridiculous head there was definite decision as to a deadline. He watched the approach of this great, strange creature— this Danger, this thing so wholly new and foreign to his experience, and doubtless to all the generations of his forbears. A black hand grasped the thorny branch six feet from his perch, and like a flash he played his next trick— the only remaining one he knew, one that set him apart from all modern land birds, as the frog is set apart from the swallow.

The young hoatzin stood erect for an instant, and then both wings of the little bird were stretched straight back, not folded, bird-wise, but dangling loosely and reaching well beyond the body. For a considerable fraction of time he leaned forward. Then without effort, without apparent leap or jump he dived straight downward, as beautifully as a seal, direct as a plummet and very swiftly. There was a scarcely-noticeable splash, and as I gazed with real awe, I watched the widening ripples which undulated over the muddy water—the only trace of the whereabouts of the young bird.

WILLIAM BEEBE from *Jungle Peace*

We bateing our hooks with flyeing fishes, and casteing them into the sea out of the sterne of our shipps by lines, the dolphins and bonettayes would presently crush them with greedines and swallow them downe, and being fastened, offer themselves to our cooke to put them out of their torment. But the greatest spoyle whereunto these flying fishes were subject to in the ayer, was that a multitude of strange birds did ever attend upon the shoals of the dolphin and bonetta in the ayer, knoweing that when they light upon the sholes of the flying fishes, they would put them upp as a covey of partridges, and they presently as hawkes fell upon them, with all violence to make havoke, and slew 1000 before they held one fast for their owne use, where with they pleasured their friends, the dolphins and bonettayes, in the sea, which received them with greedynes, lookeing for more. When the foules rushed upon anny to serve their owne turne, they soared up so high as well they might be seen, where, casting their wings abroad, they descend by degrees little and little till they have picked the bones of their purchase, and so look for fresh againe. The fowles are in bignes eagles' fellows, whereof we had strange reports from our Portugall pilott, who professed to have experience of their nature and quallityes, that is, that they cannot abyde to touch the water with their feet, and therefore being never so hunger bitt, they would not take out of the sea anny slaine bodyes of the fishes they killed themselves. Againe, when they slept they mounted up into the ayer, and casting their wings abroad, descended without wakeing, fast on sleep, till they came neare to the water, which nature abhorring, they presently awake, and flying up againe to fetch out the rest of their sleep as before. Last

Man-o'-War Birds

of all, they engender in the ayer, and never com at land, but only in the tyme of layeing their eggs, which is as it were but a moment, for with all speed the female dropps her eggs in the sands, and, covering them, presently departeth, never reparing anny more to them, but leaveth them to the heat of the sonn and the nature of the sands in the providence of God to bring them forth living creatures, like to them in their kind, without showing anny spark of naturall affection towards them.

SIR FRANCIS DRAKE from *The World Encompassed*

May 3, 1840. Favoured by a strong north-westerly breeze we advanced rapidly towards Kerguelen Island. On the morning of the 3d, when in lat. 47° 17′ S., long. 58° 50′ E., the first piece of Antarctic ice was seen by us, though so small as scarcely to deserve the name of an ice-berg, being not more than twenty feet high and evidently fast dissolving, yet it was sufficiently solid to injure seriously any vessel that might run against it. We passed several beds of floating sea-weed, and were accompanied on our course by many of the great albatross, and the large dark petrel, and still more numerously by the speckled Cape pigeon and stormy petrel, of two or three different kinds. These birds added a degree of cheerfulness to our solitary wanderings, which contrasted strongly with the dreary and unvarying stillness of the tropical region, where not a sea-bird is to be seen, except only in the vicinity of its few scattered islets, which is the more remarkable where the ocean abounds so plentifully with creatures fit for their food.

CAPTAIN SIR JAMES CLARK ROSS, R.N., from *A Voyage of Discovery and Research in the Southern and Antarctic Regions*

March 28, 1841. At noon we were in lat. 57° 21′ S., long. 127° 35′ E.: during the day we observed several large flocks of a small dark-coloured petrel, which we took to be the young of the Cape-pigeon proceeding to the north-ward: by the length of the time they took to fly past us, we estimated some of those flocks to be from six to ten miles in length, two or three miles broad, and very densely crowded together, literally darkening the sky during the two or three hours they were passing over and about us.

CAPTAIN SIR JAMES CLARK ROSS, R.N., from *A Voyage of Discovery and Research in the Southern and Antarctic Regions*.

Jan. 11, 1841. The ceremony of taking possession of these newly-discovered lands, in the name of our Most Gracious Sovereign, Queen Victoria, was immediately proceeded with; and on planting the flag of our country amidst the hearty cheers of our party, we drank to the health, long life, and happiness of Her Majesty and His Royal Highness Prince Albert. The island was named Possession Island. It is situated in lat. 71° 56′, and long. 171° 7′ E., composed entirely of igneous rocks, and only accessible on its western side. We saw not the smallest appearance of vegetation, but inconceivable myriads of penguins completely and densely covered the whole surface of the island, along the ledges of the precipices, and even to the summits of the hills, attacking us vigorously as we waded through their ranks, and pecking at us with their sharp beaks, disputing possession; which, together with their loud coarse notes, and the insupportable stench from the deep bed of guano, which had been forming for ages, and which may at some period be valuable to the agriculturists of our Australasian colonies, made us glad to get away again, after having loaded our boats with geological specimens and penguins.

CAPTAIN SIR JAMES CLARK ROSS, R.N., from *A Voyage of Discovery and Research in the Southern and Antarctic Regions.*

April 26, 1840. Land was seen at daylight this morning, bearing E. by S. at the distance of ten miles. It proved to be Penguin, or Inaccessible Island, and well deserves either of the names it bears, for it was literally covered with penguins on all the ledges of its rugged shores, nor could we anywhere see a point on which it would be possible to land. Like all other volcanic islands, its summits terminate in curiously shaped pinnacles, and not the smallest appearance of vegetation was perceptible.

CAPTAIN SIR JAMES CLARK ROSS, R.N., from *A Voyage of Discovery and Research in the Southern and Antarctic Regions.*

In Campbell Island, situated not much further south, and although less wooded than Auckland, having many of its valleys overgrown with underwood, and the general character of the vegetation similar, I did not meet with a single land bird.

These islands appear to be the favourite breeding-places of the Albatross (*Diomedea exulans*), and during our stay in the months of November and December they were so busily employed in the work of incubation, as to allow themselves to be caught, without making an effort to escape. It is an amusing scene to watch a group of these birds, a dozen or more, assembled together on the side of a hill, grotesquely waddling about, selecting their mates; this being settled, they disperse, and each pair fix upon a spot for the nest. This consists of a mound of soil, intermingled with withered leaves and grass, the average dimensions of which I found to be eighteen inches in height, twenty-seven inches in diameter at the top, and six feet at the base. The albatross, like the petrel, only lays one egg, of a white colour, averaging seventeen ounces in weight. In one instance, only, I found two eggs in the same nest (both of the full size, and one of them unusually elongated in its longest diameter), although I must have examined at least a hundred nests. The snow-white head and neck of the albatross appearing above the grass when sitting on its nest, betrays its situation at a considerable distance. When forced off its egg, it makes a resolute defence, snapping the mandibles of its beak sharply together in defiance. I have frequently found it sleeping in the day-time, with its head under its wing. Its greatest enemy is the *Lestris antarcticus*, a fierce raptorial gull, which is constantly on the watch for the bird quitting its nest, when it will instantly pounce down upon and devour the egg. So well is the albatross aware of the propensity of its enemy, that it will snap its beak loudly whenever it observes this rover hovering overhead. Three or four species of petrel were breeding in the holes of the cliffs overhanging the bay.

CAPTAIN SIR JAMES CLARK ROSS, R.N., from *A Voyage of Discovery and Research in the Southern and Antarctic Regions*

Jan 11, 1842. During the last few days we saw many of the great penguins, and several of them were caught and brought on board alive; indeed it was a very difficult matter to kill them, and a most cruel operation, until we resorted to hydrocyanic acid, of which a tablespoonful effectually accomplished the purpose in less than a minute. These enormous birds varied in weight from sixty to seventy-five pounds. The largest was killed by the Terror's people, and weighed seventy-eight pounds. They are remarkably stupid and allow you to approach them so near as to strike them on the head with a bludgeon, and sometimes, if knocked off the ice into the water, they will almost immediately leap upon it again as if to attack you, but without the smallest means either of offence or defence. They were first discovered during Captain Cook's voyage to these regions, and the beautiful unpublished drawing of Forster, the naturalist, has supplied the only figures and accounts which have been given to the public, both by British and foreign writers on natural history. Mr. Gray has, therefore, named it in the zoology of our voyage,

Aptenodytes Forsteri, of which we were fortunate in bringing the first perfect specimens to England. Some of these were preserved entire in casks of strong pickle, that the physiologist and comparative anatomist might have an opportunity of thoroughly examining the structure of this wonderful creature. Its principal food consists of various species of cancri and other crustaceous animals; and in its stomach we frequently found from two to ten pounds' weight of pebbles, consisting of granite, quartz, and trappean rocks. Its capture afforded great amusement to our people, for when alarmed and endeavouring to escape, it makes its way over deep snow faster than they could follow it: by lying down on its belly and impelling itself by its powerful feet, it slides along upon the surface of the snow at a great pace, steadying itself by extending its fin-like wings which alternately touch the ground on the side opposite to the propelling leg.

CAPTAIN SIR JAMES CLARK ROSS, R.N., from *A Voyage of Discovery and Research in the Southern and Antarctic Regions*

Wednesday, December 7.—Lat. 61° 22'. Long. 179° 56' W. Made good S. 25 E. 150; Ant. Circle 313. The barometer descended on a steep regular gradient all night, turning suddenly to an equally steep up grade this morning. With the turn a smart breeze sprang up from the S.W. and forced us three points off our course. The sea has remained calm, seeming to show that the ice is not far off; this afternoon temperature of air and water both 34°, supporting the assumption. The wind has come fair and we are on our course again, going between 7 and 8 knots.

Quantities of whale birds about the ship, the first fulmars and the first McCormick* skua seen. Last night saw "hour glass" dolphins about. Sooty and black-browed albatrosses continue, with Cape chickens.

R. F. SCOTT from *Scott's Last Expedition*

Fulmars

To-day I walked over our peninsula to see what the southern side was like. Hundreds of skuas were nesting and attacked in the usual manner as I passed. They fly round shrieking wildly until they have gained some altitude. They then swoop down with great impetus directly at one's head, lifting again when within a foot of it. The bolder ones actually beat on one's head with their wings as they pass. At first it is alarming, but experience shows that they never strike except with their wings. A

* McCormick, after whom the bird was named, was doctor-naturalist on the *Erebus* with Ross, in 1839-43.

skua is nesting on a rock between the ponies and the dogs. People pass every few minutes within a pace or two, yet the old bird has not deserted its chick. In fact, it seems gradually to be getting confidence, for it no longer attempts to swoop at the intruder.

R. F. SCOTT from *Scott's Last Expedition*

At six this morning we were well in the open sea, the sky thick and overcast with occasional patches of fog. We passed one small berg on the starboard hand with a group of Antarctic petrels on one side and a group of snow petrels on the other. It is evident that these birds rely on sea and swell to cast their food up on ice ledges—only a few find sustenance in the pack where, though food is plentiful, it is not so easily come by. A flight of Antarctic petrels accompanied the ship for some distance, wheeling to and fro about her rather than following in the wake as do the more northerly sea birds.

R. F. SCOTT from *Scott's Last Expedition*

Meares and the dogs were out early, and have been running to and fro most of the day with light loads. The great trouble with them has been due to the fatuous conduct of the penguins. Groups of these have been constantly leaping on to our floe. From the moment of landing on their feet their whole attitude expressed devouring curiosity and a pig-headed disregard for their own safety. They waddle forward, poking their heads to and fro in their usually absurd way. "Hulloa!" they seem to say, "here's a game—what do all you ridiculous things want? " And they come a few steps nearer. The dogs make a rush as far as their leashes or harness allow. The penguins are not daunted in the least, but their ruffs go up and they squawk with semblance of anger, for all the world as though they were rebuking a rude stranger—their attitude might be imagined to convey " Oh, that's the sort of animal you are; well, you've come to the wrong place— we aren't going to be bluffed and bounced by you," and then the final fatal steps forward are taken and they come within reach. There is a spring, a squawk, a horrid red patch on the snow, and the incident is closed. Nothing can stop these silly birds. Members of our party rush to head them off, only to be met with evasions—the penguins squawk and duck as much as to say, " What's it got to do with you, you silly ass? Let us alone."

With the first spilling of blood the skua gulls assemble, and soon, for them at least, there is a gruesome satisfaction to be reaped. Oddly enough, they don't seem to excite the dogs; they simply alight within a few feet and wait for their turn in the drama, clamouring and quarrelling amongst themselves when the spoils accrue.

R. F. SCOTT from *Scott's Last Expedition*

There are three groups of penguins roosting on the floes quite close to the ship. I made the total number of birds 39. We could easily capture these birds, and so it is evident that food can always be obtained in the pack.

To-night I noticed a skua gull settle on an upturned block of ice at the edge of a floe on which several penguins

Adélie Penguins and Skua Gull

YB

were preparing for rest. It is a fact that the latter held a noisy confabulation with the skua as subject—then they advanced as a body towards it; within a few paces the foremost penguin halted and turned, and then the others pushed him on towards the skua. One after another they jibbed at being first to approach their enemy, and it was only with much chattering and mutual support that they gradually edged towards him.

They couldn't reach him as he was perched on a block, but when they got quite close the skua, who up to that time had appeared quite unconcerned, flapped away a few yards and settled close on the other side of the group of penguins. The latter turned and repeated their former tactics until the skua finally flapped away altogether.

R. F. SCOTT from *Scott's Last Expedition*

Wilson went over the floe to capture some penguins and lay flat on the surface. We saw the birds run up to him, then turn within a few feet and rush away again. He says that they came towards him when he was singing, and ran away again when he stopped. They were all one-year birds, and seemed exceptionally shy; they appear to be attracted to the ship by a fearful curiosity.

R. F. SCOTT from *Scott's Last Expedition*

They [the Penguins] have lost none of their attractiveness, and are most comical and interesting; as curious as ever, they will always come up at a trot when we sing to them, and you may often see a group of explorers on the poop singing " For she's got bells on her fingers and rings on her toes, elephants to ride upon wherever she goes," and so on at the top of their voices to an admiring group of Adélie penguins. Meares is the greatest attraction; he has a full voice which is musical but always very flat. He declares that "God save the King" will always send them to the water, and certainly it is often successful.

(Dr. Wilson's Journal)

When seen for the first time, the Adélie penguin gives you the impression of a very smart little man in an evening dress suit, so absolutely immaculate is he, with his shimmering white front and black back and shoulders. He stands about two feet five inches in height, walking very upright on his little legs.

His carriage is confident as he approaches you over the snow, curiosity in his every movement. When within a

Adélie Penguins (Bathing Party)

yard or two of you, as you stand silently watching him, he halts, poking his head forward with little jerky movements, first to one side, then to the other, using his right and left eye alternately during his inspection. . . .

After a careful inspection, he may suddenly lose all interest in you, and ruffling up his feathers sink into a doze. Stand still for a minute till he has settled himself to sleep, then make sound enough to wake him without startling him, and he opens his eyes, stretching himself, yawns, then finally walks off, caring no more about you.

DR. G. MURRAY LEVICK, R.N., from *Antarctic Penguins*

By the morning of October 19 there had been a good many more arrivals, but the rookery was not yet more than one-twentieth part full. All the birds were fasting absolutely. Nest building was now in full swing, and the whole place waking up to activity. Most of the pebbles for the new nests were being taken from old nests, but a great deal of robbery went on nevertheless. Depredators when caught were driven furiously away, and occasionally chased for some distance, and it was curious to see the difference in the appearance between the fleeing thief and his pursuer. As the former raced and ducked about among the nests, doubling on his tracks, and trying by every means to get lost in the crowd and so rid himself of his pursuer, his feathers lay close back on his skin, giving him a sleek look which made him appear half the size of the irate nest-holder who sought to catch him, with feathers ruffled in indignation. . . .

The consciousness of guilt, however, always makes a penguin smooth his feathers and look small, whilst indignation has the opposite effect. Often when observing a knoll crowded with nesting penguins, I have seen an apparently undersized individual slipping quietly along among the nests, and always by his subsequent proceedings he has turned out to be a robber on the hunt for his neighbours' stones. The others, too, seemed to know it, and would have a peck at him as he passed them.

Penguin Stealing a Stone

At last he would find a hen seated unwarily on her nest, slide up behind her, deftly and silently grab a stone, and run off triumphantly with it to his mate who was busily arranging her own home. Time after time he would return to the same spot, the poor depredated nest-holder being quite oblivious of the fact that the side of her nest which lay behind her was slowly but surely vanishing stone by stone.

DR. G. MURRAY LEVICK, R.N., from *Antarctic Penguins*

During October 20 the stream of arrivals was incessant. Some mingled at once with the crowd, others lay in batches on the sea-ice a few yards short of the rookery, content to have got so far, and evidently feeling the need for rest after their long journey from the pack. The greater part of this journey was doubtless performed by swimming, as they crossed open water, but I think that much of it must have been done on foot over many miles of sea-ice, to account for the fatigue of many of them.

Their swimming I will describe later. On the ice they have two modes of progression. The first is simple walking. Their legs being very short, their stride amounts at most to four inches. Their rate of stepping averages about one hundred and twenty steps per minute when on the march.

Their second mode of progression is "tobogganing." When wearied by walking or when the surface is particularly suitable, they fall forward on to their white breasts, smooth and shimmering with a beautiful metallic lustre in the sunlight, and push themselves along by alternate powerful little strokes of their legs behind them.

DR. G. MURRAY LEVICK, R.N., from *Antarctic Penguins*

As time went on, I became certain that invariably pairing took place after arrival at the rookery. On October 23 I went to the place where the stream of arrivals was coming up the beach, and presently followed a single bird, which I afterwards found to be a cock, to see what it was going to do. He threaded his way through nearly the whole length of the rookery by himself, avoiding the tenanted knolls where the nests were, by keeping to the emptier hollows. About every hundred yards or so he stopped, ruffled up his feathers, closed his eyes for a moment, then " smoothed himself out " and went on again, thus evidently struggling against desire for sleep after his journey. As he progressed he frequently poked his little head forward and from side to side, peering up at the knolls, evidently in search of something.

Arrived at length at the south end of the rookery, he appeared suddenly to make up his mind, and boldly ascending a knoll, which was well tenanted and covered with nests, walked straight up to one of these on which a hen sat. There was a cock standing at her side, but my little friend either did not see him or wished to ignore him altogether. He stuck his beak into the frozen ground in front of the nest, lifted up his head and made as if to place an imaginary stone in front of the hen, a most obvious piece of dumb show. The hen took not the slightest notice nor did her mate.

My friend then turned and walked up to another nest, a yard or so off, where another cock and hen were. The cock flew at him immediately, and after a short fight, in which each used his flippers savagely, he was driven clean down the side of the knoll away from the nests, the victorious cock returning to his hen.

DR. G. MURRAY LEVICK, R.N., from *Antarctic Penguins*

When starting to make her nest, the usual procedure is for the hen to squat on the ground for some time, probably to thaw it, then working with her claws to scratch away at the material beneath her, shooting out the rubble behind her. As she does this she shifts her position in a circular direction until she has scraped out a round hollow. Then the cock brings stones, performing journey after journey, returning each time with one pebble in his beak which he deposits in front of the hen who places it in position.

Sometimes the hollow is lined with a neat pavement of stones placed side by side, one layer deep, on which the hen squats, afterwards building up the sides around her. At other times the scoop would be filled up indiscriminately by a heap of pebbles on which the hen then sat, working herself down into a hollow in the middle.

DR. G. MURRAY LEVICK, R.N., from *Antarctic Penguins*

On November 3 several eggs were found, and on the 4th these were beginning to be plentiful in places, though many of the colonies had not yet started to lay.

Let me here call attention to the fact that up to now not a single bird out of all those thousands had left the rookery once it had entered it. Consequently not a single bird had taken food of any description during all the most strenuous part of the breeding season, and as they did not start to feed till November 8 thousands had to my knowledge fasted for no fewer than twenty-seven days. Now of all the days of the year these twenty-seven are certainly the most trying during the life of the Adélie.

With the exception, in some cases, of a few hours immediately after arrival (and I believe the later arrivals could not afford themselves even this short respite) constant vigilance had been maintained; battle after battle had been fought; some had been nearly killed in savage encounters, recovered, fought again and again with varying fortune. They had mated at last, built their nests, procreated their species, and, in short, met the severest trials that Nature can inflict upon mind and body, and at the end of it, though in many cases blood-stained and in all caked and bedraggled with mire, they were as active and as brave as ever.

DR. G. MURRAY LEVICK, R.N., from *Antarctic Penguins*

By November 7, though many nests were still without eggs, a large number now contained two, and their owners started, turn and turn about, to go to the open water leads about a third of a mile distant to feed, and as a result of this a change began gradually to come over the face of the rookery. Hitherto the whole ground in the neighbourhood of the nests had been stained a bright green. This was due to the fasting birds continually dropping their watery, bile-stained excreta upon it. (The gall of penguins is bright green.) These excreta practically contained no solid matter excepting epithelial cells and salts.

The nests themselves are never fouled, the excreta being squirted clear of them for a distance of a foot or more, so that each nest has the appearance of a flower with bright green petals radiating from its centre. Even when the chicks have come and are being sat upon by the parents, this holds good, because they lie with their heads under the old bird's belly and their hindquarters just presenting themselves, so that they may add their little decorative offerings, petal by petal! Now that the birds were going to feed, the watery-green stains upon the ground gave place to the characteristic bright brick-red guano, resulting from their feeding on the shrimp-like euphausia in the sea; and the colour of the whole rookery was changed in a few days, though this was first notice-able, of course, in the region of those knolls which had been occupied first, and which were not settled down to the peaceable and regular family life which was to last until the chicks had grown.

DR. G. MURRAY LEVICK, R.N., from *Antarctic Penguins*

During the fasting season, as none of the penguins had entered the water, they all became very dirty and dis-reputable in appearance, as well may be imagined con-sidering the life they led, but now that they went regularly to swim, they immediately got back their sleek and spotless state.

From the ice-foot to the open water, the half mile or so of sea-ice presented a lively scene as the thousands of birds passed to and fro over it, outward bound parties of dirty birds from the rookery passing the spruce bathers, homeward bound after their banquet and frolic in the sea. So interesting and instructive was it to watch the bathing parties, that we spent whole days in this way.

As I have said before, the couples took turn and turn about on the nest, one remaining to guard and incubate while the other went off to the water.

On leaving their nests, the birds made their way down the ice-foot on to the sea-ice. Here they would generally wait about and join up with others until enough had gathered together to make up a decent little party, which would then set off gaily for the water. They were now in the greatest possible spirits, chattering loudly and frolicking with one another, and playfully chasing each other about, occasionally indulging in a little friendly sparring with their flippers.

Arrived at length at the water's edge, almost always the same procedure was gone through. The object of every bird in the party seemed to be to get one of the others to enter the water first. They would crowd up to the very edge of the ice, dodging about and trying to push one another in. Sometimes those behind would nearly succeed in pushing the front rank in, who then would just recover themselves in time, and rushing round to the rear, endeavour to turn the tables on the others. Occasionally one actually would get pushed in, only to turn quickly under water and bound out again on to the ice like a cork shot out of a bottle. Then for some time they would chase one another about, seemingly bent on having a good game, each bird intent on finding any excuse from being the first in. Sometimes this would last a few minutes, sometimes for the better part of an hour, until suddenly the whole band would change its tactics, and one of the number start to run at full tilt along the edge of the ice, the rest following closely on his heels, until at last he would take a clean header into the water. One after another the rest of the party followed him all taking off exactly from the spot where he had entered, and following one another so quickly as to have the appearance of a lot of shot poured out of a bottle into the water.

DR. G. MURRAY LEVICK, R.N., from *Antarctic Penguins*

Whilst in the water the penguins usually hunted and played in parties, just as they had entered it, though a fair number of solitary individuals were also to be seen. When a party had satisfied their appetites and their desire for play, they would swim to a distance of some thirty to forty yards from the ice-foot, when they might be seen all to stretch their necks up and take a good look at the proposed landing-place. Having done this, every bird would suddenly disappear beneath the surface, not a ripple showing which direction they had taken, till suddenly, sometimes in a bunch, sometimes in a stream, one after the other they would all shoot out of the water, clean up on to the top of the ice-foot. Several times I measured the distance from the surface of the water to the ledge on which they landed, and the highest leap I recorded was exactly five feet. The " take off " was about four feet out from the edge, the whole of the necessary impetus being gained as the bird approached beneath the water.

DR. G. MURRAY LEVICK, R.N., from *Antarctic Penguins*

The Spitzbergen Ptarmigan (*Lagopus mutus hyperboreus*) has been described as the hardiest of all birds, and for some two-thirds of the year it lives in darkness and in burrows under the snow. Even this, however, seems to be surpassed by the Emperor Penguin (*Aptenodytes forsteri*), which not only lives but breeds on the ice during the perpetual night and tremendous frost of the Antarctic winter.

A. LANDSBOROUGH THOMSON from *Problems in Bird Migration*

I was once acquainted with a *famous shooter* whose name was William Ewing. He was a barrister of Philadelphia, but became far more renowned by his gun than by his law cases. We spent scores of days together at shooting, and were extremely well matched, I having excellent dogs and caring little about my reputation as a shot, his dogs being good for nothing, and he caring more about his reputation as a shot than as a lawyer. The fact which I am going to relate respecting this gentleman ought to be a warning to young men how they become enamoured of this species of vanity. We had gone about ten miles from our home, to shoot where partridges were said to be very plentiful. We found them so. In the course of a November day, he had, just before dark, shot, and sent to the farm-house, or kept in his bag, *ninety-nine* partridges. He made some few *double shots*, and he might have had a *miss* or two, for he sometimes shot when out of my sight, on account of the woods. However, he said that he killed at every shot; and as he had counted the birds, when he went to dinner at the farm-house and when he cleaned his gun, he, just before sunset, knew that he had killed *ninety-nine* partridges, every one upon the wing, and a great part of them in woods very thickly set with largish trees. It was a grand achievement; but, unfortunately, he wanted to make it *a hundred*. The sun was setting, and, in that country, darkness comes almost at once; it is more like the going out of a candle than that of a fire; and I wanted to be off, as we had a very bad road to go, and as he, being under strict petticoat government, to which he most loyally and dutifully submitted, was compelled to get home that night, taking me with him, the vehicle (horse and gig) being mine. I, therefore, pressed him to come away, and moved on myself towards the house (that of old John Brown, in Bucks county, grandfather of that General Brown, who gave some of our whiskered heroes such a rough handling last war, which was waged for the purpose of " deposing James Madison "), at which house I would have stayed all night, but from which I was compelled to go by that watchful government, under which he had the good fortune to live. Therefore I was

Partridge

in haste to be off. No: he would kill the *hundredth* bird! In vain did I talk of the bad road and its many dangers for want of moon. The poor partridges, which we had scattered about, were *calling* all around us; and, just at this moment, up got one under his feet, in a field in which the wheat was three or four inches high. He shot and *missed*. " That's it," said he, running as if to *pick up* the bird. " What! " said I, " you don't think you *killed*, do you? Why there is the bird now, not only alive, but

calling in that wood "; which was at about a hundred
yards' distance. He, in that *form of words* usually employed
in such cases, asserted that he shot the bird and saw it
fall; and I, in much about the same form of words, asserted that he had *missed*, and that I, with my own eyes,
saw the bird fly into the wood. This was too much! To
miss once out of a hundred times! To lose such a chance
of immortality! He was a good-humoured man; I liked
him very much; and I could not help feeling for him,
when he said, "Well, *sir*, I killed the bird; and if you
choose to go away and take your dog away, so as to prevent me from *finding* it, you must do it; the dog is yours,
to be sure." "The *dog*," said I, in a very mild tone,
"why, Ewing, there is the spot; and could we not see
it, upon this smooth green surface, if it were there?"
However, he began to *look about;* and I called the dog,
and affected to join him in the search. Pity for his weakness got the better of my dread of the bad road. After
walking backward and forward many times upon about
twenty yards square with our eyes on the ground, looking
for what both of us knew was not there, I had passed him
(he was going one way and I the other), and I happened
to be turning round just after I had passed him, when I
saw him, putting his hand behind him, *take a partridge
out of his bag and let it fall upon the ground!* I felt no
temptation to detect him, but turned away my head, and
kept looking about. Presently he, having returned to the
spot where the bird was, called out to me, in a most
triumphant tone, "*Here! here!* Come here!" I went up
to him, and he, pointing with his finger down to the
bird, and looking hard in my face at the same time, said,
"There, Cobbett; I hope that this will be a *warning* to

you never to be obstinate again!" "Well," I said, "come along": and away we went as merry as larks. When we got to Brown's, he told them the story, triumphed over me most clamorously; and though he often repeated the story to my face, I never had the heart to let him know that I knew of the imposition, which puerile vanity had induced so sensible and honourable a man to be mean enough to practise.   WILLIAM COBBETT from *Rural Rides*

A quarter of an hour before sunset in springtime you go out into the woods with your gun, but without your dog. You seek out a spot for yourself on the outskirts of the forest, take a look round, examine your caps, and glance at your companion. A quarter of an hour passes; the sun has set, but it is still light in the forest; the sky is clear and transparent; the birds are chattering and twittering; the young grass shines with the brilliance of emerald. . . . You wait. Gradually the recesses of the forest grow dark; the blood-red glow of the evening sky creeps slowly on to the roots and the trunks of the trees, and keeps rising higher and higher, passes from the lower, still almost leafless branches, to the motionless, slumbering tree-tops. . . . And now even the topmost branches are darkened; the purple sky fades to dark-blue. The forest fragrance grows stronger; there is a scent of warmth and damp earth; the fluttering breeze dies away at your side. The birds go to sleep—not all at once—but after their kinds; first the finches are hushed, a few minutes later the warblers, and after them the yellow buntings. In the forest it grows darker and darker. The trees melt together

into great masses of blackness; in the dark-blue sky the
first stars come timidly out. All the birds are asleep. Only
the redstarts and the nuthatches are still chirping drowsily.
. . . And now they too are still. The last echoing call of
the pee-wit rings over our heads; the oriole's melancholy
cry sounds somewhere in the distance; then the nightingale's first note. Your heart is weary with suspense, when
suddenly—but only sportsmen can understand me—suddenly in the deep hush there is a peculiar croaking and
whirring sound, the measured sweep of swift wings is
heard, and the snipe, gracefully bending its long beak,
sails smoothly down behind a dark bush to meet your
shot.   IVAN TURGENEV from *A Sportsman's Sketches*

It must have been in the early summer of 1921 that I was
fishing the Driffield Beck in Yorkshire, and, my skill not
having equalled the cunning of the trout, I went up to
the top of the waters, to lay siege to either of two good
ones that I knew lived there.

To get to them, I had to pass through a small rather
dense copse; and I picked my way as silently as I could,
trailing my rod behind me.

So far, I had had no thought for anything but the
trout and myself, but suddenly, as I was about to step
over the stile at the far end of the copse, an intense
twittering of birds caught my attention.

I was already astride the stile, so that I could sit silently
to watch the play before me.

There was a three-strand plain wire fence between the
meadow and the stream; and to within a few yards of my

ZB

perch each strand was thronged with every small bird in the parish! Those in the best positions, on each wire, were elbowing each other and their neighbours outwards to get a more comfortable position, and a better view. Those on the outside places were constantly being dislodged, and flew back to crash into the centre of each row from which they had been evicted—the whole manœuvre being accompanied by an orchestra of piping,

Stoat

trilling, squeaking, and squawking till the audience were all seated, the circus began.

And what a circus! So far, I had had ears and eyes for nothing but the little birds; but now I looked at the performer. It was a stoat. He was almost still, just moving a foot or two at a time, right or left, facing his audience— just as a music-hall performer over his patter steps across a stage " till ready." Then the show began. Never have I

seen anything like it. Backward and forward, round and
round, somersault after somersault, an infinity of rhythmical improvisation and agility. I was as spell-bound as
the audience—themselves almost silent by now.

Round and round, up and down, went the stoat; each
turn and each jump, however, taking him inch by inch
nearer to the birds, till he was within a foot or two of
the bottom of the fence. Then he jumped! But even as
he jumped, so did the birds, who dissolved in a flurry of
small wings, leaving not even a feather behind them to
pay for their entertainment.   ANON

The places which the balbuzzard prefers to frequent, are
not the shores of the sea, but low lands bordering on
ponds and rivers, from which habit it might be termed
the fresh-water eagle. Perched on a lofty tree, or hovering
at a considerable elevation in the air, it watches the fish
from afar, descends upon it with the rapidity of lightning,
seizes it at the moment it appears on the surface of the
water, or even plunges in completely after it, and carries
it off in its talons. But this prey, the weight of which
renders the flight of the bird slow and laborious, does
not always remain the portion of the balbuzzard. On the
banks of the Ohio, where it goes to fish, when the *perca
ocellata* quits the ocean to enter the river, dwells also the
formidable pygargus. When he sees the balbuzzard arrived
to the height of his eyrie, he quits his own, pursues him
closely, until the fisher, convinced of his inferiority,
abandons the prey; then this fierce antagonist with folded
wings shoots down like an arrow, and with the most

inconceivable address, seizes the fish again before it reaches the river. The right of the strongest is the sovereign arbiter of small and great events, and governs throughout the universe with resistless sway, in the air, on the earth, and under the waters.

A still more extraordinary circumstance is related of the pygargus, by M. de Buch, in his travels in Norway and Lapland; and notwithstanding the respectable authority on which it rests, we can scarcely credit it. The pygargi of the isles of the interior sea, known under the name of *Loffoden*, not being able to attack the oxen with open force, have recourse to this stratagem. The bird plunges into the waves, and coming out all wet, rolls himself upon the shore until his plumage is all covered with sand, he then hovers over his victim, shaking the sand into his eyes, and striking him at the same time with his beak and wings. The ox blinded, and rendered desperate, runs here and there, to avoid an enemy who attacks him on all sides, and he falls at last, exhausted with fatigue, or precipitates himself from the summit of a rock. The eagle then drops upon him, and devours his prey in tranquillity.

BARON CUVIER from *The Class Aves*

April 16, 1749. This country has several kinds of swallows, viz. such as live in barns, in chimneys, and underground; there are likewise martins.

The barn swallows, or house-swallows, are those with a furcated tail. They are Linnaeus's *Hirundo rustica*. I found them in all the parts of North America which I travelled over. They correspond very nearly to the

European house-swallow in regard to their colour, however, there seems to be a small difference in the note. I took no notice this year when they arrived: but the following year, 1750, I observed them for the first time, on the

Swallows

Tenth of April (new style); the next day in the morning, I saw great numbers of them sitting on posts and planks, and they were as wet as if they had just come out of the sea.[1]

It has been a subject of contest among naturalists, to determine the winter retreat of swallows. Some think,

[1] Note by John Reinhold Forster, 1772.

they go to warmer climates when they disappear in the Northern countries; others say, they creep into hollow trees, and holes in clefts of rocks, and lie there all the winter in a torpid state: and others affirm, that they take their retreat into water, and revive again in the spring. The two first opinions have been proved, and it seems have found credit; the last has been treated as ridiculous, and almost as an old woman's tale. Natural history, as all the other histories, depends not always upon the intrinsic degree of probability, but upon facts founded on the testimony of people of noted veracity.—Swallows are seldom seen sinking down into the water; swallows have not such organs as frogs or lizards, which are torpid during winter, *ergo*, swallows live not, and cannot live under water.—This way of arguing, I believe, would carry us, in a great many cases, too far; for tho' it is not clear to every one, it may however, be true; and lizards and frogs are animals of a class widely different from that of birds, and must therefore of course have a different structure; hence it is they are classed separately. The bear and the marmot are in winter in a torpid state, and have however not such organs as lizards and frogs; and no body doubts of their being, during some time, in the most rigid climates in a torpid state; for the *Alpine* nations hunt the marmots frequently, by digging their holes up, and find them so torpid, that they cut their throats, without their reviving or giving the least sign of life during the operation; but when the torpid marmot is brought into a warm room and placed before the fire, it revives from its lethargy. The question must therefore be decided by facts; nor are they wanting here; Doctor Wallerius, the celebrated Swedish chemist, wrote in 1748, September

the 6th O.S., to the late Mr. Klein, secretary to the city
of Dantzick: " That he has seen, more than once, swallows
assembling on a reed, till they were all immersed and went
to the bottom; this being preceded by a dirge of a quarter
of an hour's length, he attests likewise that he had seen
a swallow caught during winter out of a lake with a net,
drawn, as is common in northern countries, under the
ice; this bird was brought into a warm room, revived,
fluttered about, and soon after died."

Mr. Klein applied to many *Fermiers generaux* of the
King of Prussia's domains, who had great lakes in their
districts, the fishery in them being a part of the revenue;
in winter the fishery thereon is the most considerable
under the ice, with nets spreading more than 200 or 300
fathoms, and they are often wound by screws and engines,
on account of their weight. All the people questioned
made affidavits upon oath before the magistrates. First,
the mother of the Countess Lehndorf said, that she had
seen a bundle of swallows brought from the *Frish-Haff*
(a lake communicating with the Baltic at Pillau) which
when brought into a moderately warm room, revived and
fluttered about. Secondly, Count Schlieben gave an instrument on stamped paper, importing, that by fishing
on the lake belonging to his estate of Gerdauen in winter,
he saw several swallows caught in the net, one of which
he took up with his hand, brought it into a warm room,
where it lay about an hour, when it began to stir, and
half an hour after it flew about in the room. Thirdly,
Fermier general (Amtman) Witkowski made affidavit,
that in the year 1740, three swallows were brought up
with the net in the great pond at Didlacken; in the year
1741, he got two swallows from another part of the pond,

and took them home (they all being caught in his presence); after an hour's space they revived all in a warm room, fluttered about, and died three hours after. Fourthly, *Amtman Bönke* says, that having had the estate Kleskow in farm, he had seen nine swallows brought up in a net from under the ice, all of which he took into a warm room, where he distinctly observed how they gradually revived; but a few hours after they all died. Another time his people got likewise some swallows in a net, but he ordered them again to be thrown into the water. 5thly, Andrew Rutta, a master fisherman, at Oletsko, made affidavit, 1747, that 22 years ago, two swallows were taken up, by him, in a net, under the ice, and being brought into a warm room, they flew about. 6thly, Jacob Kosiulo, a master fisherman at Stradauen, made affidavit, that in 1736, he brought up in winter, in a net, from under the ice of the lake at Raski, a seemingly dead swallow, which revived in half an hour's time, in a warm room, and he saw, a quarter of an hour after, the bird grow weaker, and soon after dying. 7thly, I can reckon myself among the eye witnesses of this *paradoxon* of natural history. In the year 1735, being a little boy, I saw several swallows brought in winter by fishermen from the River Vistula, to my father's house, where two of them were brought into a warm room, revived, and flew about. I saw them several times settling on the warm stove (which the Northern nations have in their rooms,) and I recollect well that the same forenoon they died, and I had them, when dead, in my hand.

In the year 1754, after the death of my uncle Godfrey Wolf, Captain in the Polish regiment of foot-guards; being myself one of his heirs, I administered for my co-heirs, several estates called the Starosty, of Dirschau, in Polish Prussia, which my late uncle farmed under the king. In January the lake of Lybshau, belonging to these estates, being covered with ice, I ordered the fishermen to fish therein, and in my presence several swallows were taken; which the fishermen threw in again; but one I took up myself, brought it home, which was five miles from thence, and it revived, but died about an hour after its reviving. These are facts, attested by people of the highest quality, by some in public offices, and by others, who, though of low rank, however made these affidavits upon oath. It is impossible to suppose indiscriminately that they were prompted by views of interest, to assert as a fact, a thing which had no truth in it. It is therefore highly probable, or rather incontestably true, that swallows retire in the Northern countries during winter, into the water, and stay there in a torpid state, till the return of warmth revives them again in spring. The question therefore I believe ought for the future to be thus stated: The swallows in Spain, Italy, France, and perhaps some from England, remove to warmer climates; some English ones, and some in Germany and other mild countries, retire into clefts and holes in rocks, and remain there in a torpid state. In the colder Northern countries the swallows immerse in the sea, in lakes, and rivers, and remain in a torpid state, under ice, during winter. There are still some objections to this latter assertion, which we must remove. It is said, Why do not rapacious fish, and aquatic quadrupeds and birds devour these swallows? The answer is obvious. Swallows choose only such places in the water for their winter retreat as are near reeds and rushes; so that sinking down there between them and

their roots they are by them secured against the rapacious-
ness of their enemies. But others object, Why are not
these birds caught in such waters as are continually
harassed by nets? I believe the same answer which has
been made to the first object will serve for this likewise.
Fishermen take care to keep off with their nets from
places filled with reeds and rushes, for fear of entangling
and tearing their nets; and thus the situation of swallows
under water, is the reason that they are seldom disturbed
in their silent winter retreats. What confirms this opinion
still more is, that swallows were never caught in Prussia,
according to the above-mentioned affidavits, but with
those parts of the net which passed near to the reeds and
rushes; and sometimes the swallows were yet fastened
with their feet to a reed, when they were drawn up by
the net. As to the argument taken from their being so
long under water without corruption, I believe, there is
a real difference between animals suffocated in water, and
animals being torpid therein.

PETER KALM from *Travels into North America*

When quails come to land, if it be fair weather or if a
north wind is blowing, they will pair off and manage
pretty comfortably; but if a southerly wind prevail they
are greatly distressed owing to the difficulties in the way
of flight, for a southerly wind is wet and violent. For this
reason bird-catchers are never on the alert for these birds
during fine weather, but only during the prevalence of
southerly winds, when the bird from the violence of the
wind is unable to fly. And, by the way, it is owing to

the distress occasioned by the bulkiness of its body that the bird always screams while flying: for the labour is severe.

ARISTOTLE from *Historia Animalium*
Trans. D'Arcy Wentworth Thompson

Of birds, the crane, as has been said, migrates from one end of the world to the other; they fly against the wind. The story told about the stone is untrue: to wit, that the bird, so the story goes, carries in its inside a stone by way of ballast, and that the stone when vomited up is a touchstone for gold.

ARISTOTLE from *Historia Animalium*
Trans. D'Arcy Wentworth Thompson

The halcyon is not much larger than the sparrow. Its colour is dark blue, green and light purple; the whole body and wings, and especially parts about the neck, show these colours in a mixed way, without any colour being sharply defined; the beak is light green, long and slender: such, then, is the look of the bird. Its nest is like sea-balls, i.e., the things that go by the name of halosachne or sea-foam, only the colour is not the same. The colour of the nest is light red, and the shape is that of the long-necked gourd. The nests are larger than the largest sponge, though they vary in size; they are roofed over, and great part of them is solid and great part hollow. If you use a sharp knife it is not easy to cut the rest through; but if you cut it, and at the same time bruise it with your hand, it will soon crumble to pieces, like the halosachne. The opening is small, just enough for a tiny entrance, so that even if the nest upset the sea does not enter in; the hollow channels are like those in sponges. It is not known for certain of what material the nest is constructed; it is possibly made of backbones of the gar-fish; for, by the way, the bird lives on fish. Besides living on the shore, it ascends fresh-water streams. It lays generally about five eggs,

Swan

and lays eggs all its life long, beginning to do so at the age
of four months.   ARISTOTLE from *Historia Animalium*
            Trans. D'Arcy Wentworth Thompson

Swans are web-footed, and live near pools and marshes;
they find their food with ease, are good-tempered, are
fond of their young, and live to a green old age. If the
eagle attacks them they will repel the attack and get the
better of their assailant, but they are never the first to
attack. They are musical, and sing chiefly at the approach
of death; at this time they fly out to sea, and men, when
sailing past the coast of Libya, have fallen in with many
of them out at sea singing in mournful strains, and have
actually seen some of them dying.

                          ARISTOTLE from *Historia Animalium*
                Trans. D'Arcy Wentworth Thompson

The cepphus is caught by means of sea-foam; the bird
snaps at the foam, and consequently fishermen catch it
by sluicing with showers of sea-water. These birds grow
to be plump and fat; their flesh has a good odour, excepting the hinder quarters, which smell of shore-weed.

                          ARISTOTLE from *Historia Animalium*
                Trans. D'Arcy Wentworth Thompson

Storks, and all other birds, when they get a wound fighting,
apply marjoram to the place injured.

                          ARISTOTLE from *Historia Animalium*
                Trans. D'Arcy Wentworth Thompson

A great number of birds also go into hiding; they do not all migrate, as is generally supposed, to warmer countries. Thus, certain birds (as the kite and the swallow) when they are not far off from places of this kind, in which they have their permanent abode, betake themselves thither; others, that are at a distance from such places, decline the trouble of migration and simply hide themselves where they are. Swallows, for instance, have been often found in holes, quite denuded of their feathers, and the kite on its first emergence from torpidity has been seen to fly from out some such hiding-place.

ARISTOTLE from *Historia Animalium*

Trans. D'Arcy Wentworth Thompson

New Jersey, Raccoon, May 19, 1749. When the snake lies under a tree, and has fixed his eyes on a bird or squirrel above; it obliges them to come down, and to go directly into its mouth. I cannot account for this, for I never saw it done. However, I have a list of more than twenty persons, among which are some of the most creditable people, who have all unanimously, though living far distant from each other, asserted the same thing; they assured me upon their honour that they have seen (at several times) these Black Snakes fascinating squirrels and birds which sat on the tops of trees, the snake lying at the foot of the tree, with its eyes fixed upon the bird or squirrel, which sits above it, and utters a doleful note; from which it is easy to conclude with certainty that it is about to be fascinated, though you cannot see it. The bird or squirrel runs up and down along the tree continuing its plaintive song, and always comes nearer the snake, whose eyes are unalterably fixed upon it. It should seem as if these poor creatures endeavoured to escape the snake, by hopping or running up the tree; but there appears to be a power which withholds them: they are forced downwards, and each time that they turn back, they approach nearer their enemy, till they are at last forced to leap into its mouth, which stands wide open for that purpose.

PETER KALM from *Travels into North America*

March 9, 1772. As a gentleman and myself were walking on the fourth of last November round the sea-banks at Newhaven, near the mouth of the Lewes river, in pursuit of natural knowledge, we were surprised to see three house-swallows gliding very swiftly by us. That morning was rather chilly, with the wind at north-west; but the tenor of the weather for some time before had been delicate, and the noons remarkably warm. From this incident, and from repeated accounts which I meet with, I am more and more induced to believe that many of the swallow kind do not depart from this island; but lay themselves up in holes and caverns; and do, insect-like and bat-like, come forth at mild times, and then retire again to their *latebrae*. Nor make I the least doubt but that, if I lived at Newhaven, Seaford, Brighthelmstone, or any of those towns near the chalk-cliffs of the Sussex coast, by proper observations, I should see swallows stirring at periods of the winter, when the noons were soft and inviting, and the sun warm and invigorating. And I am the more of this opinion from what I have remarked during some of our late springs, that though some swallows did make their appearance about the usual time, viz., the thirteenth or fourteenth of April, yet meeting with an harsh reception, and blustering cold north-east winds, they immediately withdrew, absconding for several days, till the weather gave them better encouragement.

GILBERT WHITE from *Selborne*

ACKNOWLEDGMENTS

I wish to thank the authors or their executors or literary representatives and the publishers for permission to include the following copyright poems or prose passages. If inadvertently omissions have been made, I offer the authors and publishers concerned my apologies.

Mr. W. B. Alexander	for	*Birds of the Ocean.* (G. B. Putnam's Sons, New York).
Mr. Martin Armstrong	,,	*The Buzzards.* (Martin Secker & Warburg
Mr. Charles S. Bayne	,,	An article in the Report of the Committee on Bird Sanctuaries in Royal Parks (England) 1935. (H.M. Stationery Office.)
Mr. William Beebe	,,	*Jungle Peace.* (The Modern Library, New York, and Messrs. Henry Holt & Co., New York.)
The Exors. of the late Mr. A. C. Benson		*Lord Vyet and other Poems,* and *The Hawk.* (John Lane the Bodley Head.)
Mr. Edgar Chance	,,	*The Cuckoo's Secret.* (Sidgwick & Jackson.)
Mr. F. Spencer Chapman	,,	*Watkins' Last Expedition.* (Chatto & Windus.)
Mrs. Frances Cornford	,,	*The Hills.*
Mr. Howard Corning	,,	*Letters of John James Audubon* 1826-1840. (The Club of Odd Volumes, Boston.)
The Exors. of the late Mr. T. A. Coward	,,	*The Birds of the British Isles and their Eggs.* (Frederick Warne & Co. Ltd.)

AAb

Mr. W. H. Davies	for	*Collected Poems of W. H. Davies.* (Jonathan Cape Ltd.)
Mr. Walter de la Mare	,,	*Poems 1901-1918.* (Constable & Co.)
Miss Camilla Doyle	,,	(Sampson Low Marston.)
Mr. Peter Freuchen	,,	*Arctic Adventure.* (Wm. Heinemann, Ltd.)
Mr. Robert Frost	,,	(Longmans Green & Co. Ltd. and Henry Holt & Co. N.Y.)
Mr. Wilfred Wilson Gibson	,,	*Collected Poems 1905-1935.* (Macmillan & Co. Ltd.)
Mr. J. H. Gurney	,,	*The Gannet.* (Witherby & Co.)
Mr. Laurence Housman	,,	(Sidgwick & Jackson.)
The Exors. of the late Mr. W. H. Hudson	,,	(J. M. Dent & Son Ltd.
Mr. Ford Madox Hueffer	,,	*The Starling.* (Martin Secker and Warburg, Ltd.)
Mr. Aldous Huxley	,,	*Beyond the Mexique Bay.* (James B. Pinker & Son.)
Mr. Julian Huxley	,,	*Bird Watching and Bird Behaviour.* (James B. Pinker & Son.)
do.	,,	*Africa View.* (Chatto & Windus.)
Mr. E. C. Keith	,,	*Woodcock and Snipe.* (Philip Allan & Co.)
Dr. G. Murray Levick, R.N.	,,	*Antarctic Penguins.* (Wm. Heinemann Ltd.)
Mr. R. M. Lockley	,,	Article *On the Breeding Habits of the Manx Shearwater with Special Reference to its Incubation and Fledging Periods.* (British Birds. Witherby & Co.)
Dr. Lorenz	,,	*Friendships with Free Birds.* (The Countryman.)
Mr. Robert Lynd	,,	*Solomon in all his Glory.* (The Richards Press Ltd.)

Mr. Robert Lynd	for	(News-Chronicle.)
Rear-Admiral H. Lynes, C.N.G.	,,	*British Birds.* (Witherby & Co.)
Mr. J. A. Mackareth	,,	
The Exors. of the late Mr. George Meredith	,,	*Poetical Works.* (Constable & Co.)
Miss Edna St. Vincent Millay	,,	*The Buck in the Snow* and *Other Poems.* (Harper & Bros. and A. M. Heath & Co.)
Mrs. Munro for the late Harold Munro	,,	(Cobden-Sanderson Ltd.)
Mr. Alfred Noyes	,,	(Wm. Blackwood & Sons.)
Mr. Donald Culross Peattie	,,	*Singing in the Wilderness.* (G. B. Putnam's Sons, New York.)
do.	,,	*An Almanac for Moderns.* (Geo. Allen & Unwin Ltd.)
Miss Ruth Pitter	,,	*Edwardian Poetry I* 1936. (The Richards Press Ltd.)
Mr. Seigfried Sassoon	,,	*War Poems.* (Wm. Heinemann Ltd.)
The Exors. of the late Captain Robert Falcon Scott	,,	*Scott's Last Expedition.* (John Murray.
Mr. Edmund Selous	,,	*A Bird Watcher in the Shetlands.* (J. M. Dent & Sons Ltd.)
do.	,,	*Realities of Bird Life.* (Constable & Co.)
Mr. J. W. Seigne	,,	*Woodcock and Snipe.* (Philip Allan & Co.)
Miss Fredegond Shove	,,	*Dreams and Journeys.* (Blackwell).
Sir J. C. Squire	,,	*The Birds and other Poems.* (Wm. Heinemann Ltd.)
Miss Freya Stark	,,	*The Southern Gates of Arabia.* (John Murray)
Mr. George Miksch Sutton	,,	*Birds in the Wilderness.* (Macmillan & Co.)
Mr. A. Landsborough Thomson	,,	*Problems of Bird Migration.* (Witherby & Co.)

Mr. J. W. and Miss Anne Tibble	for	*John Clare, A Life.* Cobden-Sanderson Ltd.)
Mr. H. M. Tomlinson	,,	*The Sea and the Jungle.* (Duckworth & Co.)
Miss E. L. Turner	,,	*Broadland Birds.* (Country Life.)
Mrs. Dorothy Whipple	,,	*The Other Day.* (Michael Joseph Ltd.)
Mr. H. F. Witherby	,,	*Secrets of the Long-tailed Tit's Architecture.* (The Countryman).
do.	,,	*Bird Hunting on the White Nile.*

INDEX OF AUTHORS

INDEX OF BIRDS